Re-Inventing the Book

CHANDOS

INFORMATION PROFESSIONAL SERIES

Series Editor: Ruth Rikowski
(email: Rikowskigr@aol.com)

Chandos' new series of books is aimed at the busy information professional. They have been specially commissioned to provide the reader with an authoritative view of current thinking. They are designed to provide easy-to-read and (most importantly) practical coverage of topics that are of interest to librarians and other information professionals. If you would like a full listing of current and forthcoming titles, please visit www.chandospublishing.com.

New authors: We are always pleased to receive ideas for new titles; if you would like to write a book for Chandos, please contact Dr Glyn Jones on g.jones.2@elsevier.com or telephone +44 (0) 1865 843000.

Re-Inventing the Book

Challenges from the Past for the Publishing Industry

Christina Banou

AMSTERDAM • BOSTON • HEIDELBERG • LONDON
NEW YORK • OXFORD • PARIS • SAN DIEGO
SAN FRANCISCO • SINGAPORE • SYDNEY • TOKYO
Chandos Publishing is an imprint of Elsevier

CHANDOS
PUBLISHING

Chandos Publishing is an imprint of Elsevier
50 Hampshire Street, 5th Floor, Cambridge, MA 02139, United States
The Boulevard, Langford Lane, Kidlington, OX5 1GB, United Kingdom

Notices
Knowledge and best practice in this field are constantly changing. As new research and
experience broaden our understanding, changes in research methods, professional practices,
or medical treatment may become necessary.

Practitioners and researchers must always rely on their own experience and knowledge in
evaluating and using any information, methods, compounds, or experiments described herein.
In using such information or methods they should be mindful of their own safety and the
safety of others, including parties for whom they have a professional responsibility.

To the fullest extent of the law, neither the Publisher nor the authors, contributors, or
editors, assume any liability for any injury and/or damage to persons or property as a
matter of products liability, negligence or otherwise, or from any use or operation of any
methods, products, instructions, or ideas contained in the material herein.

Library of Congress Cataloging-in-Publication Data
A catalog record for this book is available from the Library of Congress

British Library Cataloguing-in-Publication Data
A catalogue record for this book is available from the British Library

ISBN: 978-0-08-101278-9 (print)
ISBN: 978-0-08-101279-6 (online)

For information on all Chandos Publishing publications
visit our website at https://www.elsevier.com/

  Working together
to grow libraries in
developing countries

www.elsevier.com • www.bookaid.org

Publisher: Glyn Jones
Acquisition Editor: George Knott
Editorial Project Manager: Tessa De Roo
Production Project Manager: Debasish Ghosh
Designer: Vicky Pearson Esser

Typeset by TNQ Books and Journals

To my daughter Mary,
Because she has re-invented my Time,
Keeping me rediscovering words,
Reimagining worlds…

Contents

Foreword

It is now commonplace to talk of the changes that are happening to the publishing industry and the book itself. Frequent references are made to Gutenberg as we absorb the impact of the major shifts that have occurred in all areas of publishing, with changing roles for authors, readers and the different players in the value chain. That is why it is so timely to read this book by Christina Banou, which places contemporary change in the context of the book's history, revealing how current trends can be traced back to the past.

Banou moves expertly between present developments in the industry and previous periods in the chronology of the book, offering a number of examples. She draws a comparison between patronage in Renaissance Italy, when special editions were prepared for wealthy book collectors, and today's crowdfunding of editions featuring the donor's name. During the Renaissance, the printer offered personalized copies to satisfy the needs and expectations of powerful readers – today we can have printed or digital copies of, say, a children's story which features an individual child.

Modern day publishers send selected readers advance copies of new books, and look to build online communities around their publishing lists. Readers may be encouraged to participate in the development of fiction, with authors seeking feedback on early drafts and plot development. Literature sites feature a variety of genre and fan fiction, which are trawled by publishers seeking the next big thing. Banou looks back to the case of Pietro Aretino, who in the 16th century saw himself as the 'secretary of the world', and who cultivated a direct relationship with his readers. He promoted his work and profile to leverage financial support, fame and money; and he gathered feedback from his readers and thereby added value to his work.

The serialization of stories is back in fashion today, alongside an interest in shorter works, especially for digital publication, and Banou recalls how in the 19th century, the French publisher Louis Hachette created seven special series of shorter works designed for the new railway bookshops. Hachette opened a bookstore at every railway station in France, and his company came to own 750 shops by the end of the century.

Banou ably meets her objective to provide a methodological and theoretical background to explain current issues and trends. Her book provides much food for thought about the direction of the contemporary industry, and it is surely instructive to discover that much of the change we can see merely echoes the past.

Angus Phillips
Director of the Oxford International Centre for Publishing Studies

Preface and Acknowledgements

This book is part of my research and study that goes back in time. The love for books since I was a child has obviously been the starting point leading to pages, books, studies, journeys, conversations, research, papers and questions regarding boundaries and challenges, myths and realities, certainties and uncertainties. Since belonging to a generation that has successfully passed from printed to digital combining and converging all forms of the book, using daily many devices from paper to screen and vice versa, and been mostly satisfied with that, I have also wondered about 'new' and 'old'.

Interested initially in the history and art of the printed book and then in the publishing industry nowadays, I was convinced that the past of the publishing industry can – among other tools and theories – constitute a method, a theory, a framework not only for explaining and understanding current trends of our constantly changing era, but also for introducing and developing strategies and policies. Thus, I have always been concerned and challenged by the twofold: first, by the extension of the boundaries of the book and of the publishing activity, and second, by the correlation and convergence of the old and new.

Furthermore, common values and features in publishing demonstrate that the past is not a matter only of history but also of other fields and concepts creating thus a multidisciplinary and often privileged approach and method for studying, researching, exploring issues. In that framework, the book – whether printed or not, tangible or not – has to be studied both in its content and artistic identity. As publishing experiences from Renaissance and the Baroque era may be of value nowadays, the 'transformations' of the book, as well as structural changes in the publishing chain and industry, have to be rediscovered and reconsidered in a competitive, hybrid environment.

Certainly, there is always something more to be studied and to be written; when the work is finished and the manuscript sent to the publisher, the author has to cope with what wants and should be done in the future, with the material that was not included, the pages that could have been written. That is certainly the challenge for future discoveries and rediscoveries along with the satisfaction of the already completed work and the delight of the publishing process ahead.

Coming to the end of this book in late July 2016, I would like to cordially thank Angus Phillips, Head of the School of Arts and Director of the Oxford International Centre for Publishing Studies, Oxford Brookes University, for writing the foreword and seeing the manuscript. I am grateful for his precious concern, encouragement and collaboration not only in this book but also before and beyond it.

A diachronic acknowledgment is owed to those friends and colleagues who accompanied me in privileged conversations regarding books, art and time, some of them going back in previous decades; but a book is a work of time as well.

My sincere thanks have to be expressed to my students, postgraduate and undergraduate, who during the last 15 years through their questions and queries have broadened the scientific and bookish boundaries by setting new questions and offering different and often rediscovered options and points of view.

I would like to sincerely thank George Knott of Chandos Publishing, Elsevier, for his collaboration and interest since the book proposal, and for his comments on the text, as well as Dr Tessa de Roo, Chandos Publishing, for her collaboration and for always having the answers concerning the journey of my book.

My husband Petros Kostagiolas has always offered me another point of you; and I thank him for this. My 7-year-old daughter Mary shows me daily other ways for exploring words and worlds; the dedication and my great thank you is to her wishing these pages of my in-books life to meet her time someday.

Introduction: the continuing revolution of Gutenberg

1

1.1 The continuing revolution of Gutenberg: the publishing industry at a turning point

The love for books may be the starting point when readers talk about them; this love probably transforms the publishing activity into a semifictional and 'romantic' process where the author writes a book, the publisher reads this manuscript and then oversees the entire production activity, the editor edits, the contract is signed, collaborations are checked, the bookseller promotes the title and finally the success of the work is celebrated. Real life is usually more complicated and far from what the readers have in mind. Obviously, stereotypes are derived from the time the book has been regarded through the centuries as a semisacred object; fiction and films often offer a simplified aspect of the publishing activity.

We have to remember that publishing has always been a business, an industry, certainly a creative and unique one – due to the reasons mentioned – in a highly competitive environment. The publishing value chain is so called due to the added value by all stakeholders, whose roles have been redefined according to the social, technological, cultural, financial and political conditions. Probably, the still 'romantic' concept of publishing, the surprise for the competition and for the strategies used, as well as for the changes that technology has brought about may be attributed to the unique identity of the industry, which is part of both the creative and the information ones.

During the last four decades, significant changes have taken place in the publishing industry altering the publishing value chain, the publishing activity and the structure of the industry whereas the book per se is often being transformed. In a hybrid world, new forms of the book coexist with the older, traditional ones; for example, reading books (whether small forms or not) on tablets and mobiles has resulted in deep changes in reading and consumer behaviour, in communication, in writing cultures, offering at the same time new aesthetic and reading experiences. Undeniably, the rapid advances in technology and the convergence of media are a reality, social media and networking provide the framework for viable and successful promotion and marketing strategies, feedback from the readers is offered more than ever and the role of the reader is upgraded. Challenges are considered to be many due to new information and communication technologies that offer a variety of tools, methods and opportunities to be explored.

Thus, the publishing industry seems often to be at a cross-road, at a constant turning point. Undeniably, nowadays it faces several and important challenges that force it to redefine values, redevelop strategies, rediscover methods and obviously re-create taste. Emerging opportunities offer to the publishers a variety of strategies

Re-Inventing the Book. http://dx.doi.org/10.1016/B978-0-08-101278-9.00001-2

and methods, whereas new concepts and issues provide the framework for innovation and experiment.

We have though to note that among the diachronic features of publishing innovation, risk and experiment are recognized. The printed book has been since its invention by Gutenberg in the mid-15th century a unique product: more precisely, a mass product and an information medium, a work of art and a commodity, a symbol of knowledge and of prestige, a commercial product and a propaganda medium (Eisenstein, 1983; Johns, 1998). Books are the magnifying mirror of each period reflecting and at the same time enhancing social, cultural, political, educational, financial, scientific conditions and concepts.

In our globalized and digital world where innovation and tradition still go hand in hand, challenges are many, augmenting day by day, running even faster than our needs, desires and expectations. The exploitation of new information and communication technologies ought to be counted as one of the peak points for the publishing industry. Among the challenges we may also recognize the emergence of new publishing and business models, the role of social media in building reading communities as well as in promoting books, the emergence of new forms of the book, the important role of the aesthetics in publishing, reader engagement and reader-centred marketing and promotion strategies. Meanwhile, we have to consider that publishing has been far from being a simple, easy to measure, even in cases to be described, activity.

The publishing business has been since its origins in Renaissance a competitive business, highly risky, tentative but rewarding, innovative and at the same time based on the already tested and successful. Collaborating with the 'world movers and world shakers', as Schuster had stated (Gross, 1985, p. 28), seemed and seems to be a strong reward itself. Even recently, although changes in the field are sweeping, the creative aspect of the industry provides it with a unique, privileged identity. Obviously, publishing as a 'work of a gentleman' in the 'good old days' is nostalgia for an ideal past that we seriously wonder if it really existed. We have though to recognize that the publishing industry always explored, exploited, experimented, enhanced and tried to expand, enforcing at the same time readers and authors to certain experiences altering thus the publishing chain, developing literary taste, giving access to information and providing new opportunities.

After the invention of printing, the printed book revolutionized all forms of learning and communication. It was a mass medium that offered access to information, bringing about significant changes in knowledge dissemination, scholar communication, education, propaganda and communication (Eisenstein, 1983; Richardson, 1999; Chartier, 1994). Furthermore, the book as a material object led to the development and democratization of taste, whereas as an object with both tangible and intangible characteristics it has in its evolution been transformed according to the social, economic, cultural, educational, scientific and political conditions related to the publishing policy of each publishing company.

Undeniably, the publishing history is a history of challenges, surprises and innovations, of needs and desires, of privileged and often troubled relationships. It is a history not mainly and not always of discoveries but often of rediscovering, reconsidering, redeveloping, reusing, reengaging and reimagining. But the knowledge of the past goes beyond history; it is a study of the typology of the book and of the construction and function of the publishing industry leading to the understanding of strategies, issues, concepts, trends and providing as well the framework for setting new strategies.

Nowadays, in a rapidly changing world, the book publishing industry is among the ones that flourish and change although it has to overcome difficulties facing strong competition from other powerful media even at the same device. It is in this complex environment that questions concerning the structure and function of the industry, the role of stakeholders and the nature of the book emerge. As Greco et al. (2013, p. 5) state, 'Book publishing in the United States in the 21st century is a frenetic fast-paced world of thousands of publishing companies employing more than 95,000 individuals, issuing more than one million new titles annually, keeping over five million distinct titles in print, and generating approximately +27 billion annually in net publishers' revenues'. Phillips (2014, p. i) writes that: 'this is an exciting period of the book, a time of innovation, experimentation, and change. It is also a time of considerable fear within the book industry as it adjusts to changes in how books are created and consumed'.

During the past four decades, mergers and acquisitions of the publishing companies have definitely changed the structure of the industry and the publishing activity leading not only to the dominance of large publishing companies and conglomerations, but also to the development of bestselling cultures, to changes in promotion, distribution and retail. In that framework, the role of the agent and of the reader is upgraded. Additionally, new business and publishing models set the scene for changes in the book, and in the publishing process and chain. Social media and networking introduce and develop cultures of communication, tools for promotion and marketing, methods for reader participation. In that context, the publisher is further empowered although publishing models, such as self-publishing and open access, appear to threaten him/her: publishing companies develop strategies, methods and policies based on new information technologies and deriving from the common ground of the industry; these strategies are thriving.

As mentioned, information technologies constitute already an advantage and a challenge for publishing. Technology is usually an ally providing the methods and tools for discovering but also for redeveloping, reusing and reviving older and tested strategies. We have though to admit that technology runs extremely fast, faster sometimes than our desires, needs and expectations. For example, gamification, storytelling, and the use of multimedia in publishing are promising but the majority of readers are not yet familiar with them. It is noteworthy that the printed book not only coexists with the electronic one and the digital publications but its sales are increasing. In the UK in 2015, according to the Publishers Association's Statistics (13 May 2016), 'sales of physical books from publishers increased for the first time in four years while digital sales fell for the first time since the PA started collecting figures' (The Publishers Organization, 2016). The same is to be pointed out, according to the Association of American Publishers, for the USA where both paperback and hardback saw growth (AAP, 2016). This 'resurgence' or thriving of the printed book is to be further discussed in a wider framework.

At the same time, readers tend to read on devices that they carry with them, such as mobiles (smartphones) and tablets. An opportunity and a need for the publishers is to provide editions for mobiles: this means changes not only in content (for example, short forms, serialization) but also in the aesthetics of the book, which, as discussed in the next chapter, is of great significance. The question should be not only for the 'content' but for works, books or editions.

Questions raised inevitably include the relationship between technology and publishing, the typology and the aesthetic value of the books published, the nature of reading and communicating, the consumer behaviour, the impact of technology on the publishing activity, the role of social media in building communities of readers, the development of marketing strategies, the communication between stakeholders, reader engagement, the role of information in the publishing process, the development of taste and of creation of book policy.

It seems that there is always a turning point in each era of publishing; publishers had and have to cope with problems and exploit the new opportunities so as to innovate and introduce new issues. Beyond these, we have to recognize the need for surprise and more specifically the desire for the unexpected; it is though noteworthy that the unexpected is often seen as an evolution of the already tested, tried and loved.

Furthermore, there is abundance of information and abundance of titles; in that world, readers need specific information to get access, evaluate and finally discover the information they are seeking. Publishers offer this information, from their specific point of view, together with booksellers, libraries, communities of readers and social media. Among all the intermediaries involved in the publishing industry, the publisher is the one who has the privilege and the advantage of (1) providing the book after deciding, choosing and overseeing the publishing process; (2) providing access to books; (3) providing information that leads to the discovery of titles; (4) being a player in the discoverability of the readers; (5) taking advantage of all the available opportunities; (6) collaborating with other stakeholders; (7) deciding on the information provided according to aims, values and publishing policies.

This constant turning point of the publishing activity reflects the dynamic nature of the industry. Continuity and evolution depend on the exploitation and exploration of the 'new'; innovation goes hand in hand with tradition in the broader economic, cultural, social, political and academic background. Readers of the first printed books needed and expected faster and better access to the text, more friendly and economic books (in regard to the manuscript book that was expensive, rare, unique) which at the same time have aesthetic value. Certainly the printed book as mass medium offered access and changed concepts of communicating, thinking, collaborating, understanding, interpreting, researching, writing, reading and sharing. The typology of the printed book changed according to the needs, expectations and desires of the stakeholders; the printed page developed its own information mechanisms, whereas illustration and decoration cultivated taste offering a precious and privileged medium of aesthetic trends.

It seems that nowadays needs, expectations and desires of the readers are the same: they need and want immediate access to information and knowledge, as well as sharing and communicating through friendly and economic books with aesthetic value.

Technology alters the media and the time required, but expectations are the same. From this point of view, in a different economic, technological, social and cultural context, the revolution that begun with Gutenberg is still continuing being also reenforced with new tools and methods.

1.2   New worlds for old strategies, new words for old values

There seem to be new worlds in publishing in which older strategies and policies are rediscovered and redeveloped; technology often gives an advantage to older, used and usually successful concepts and strategies that are revived today. In that framework, new words, new terms are used so to describe and discuss older values and features that are reemerging. These globalized and converged worlds inevitably offer a variety of choices to all stakeholders in the publishing chain. The knowledge of the past adds value to publishing strategies and policies leading to successful list-building and marketing.

Main features of the publishing industry nowadays have been discussed and highlighted in a number of works (Thompson, 2010; Phillips, 2014; Clark and Phillips, 2014; Miller, 2007; Striphas, 2009; Epstein, 2001; Greco et al., 2013) and may be synopsized as follows:

- Mergers and acquisitions of publishing houses during the last four decades,
- Dominance of large publishing companies and conglomerations,
- Emerging role of new information and communication technologies in publishing,
- Online communities of readers,
- Social media in publishing,
- Social media marketing,
- New marketing tools,
- Changes in the publishing value chain,
- Redefinition of old roles and emergence of new ones (role of the publisher, authorship redefined, upgraded role of the agent, etc.),
- New stakeholders in the publishing chain,
- New publishing models (such as self-publishing, Open Access),
- New business models,
- Reader/user engagement,
- Changes in consumer cultures,
- Changes in reading cultures,
- Crowdfunding,
- Use of multimedia in the book,
- Gamification in publishing,
- Storytelling,
- Bestselling cultures,
- Changes in retail, in brick and mortar sales (Independent bookstores: difficulties and challenges. The independent bookstores, after their decline, get a step forward while experts point out their influential role. Emergence of other retail points.),
- Emergence of online bookstores. Leading role of Amazon and other electronic bookstores,

- Transformations of the book. Re-defining the boundaries of the book with the use of gamification, multimedia…,
- The role of libraries – information services (use of social media).

Among the key values and concepts of the publishing industry the following may
be recognized:

- Globalization
- Convergence
- Access
- Innovation
- Risk
- Experiment
- Competition
- Disintermediation (Phillips, 2014)
- Discoverability (Phillips, 2014; Michaels, 2015)
- Reader engagement
- Communication between stakeholders
- Friendly books
- Redefinition of old roles and emergence of new ones

Main topics, trends, challenges and opportunities that will be explored and discussed in this book include the following:

- Aesthetics in publishing (whether in printed or electronic/digital books), artistic identity of
the book nowadays,
- Reader engagement,
- Communities of readers and the role of social media/networking,
- Personalized publishing services,
- Role of the (both verbal and visual) paratext in both printed and digital/electronic books,
- Convergence of media,
- Direct communication between stakeholders in the publishing chain,
- Short forms,
- New forms of the book (with multimedia, gamification, etc.),
- Serialization,
- Personalized copies,
- Preorders,
- Crowdfunding,
- 'New' marketing strategies,
- 'New' promotion methods,
- The role of information in the publishing chain,
- Information mechanisms of the page, whether printed or not,
- …

Nowadays, the framework is set by new information and communication technologies that push forward the reevaluation of strategies and aims. Publishers have to
rediscover, redevelop, reinvent, reuse, re-create and reevaluate. Multiple opportunities
offer to them a variety of choices and new business and publishing models that may
adopt according to their profile, tradition, history, fame, backlist, aims and specializa-
tion. Certainly, this is a more than an interesting period for publishing; but this is not

the first time. Renaissance was a much challenging and experimental period for the printed book. Difficulties also exist but as Roberto Calasso (2015, p. 13) says 'there are always hard times in publishing'. Opportunities are provided too. The printed book as known for centuries is still produced and read but new intangible forms of the book call for new proposals, methods, design and strategies; aesthetics of the book, the book as an object of art and desire is always of value whether in paper or on the screen, whether on the ebook device or on the tablet and smartphone. And that is a challenge for the publishers deriving from older and tested methods, from existing behaviours and strategies that call for their exploitation in a world in which 'amazing' opportunities seem to set the scene.

Challenges and opportunities of our digital, globalized era – that in most cases seem to be innovative, new, revolutionary – have their origins in the past of the publishing industry deriving from strategies, ideas, perceptions, issues and values even since Renaissance. Gutenberg's invention not only revolutionized all forms of learning but offered a democratic medium of information, communication and transmission of knowledge providing at the same time innovative models for producing, acquiring, promoting, advertising, distributing and selling books. Thus patterns of book consumption, reading, writing, researching and thinking were altered. Furthermore, the printing press led to the democratization of knowledge and of taste. From this point of view, the production and distribution of texts and images, the dissemination of ideas and of information led to the recognition of access as an enduring value in a challenging and changing era such as Renaissance. It is noteworthy that access and communication were counted among the advantages of the printing process since the invention of printing.

Initially, Febvre–Martin (1990, first edition in French in 1957) and Eisenstein (1983) referred to the changes brought about by the printing technology. Richardson (1994, 1999), Chartier (1994), Johns (1998), Darnton (1996, 2009), Lowry (1979), Barbier (2000), Finkelstein and McCleery (2001, 2012), Robertson (2013), Howard (2009) and others have studied the publishing activity in its evolution focussing often in specific issues and eras, setting the methodology and examining the impact of typography on several aspects (such as social, cultural, etc.).

The printed book was outlined and praised as an information medium that provided access to readers changing education, scholar communication, science and everyday life by democratizing both knowledge and taste. Giorgio Vasari in the second edition of the *Vite* at the end of the life of Marcantonio Raimondi (Bolognese) wrote regarding the benefits of the prints that 'they brought to light many histories and works by excellent masters and gave the opportunity to see the various inventions and styles of painters to those who are unable to go to the places where the principal works are' (Gregory, 2012, p. 46). The value of these engravings as information resources is further outlined when Vasari mentions that '... although many plates have been [113] badly executed through the avarice of the printers, eager more for gain than for honour, yet in certain others, besides those that have been mentioned, there may be seen something of the good'.[1] It is noteworthy that publishers are to be blame for

---

[1] http://www.gutenberg.org/files/28422/28422-h/28422-h.htm#Page_95.

avarice and gaining profit (a rather common accuse when talking about the publishing activity) and engravings are recognized as valuable information resources. That is why Vasari admits that 'I have thought it right to give this long but necessary account, in order to satisfy not only the students of our arts, but also all those who delight in works of that kind' setting also other issues of taste, dissemination, collections, etc.

In this book, features, values, strategies, opportunities and challenges will be discussed and investigated; the book aims to provide a methodological and theoretical framework with the twofold aim: (1) to understand and explain current trends and issues and (2) to introduce and propose strategies, methods and policies for publishers. The book takes as key element and starting point that publishing values, aims and strategies have been mostly common since Renaissance.

The invention of printing by Gutenberg implied different ways of book production, promotion, distribution and marketing developing the publishing chain as known till now. The aims and values of the publishing industry have not really changed. Readers want to read, learn, be informed, be entertained, teach, communicate, do research, search, enjoy, share and discover. The publishing industry has always exploited the new opportunities for producing, distributing, promoting, advertising the books and reaching existing and potential audiences. There are also significant and more than interesting turning points of both continuity and innovation where older and new trends coexisted: printed and manuscript, oral and printed tradition, word and image, hand illumination and printed illustration in different copies of the same edition. In that context, the printed book and the publishing activity gained their identity in a world of multiple choices in which the stakeholders defined their strategies and values. The systemization in book production and in the organization of the publishing process that took place in Renaissance led to the discovery and exploitation of promising issues.

The capitals of the publishing industry that developed gradually since Renaissance are identified as follows (Thompson, 2010, pp. 3–10):

- Intellectual
- Symbolic
- Economic
- Human
- Social

To the above we may add in this book the aesthetic capital. The book as material object, as a mass (potential or not) work of art, has its own dynamic identity and its significant role in (1) developing the typology of the page, (2) introducing new promotion and marketing methods, (3) being an advertisement of itself, (4) creating 'celebrities' in the publishing chain, (5) developing taste and (6) developing the identity of the publishing company. The typology and the identity of the printed book had been gradually developed during the first decades of printing in Renaissance. This identity was further enriched and constantly developed according to the art of the era, the printing and illustration techniques, the readers' needs, the social and cultural conditions, etc. Nowadays, aesthetics in publishing regarding new forms of the book with no tangible features define a field of new opportunities and challenges in which tools, methods and strategies from the past may be explored.

The understanding of the above capitals, even with other name or with no specific name during the early centuries of printing and publishing, led to the development of (1) specific strategies and publishing policies, (2) promotion methods, (3) collaborations, synergies and (4) the typology of the book both as content and as object. For example, the symbolic capital was demonstrated by the printer's mark, and by introductions, prologues and other paratext material that pointed out the publisher's work. The quality of the book as content was exhibited through the praise of the text itself and of the edition, translation etc., pointing out the work of the collaborators, such as editors, artists, translators and other scholars.

Terms used may have changed and developed, whereas new ones, such as gamification, are adopted due mainly to the introduction of concepts and methods by information and communication technologies. For example, what was meant in publishing by the words 'instinct' or 'taste' of the publisher implied actually the systemized knowledge of the book market and of the needs and expectations of the readers. Publishing terms were gradually introduced and established according to the needs of the stakeholders who had to organize the publishing procedure, to set the framework in their printing shop/publishing house, to cope with competition, to overcome emerging difficulties and certainly to exploit all the opportunities provided. From the first manuals of typography, such as those by Joseph Moxon, Martin-Dominique Fertel, Giambattista Bodoni and Zefirino Campanini, to modern manuals, guides and dictionaries of publishing and printing, we can recognize the evolution and identify the emerging needs. As Phillips states (2014): 'we have a whole new range of terminology around the book, brought about by digital developments'.

In our hybrid digital era, keywords include on the one hand globalization, convergence, democratization, access, information, discoverability, expanded audiences, the need for friendly – readable – desirable books, the quest for access to information and on the other the desire for personalized copies, the need for desirable books and sometimes the demand for personalized publishing services. The same trends have been in use since Renaissance and we will argue for this. The 'globalized worlds' existed from the printing's beginning since books were produced and distributed to multilingual and multicultural audiences. The publishing activity had been broader than the boundaries of place and of time set each time, widening thus the boundaries of the book and of audiences. From this point of view, changes nowadays in the book and in the publishing value chain, from author to the reader, are enlightened and studied taking into consideration common values.

In that framework, myths and reality are to be investigated and further studied; on the one hand, myths of a romantic age and a romantic concept of the book and the publishing activity and on the other myths of our age related to the absolute power of technology. When we read about hard competition, marketing and advertisement, we seem to forget what Kurt Wolff has written (1991, p. 31): 'Georg Heinrich Meyer was constantly after me with one message: advertise, advertise, advertise – this is the only way to sell books'.

Undeniably, it is a challenging period for publishing. Although competitive media battle at the same device for recognition, the book in all its forms thrives going a step forward where tested and used 'lessons from the past' may lead to innovative strategies.

1.3   Toward a methodological and theoretical framework for publishing

In this book 're-' seems to be the key issue: reinvent, reimagine, redevelop, redefine, reuse, re-create, reconstruct, reconsider, repropose, etc., whereas new terms introduced attempt to offer to the study and policy making of the publishing industry. More specifically, a methodological and theoretical framework is set for

1. Understanding, explaining, interpreting current issues and trends.
2. Exploring opportunities, developing strategies and policies. These strategies and methods inevitably adopt updated methods and information tools. Undeniably, new technologies play a key role but they have to be exploited, evaluated and used in a specific 'publishing framework' as it will be discussed.

Certainly, publishing is a challenging, dynamic, interdisciplinary field (Greco et al., 2013; Hartley et al., 2012) drawing from book history, art history, history of reading, marketing, management, economics of publishing, information science, social sciences, literature, media and communication studies. They all contribute and lead to a creative dialogue, 'a kind of embedded capital, carrying a history of debate, development and application within the terminology without which it is hardly possible to make sense, let alone to make progress in solving problems' (Hartley et al., 2012, p. ix). This interdisciplinary approach and methodology is tried to be clearly explained in this book. For example, in the chapter focused on the aesthetics in publishing an interdisciplinary approach has to be used on the basis of book history and art history with methodology also from media studies, marketing, literature and information science.

'A theory of publishing is a theory of mediation, of how and why cultural goods are mediated. It is the story behind media rather than the story of a medium itself, and has a big role to play in our understanding of communications' (Bhaskar, 2013, p. 4). That is true but a theory of publishing also goes beyond this, incorporating methodologies and concepts from other disciplines such as book history and art history. 'Publishing has been thoroughly explored, both historically and in the present, but not adequately theorized', says Bhaskar (2013, pp. 4–5) recognizing that a theory of publishing has, among others, to account for divergent historical understandings and publishing's past and for how it informs its engagement with digital media in the present. Thompson (2010, p. 11) recognized the nature of publishing: 'while many fields of activity are intensively competitive, the publishing field has a competitive structure that is distinctive in some respects. In terms of their competitive position, most publishers are janus-faced organizations: they must compete both in the *market for content* and in the *market for customers*'.

'Book history favors a synthetic approach', according to Robertson (2013, p. 5) and this approach has to be taken into consideration in the study of contemporary publishing activity. According to Rosen (2003, p. 12) 'book studies would bring together, under one interdisciplinary umbrella, specialists in book history, the book arts, publishing education, textual studies, reading instruction, librarianship, journalism, and the Internet, and teach all these studies in an integrated whole'. Stepanova (2007) identifies book studies as an emerging field that encompasses book history and book arts whereas Murray (2007) investigates the relation between publishing studies and other disciplines (history of the book, media, cultural studies and other) having considered also the role of texts deriving from professional experience (such as memoirs, autobiographies, 'bibliophile books', house histories); when providing future directions for publishing research he exhibited contemporariness, cross-media flows and cultural politics. Baverstock (2012) provided an overview of the features and opportunities (both research and professional) of publishing programmes in the UK.

It must be pointed out that a publishing framework has to be used for incorporating and combining theories, concepts, methodology and tools from other disciplines. For example, Squires (2007, p. 3) writes about marketing that 'for marketing it is conceived as a form of representation and interpretation, situated in the spaces between the author and the reader –but which authors and readers also take part in – and surrounding the production, dissemination and reception of texts'. More specifically, taste needs to be investigated in the publishing framework taking into consideration art history, marketing and technology issues as well.

Certainly, publishing studies and theories go beyond history; it is also true that the study of the past of the publishing industry provides tools from both book history and art history for explaining and constructing new approaches. But these approaches actually emerge from a combination of media, theories and scientific fields that (1) lead to concepts of redevelopment, reconstruction and reconsideration and (2) introduce theories, strategies, methodology and models. Thus, the publishing activity and chain are under the scrutiny of common, globalized values and different approaches – such as, for example, by economists or art historians – that offer a privileged and poly-prismatic point of view. This is related to the nature of the book (content – object, tangible – intangible aspects) and to the adding value in the publishing chain.

In that context, certain questions are raised: Why do we need publishing studies? Why the past of the publishing activity is of interest? Which is the practical value to implement for students, researchers–academics and staff of the publishing industry? What is exactly a methodological and theoretical framework in publishing? As already mentioned, our first aim is to understand, explain and interpret current issues by introducing a methodological and theoretical framework that provides new approaches based on the historical evolution and explanation. Baxandall (1985) used the term 'the historical explanation of pictures' for art history; in the book, this historical explanation is introduced concerning the publishing industry. The second aim of this book is to propose and offer to the development and planning of new strategies, policies and business models.

Going a step forward, we can actually transform what Baxandall (1985, p. 1) said from 'we do not explain pictures but remarks about pictures...' into 'we do not explain books/editions but remarks about editions', relating these remarks (1) to the culture, taste, reading and consumer behaviour, (2) to economic, social, political conditions and (3) to the specific point of view of the stakeholder. This book attempts to provide a diachronic approach to publishing, and tries to investigate the origins, evolution, development and typology of publishing.

In this framework, the 'historical explanation' of publishing and of books will be introduced using methodology and theory from book history, art history, literature, marketing, management, history of reading and media studies. This is not a book about the past of the publishing industry but about its present and future; thus the past of the publishing industry is studied as a tool with applied methodology from other scientific fields. We go back in time when needed to identity the origins and the precedents of contemporary, or 'new', issues and challenges in order to understand, explain and use them successfully.

Technology is fast, faster than our needs and expectations (or of what we think we need and expect). So, how can we quickly understand, evaluate, compare and then use these new tools, concepts, challenges developing strategies? Knowledge of the past may offer not only a tool but also a methodological and theoretical framework and help towards a theory of publishing for continuing and succeeding in complex environments.

Among the key issues of the book is the discussion of aesthetics in publishing introducing the term 'aesthetic capital' of publishing. The artistic identity of the book, whether printed or not, is investigated in the second chapter with the aim to offer a specific methodological framework for the explanation of current trends, and mainly for introducing promotion methods, marketing strategies and publishing policies for product development.

Publishing has always been a business of innovation and risk, a creative industry based on the book both as content and as object. Although content is considered to be the bedrock of the publishing activity and nowadays there is much concern about it, we will argue that the book as material object and as a potential, usually mass, art object always mattered and still matters. Furthermore, exceeding the borders of the printed book and thus of what was used and known presupposes the development of new methodologies and theories. The book, although nowadays not tangible in its new forms (electronic, virtual), always has aesthetic value; aesthetics in publishing, as discussed thereafter, is of importance not only for artistic but also for marketing and promotion issues and strategies.

Undeniably, publishing is a complicated and challenging activity; the study of the past of the publishing industry highlights also issues of reading habits, consumer behaviour, reader participation, reading policy, advertisement and the role of libraries-information services. Publishing is considered to be the first information business. Publishing culture, a term broader than print culture, changed everyday life, and this has to be exhibited too. 'The free circulation of words and images offered by print did not just raise anxieties about access to knowledge and education, but also about access to culture in the most elevated sense' (Robertson, 2013, p. 13). Nowadays access to culture and communication through a convergence of media goes certainly beyond information. In this book the term 'information publishing chain' is introduced with the aim to explore the impact of information on the publishing activity.

The book as a mass product with aesthetic merit can be personalized and redefined in different environments. Expanding the boundaries of the book and providing personalized publishing services are key issues that go beyond the twofold printed–digital, undertaking concepts of taste and expressions of privilege.

1.4   The structure of the book

The second chapter, by far the largest, focuses on the artistic identity of the book, whether printed or not, from Renaissance to our Digital Age with the aim to exhibit and discuss the importance of the aesthetics in publishing; in that context, the chapter aims to introduce a methodological framework and approach for the understanding of current trends in the field and to propose new methods and strategies for product development, marketing, promotion and reader engagement in aesthetics. The book argues that, apart from the democratization of knowledge, publishing led to the democratization of taste through the development of the artistic identity of the book and the cultivation of taste to gradually wide audiences.

Nowadays, new information technologies and multimedia are constantly bringing about changes in the book in all its forms; the artistic identity of the book, whether on tangible material or not, whether on paper or on the screen of various devices, is of major significance for a number of reasons that will be explained. Initially, the second chapter enlightens and discusses issues of book illustration and decoration providing an overview of the development and evolution of the artistic identity of the book since Renaissance. The book is examined as a visual, valuable and viable object taking into consideration information and consumption cultures. Furthermore, the visual information and experience is outlined in terms of early 'social media' as observed in the case of the early printed editions. In that framework, the aesthetics of publishing chain-circle-circuit in its evolution is discussed. The term 'circle' / "circuit" has been added as the term 'chain' may be linear; it is rather a circuit since the author gains feedback and has direct communication with the reader. More specifically, the evolution of the aesthetics publishing chain-circle-circuit since Renaissance will be studied.

The key element of the second chapter is the artistic identity of the book, whether printed or electronic/digital, and is more than significant for issues including information, marketing, reader engagement, taste making, reading and consumer behaviour. For example, the artistic identity can be a means of promotion, the study of which incorporates methodology from different fields.

Thereafter, the role and value of the paratext (both verbal and visual) is studied as an introduction to the text that also contributed since the Renaissance to the creation of the book's identity and constituted a marketing and promotion method. Apart from the front matter (title page, cover, frontispiece, dedicatory letters, etc.) emphasis is given to the development of the printed page pointing out its commercial, artistic, informative value, whereas specific issues, such as patronage, are pointed out. In the chapter the term 'patronage paratext' is introduced for describing and investigating the role of patronage in the aesthetic capital of the printed book. Nowadays, the borders of the visual paratext in the digital/electronic forms of the book are extended due to the opportunities provided by multimedia; this paratext is also of value for marketing, promotion strategies and reader engagement.

The origins of 'personalized copies' and personalized publishing services are recognized in the hand-illuminated copies of the Renaissance period that are studied, enlightening thus aspects of production, distribution, prestige as well as the nature and function of books. Reader engagement in book illustration and decoration is examined mainly during the Renaissance and the Baroque era with the aim to identify the common ground and discuss marketing and aesthetic models that are still emerging. The upgraded role of the reader nowadays is not as new as it is considered to be and this is discussed in the second chapter. Personalized copies then and now are studied, whereas if we move from dedicatory letters of the Renaissance period to dedicatory copies and editions of our Digital Age we can better explain issues of book production, promotion and consumption. In that context, a business and publishing model for the participation of the reader in the artistic identity of the book is introduced. This approach as well as the proposed framework may serve to further explore technologies in the light of both book history and art history.

Thereafter, the second chapter focuses on the expansion of the boundaries of the book due to the convergence of media that leads to the convergence of cultures. The use of multimedia (gamification and other opportunities) is examined as it has transformed the artistic identity of the book bringing about changes in the publishing chain. The success of colouring books for adults is also examined; it is noteworthy that the colouring books, which are thriving, derive from painted prints and concepts of printing on the use and addition of colour during the first decades of printing; this addition of colour was supposed to offer not only enjoyment, product development and aesthetic merit but also reader engagement.

Conclusions of the second chapter focus on the importance of the aesthetic capital in publishing regarding the publishing process as a whole (product development, promotion, marketing, advertisement, etc.). Aesthetics in publishing offer a privileged field for the combination of technology and decorative/illustrative tradition, of innovative and tested, text and image, sound and words.

The third chapter investigates reader/user engagement that seems to be among the key points of the publishing industry nowadays, often discussed and prevailed. There is much concern about the upgraded role of the reader who is further encouraged to participate in the publishing process, especially in the promotion of the book. Although this is not something new as readers have always participated in the publishing process, a frontlist has been developed according to their needs and expectations, and their consumer and reading habits influenced and in turn have been influenced by the publishers.

In our digital era, undeniably the role of the reader in the publishing chain is becoming more active and dynamic compared to the past mainly due to new information and communication technologies, social media being an important agent of change; publishers exploit these opportunities by developing strategies for reader engagement so as to have direct communication with the readers, gain feedback from them, promote books and augment sales (whether direct or not). Case studies from the Renaissance and the Baroque are provided with the aim to offer a historical background and a methodological tool for understanding, discussing and further exploiting opportunities for reader engagement.

The third chapter also focuses on publishing strategies used in the past. These strategies are rediscovered, revived and reused. Initially, preorders are studied in their evolution and redevelopment identifying as their precedent subscriptions and preorders since the 17th century. Next, crowdfunding is examined as not only the democratized evolution of patronage but also in regard to personalized publishing services and storytelling. In that framework, short forms related to new virtual forms of the book are discussed, whereas serialization as a rediscovered (deriving from the Victorian Age) and emerging publishing strategy in the digital environment is also enlightened.

Thereafter, other business and publishing models related to reader engagement are discussed including complimentary copies, giveaways, embedded advertisements, bundling, advanced reading copies, membership and the role of communities – usually online – of readers. Building communities of readers goes back in time to the academies of the Renaissance, to reading societies and book clubs of the 19th century. The third chapter considers briefly the evolution of these communities and their influence on the publishing activity and on reading–consumer behaviour as well as on bookselling and publishing cultures. In that context, the impact of social media as well as of new technologies on building communities is noted as a means that enforces the dynamic, active role of the reading audience.

Inevitably, questions raised include the role of the reader and of the publisher, the value gained according to different points of view (publisher's, reader's, etc.), boundaries of reader engagement, use of social media, new marketing tools and strategies. One of the key questions obviously is the extent and the way by which publishers try to exploit reader engagement. In this book, the term 'reader sourcing' is introduced and the 'unexpected' in publishing is discussed as an important element in the broader framework of the publishing activity and policy that goes deeper in the structure and nature of publishing.

In the fourth chapter, the value of information in the publishing industry is discussed as an agent of change taking into consideration that access to information, information sharing, information seeking behaviour, information management and evaluation lead to the development of promotion, marketing and publicity methods. From this point of view, the book introduces the publishing chain as information chain-circle-circuit; it is generally recognized that information adds value to the publishing activity, enables direct and successful communication between stakeholders, develops promotion and marketing methods, leads to innovative and creative synergies. Different aspects and needs for information may force the development of the appropriate publishing policy and promotion strategies based on information sharing and giving. The fourth chapter explains that information has always been a value, a need and an aim for publishing and sets the framework for further future investigation by the author of the 'information mechanisms' of the page.

The role of data in developing strategies and reaching audiences is then noted. Thus, the information publishing chain-circle-circuit is introduced offering a specific point of view and an additional methodological background for the study and discussion of current publishing issues.

The fifth chapter provides a synopsis on the challenges from the past that were investigated and discussed in the previous chapters with the aim to focus on specific publishing opportunities and strategies that can be exploited in the context – but not only – of new information and communication technologies. It also comments on issues of publishing activity, including how the book nowadays seems to be constantly redeveloped and reinvented: these issues include the aesthetic capital in publishing, convergence, reader engagement and reader sourcing, the role of the publisher. The common factors between the past and the present publishing values and strategies are also looked at. In that framework, transformations of the book and of the publishing value chain are considered.

Conclusions of the fifth chapter may further serve the methodological and theoretical framework set in this book and raise questions of future research interest regarding the boundaries of various aspects of the publishing activity and book market. They may also help to epitomize on the methodological and theoretical framework proposed in this book with regard to terms and methods introduced. These introduced approaches may be implemented both theoretically and practically, although the book does definitely not claim to be a business manual. Literature review is used and case studies are provided when needed.

Reinventing the book implies reimagining it; this seems not so difficult since it is obvious that even from Renaissance all stakeholders kept on reimagining and redesigning the book as a commodity, a product, an art object, an object of desire with practical implementation. In that context, new reading, consumer and aesthetic experiences are studied.

It is true that in a competitive world where too many titles are published, discoverability is a feature, a demand, a concern and a value. Simply access to information is not the key for discovering; the publisher has to actually provide, filter, evaluate information so as to encourage the reader to participate. The publishing industry diachronically goes beyond this. The elements of surprise, satisfaction, taste and augmented desire for the next title and the next publishing step are steady features and values. The publisher is still the one that decides and introduces, whereas the augmented role of the reader, the agent, the bookstores, the online reading communities has to be further examined.

The epilogue consists of a comment on the complicated relationship between the book and the time as approaches in this book resemble a poly-prismatic mirror which offers a privileged image to each issue and feature that finally constitutes and reconstructs the phenomenon as a whole. Probably this may be attributed to the fact that each book competes with the time: personal time and objective time, the time of the book and the time of the author or the reader. Reinventing the book means to a large extent to reinvent ourselves; and before this, reimaging the book means to reimagine the world and our lives.

References

Association of American Publishers (AAP) StatShot Annual Survey, July 11, 2016. US's Publishing Industry's Annual Survey Reveals Nearly 28 Billion in Revenue in 2015. http://newsroom.publishers.org/us-publishing-industrys-annual-survey-reveals-nearly-28-billion-in-revenue-in-2015/; Also: Harvey, Helen, July 12, 2016. "2015 US Publishing Revenue Flat; Print Sales Rise as Ebook Sales Decline". Book Business, Available at: http://www.bookbusinessmag.com/article/2015-u-s-book-publishing-revenue-flat-print-sales-rise-ebook-decline/.

Barbier, F., 2000. Histoire du Livre. Armand Colin, Paris.

Baverstock, A., 2012. Are publishers born or made? Symposium at Kingston University, January 2012. Logos 23 (1), 30–37.

Baxandall, M., 1985. Patterns of Intention. On the Historic Explanation of Pictures. Yale University Press, New Haven and London.

Bhaskar, M., 2013. The Content Machine. Towards a Theory of Publishing from the Printing Press to the Digital Network. Anthem Press, London and New York.

Calasso, R., 2015. The Art of the Publisher (Richard Dixon, Trans.). Penguin, London.

Chartier, R., 1994. The Order of Books. Readers, Authors and Libraries in Europe between the Fifteenth and Eighteenth Centuries (Lydia Cochrane, trans). Polity Press, Cambridge, (first edition in French: 1992).

Clark, G., Phillips, A., 2014. Inside Book Publishing, fifth ed. Routledge, London and New York.

Darnton, R., 1996. The Forbidden Bestsellers of Pre-revolutionary France. Norton, New York and London.

Darnton, R., 2009. What is the history of books? In: The Case for Books. Past, Present and Future. Public Affairs, New York, pp. 175–206.

Eisenstein, E., 1983. The Printing Revolution in Early Modern Europe. Cambridge University Press, Cambridge.

Epstein, J., 2001. Book Business. Publishing. Past, Present and Future. W. W. Norton & Company, New York and London.

Febvre, L., Martin, H.-J., 1990. The Coming of the Book. The Impact of Printing. 1450-1800 (Gerard, D., trans.). Verso, London and New York. [first edition in French, (L' apparition du Livre) 1957, first edition in English 1976].

Finkelstein, D., McCleery, A. (Eds.), 2001. The Book History Reader. Routledge, New York and London.

Finkelstein, D., McCleery, A., 2012. An Introduction to Book History, second ed. Routledge, New York and London.

Greco, A., Milliot, J., Wharton, R., 2013. The Book Publishing Industry, third ed. Routledge, New York and London.

Gregory, S., 2012. Vasari and the Renaissance Print. Ashgate Publishing, Surrey.

Gross, G. (Ed.), 1985. Editors on Editing. An Inside View of What Editors Really Do. Harper and Row Publishers, New York.

Hartley, J., et al., 2012. Key Concepts in Creative Industries. Sage, London.

Howard, N., 2009. The Book. The Life Story of a Technology. The John Hopkins University Press, Baltimore.

Johns, A., 1998. The Nature of the Book. Print and Knowledge in the Making. The University of Chicago Press, Chicago and London.

Lowry, M., 1979. The World of Aldus Manutius. Business and Scholarship in Renaissance Venice. Blackwell's, Oxford.

Michaels, K., 2015. The evolving challenges and opportunities in global publishing. Publishing Research Quarterly 31, 1–8.

Miller, L.J., 2007. Reluctant Capitalists. Bookselling and the Culture of Consumption. The University of Chicago Press, Chicago and London.

Murray, S., 2007. "Publishing studies" critically mapping research in search of a discipline. Publishing Research Quarterly 23, 3–25.

Phillips, A., 2014. Turning the Page. The Evolution of the Book. Routledge, Abington, Oxon, and New York.

Richardson, B., 1994. Print Culture in Renaissance Italy. The Editor and the Vernacular Text, 1470–1600. Cambridge University Press, Cambridge.

Richardson, B., 1999. Typography, Writers and Readers in Renaissance Italy. Cambridge University Press, Cambridge.

Robertson, F., 2013. Print Culture. From Steam Press to Ebook. Routledge, New York and London.

Rosen, J., 2003. The horizon of a new discipline: inventing book studies. Publishing Research Quarterly 19, 11–19.

Squires, C., 2007. Marketing Literature. The Making of Contemporary Writing in Britain. Palgrave Macmillan, New York.

Stepanova, M., 2007. Disciplinary duality: the contested terrain of book studies. Publishing Research Quarterly 23, 105–115.

Striphas, T., 2009. The Late Age of Print. Everyday Book Culture from Consumerism to Control. University of Columbia Press, New York, Chichester, and West Sussex.

The Publishers Organization, May 13, 2016. Strong Year for UK Publishing Industry as It Grows to 4.4 Billion Pounds. Available at: http://www.publishers.org.uk/policy-and-news/news-releases/2016/strong-year-for-uk-publishing-industry-as-it-grows-to-44bn/.

Thompson, J.B., 2010. Merchants of Culture. The Publishing Business in the Twenty-First Century. Polity Press, Cambridge.

Wolff, K., 1991. Kurt Wolff. A Portrait in Essays & Letters. The University of Chicago Press, Chicago & London.

Reimagining the book: aesthetics in publishing

2

2.1 Setting the scene: from illustration to new multimedia technologies. Approaches and trends

The artistic identity of the book has always been more than significant for the publishing activity and policy as well as for reading behaviour and consumer cultures. The printed book has been a product and a medium based on content (intangible asset) and material object (tangible features), text and typographic form (Thompson, 2010). Since Renaissance it was understood that the book is a powerful information medium and a work of art. Apart from book illustration and decoration, the artistic identity of the book is also and strongly related with other elements and parts of the book such as the title page, the cover, the headings, ornaments (such as printers' flowers, borders), visual paratext and the typology of the page as a whole. In that framework, the book as an artistic object enables the publisher to create a recognizable profile and the reader to read, enjoy and be engaged, being thus satisfied with both content and object. The book has to be desirable, apart from being readable.

Nowadays, the role of the artistic identity of the book is becoming more complicated, challenging and certainly significant not only due to new information technologies but also due to the readers' needs, expectations and desires that are constantly changing and redeveloping. Reading on mobiles, tablets, ebooks, etc., implies, apart from new tools and devices, new reading and aesthetic experiences that are still under consideration and development. Meanwhile, new technologies lead to new forms of the book altering its nature and artistic identity. But even the book with no physical existence, the digital–electronic publication, also has to be desirable and readable and a potential work of art promising and promoting itself. Furthermore, this artistic identity further encourages reader engagement being at the same time a marketing tool for the publisher. In that framework, traditional book illustration and decoration have been transformed due to new experimental multimedia technologies. For example, the use of gamification or augmented reality alters the identity of the book as well as reading and consumer behaviour. In turn, desires of readers–consumers are redefined by new technologies which sometimes is true that run faster than their needs and expectations (Danet, 2014); and this is a major research point as well.

In the chapter we will focus on the development of the artistic identity of the book since Renaissance and the Baroque era with the aim to recognize key concepts and values as well as strategies and methods that enabled the book to be a viable, valuable and visual object. Key point is that the artistic identity of the book whether printed or electronic-virtual is really significant nowadays in terms of not only product development but also of marketing and promotion issues. Intangible forms of the book require also a certain artistic development exhibiting the central role of the aesthetics

Re-Inventing the Book. http://dx.doi.org/10.1016/B978-0-08-101278-9.00002-4

in publishing nowadays as both value and strategy. Ebooks, publications that we read on tablets and mobiles, do have and do need and require artistic identity which has many and complex functions and opportunities as it will be discussed below.

Initially, the development of the artistic identity of the book, the role of book illustration and decoration are outlined taking as key element that printing led to the democratization of taste. The aesthetics publishing chain-circle-circuit is then introduced and discussed taking the illustration publishing chain a step forward. Thereafter, the role of the paratext, both visual and verbal, will be studied so as to investigate issues of promotion, communication and networking through the artistic development of the printed book. The term 'patronage paratext' and 'obscure patronage' will also be introduced so as to enlighten specific methods and publishing policies as well as issues of the nature and function of the book. The chapter will also focus on the emergence and development of reader/user engagement in the aesthetics of the book. In that context, hand painted illumination and personalized copies that led and lead to personalized publishing services will be discussed as well as convergence of media with a comment on colouring books which are thriving today.

Thus, common (between the past and the present) features and values will be outlined so as to study and further discuss challenges, opportunities and trends of our era with the aim to propose and synopsize new strategies. Aesthetics create the aesthetic capital in publishing that can be added to the other capitals of publishing. Undeniably, aesthetics may serve as

1. a medium-tool for publishers so as to create marketing and promotion strategies, apart from a recognizable identity
2. a methodological approach for researchers so as to understand, explain, evaluate and propose.

We shall focus on the artistic identity of the book as a whole, taking into consideration book illustration and decoration, title pages and covers, headings, borders, visual paratext, and other visual or even verbal material related to the aesthetics of the book. The impact of new information and multimedia technologies as well as the role of social media in creating communities of readers will be discussed in a broader framework so as to investigate marketing strategies, promotion methods, product development, co-creation, as well as building communities of readers, developing consumer behaviour and creating taste.

Inevitably, questions that arise when studying the artistic identity of the book include its commercial and promotion value, influences from the art of the era, the role of the artists, the collaborations between the stakeholders (author, printers/publishers, artists, editors), the role of the reading audience and more specifically the participation of the reader, the relationship of content with images, the development of reading and consumer behaviour, the making of publishing policies. Undoubtedly, the aesthetics of the book enables us to study and understand the role of all stakeholders in the publishing chain-circle-circuit from a specific and in time privileged point of view. Furthermore, we can approach and understand current trends related with public taste, bestsellers, communication and visual information in the publishing chain, and thus we can introduce strategies based on the already used and tested.

Multimedia technologies and gamification offer to the reader new ways of understudying and enjoying the content creating at the same time a new relationship between text and image, between author and reader, between publisher and reader changing the roles and rules in the publishing chain. At the same time they offer to the publishers a new marketing tool, a strong communication medium with the readers and an effective promotion method.

Hartley et al. (2012, pp. 1–2) states that 'aesthetics may appear to be an abstract, philosophical concept but in the creative industries it is a major coordinating mechanism for combining A. A production apparatus, which includes the practitioners and organizations in the specific craft, and their education, training and upkeep, B. Works; the "textual" or object/artifact element of creative enterprise, C. Demand, including nonmarket patronage…, D. a regulatory of state-sponsored component…'. That is true in the case of the publishing industry; but much has to be added to the above taking into consideration specific features.

More specifically, aesthetics in publishing may be studied between book history, art history, communication and media studies, marketing, management, history of science: the artistic identity of the book is undoubtedly related to the satisfaction of all stakeholders (author, reader, publisher, bookseller), to the creation of taste in each era and to the book promotion and marketing. Moreover, the artistic identity of the book had a strong informative function and a more complex aspect related to the creation of the symbolic capital and to the value added to all stakeholders, from publisher to patron and to the reader depending on the case. The book has always been bought because it has been both useful and desirable, expected and surprisingly unexpected, applying to what the readers, consciously or not, waited and proclaiming as a valuable and viable object.

Thus, every book can be a work of art? Certainly, every book can take another meaning in the hands of each reader; every book can make the difference to the reader; every publisher may make the difference by giving a specific form to the text, by innovating, combining, reviving or introducing new concepts. The role of the publishing company is central in deciding and defining the artistic identity of the company and the aesthetic expectations of the reading audience taking into consideration artistic, cultural, political, social, educational and economic conditions of the era.

For understanding aesthetics in publishing (role, influences, trends, methods, patterns), methodology is used mainly from book history and art history and then from other disciplines. It is more than interesting what Anthony Griffiths said in 2003 at the Panizzi lectures in the British Library: 'I think it is in general true to say that art historians usually ignore prints, print historians usually ignore books, while book historians rarely seem able to cope with the prints that appear on their pages' (Ionescu, 2011, p. 10). Ionescu (2011, p. 29) identifies that 'there is no consensus on which disciplines can serve best a word and image approach to illustration, an perhaps paradoxically, given the prolific scholarship on the subject, no commonly accepted or universally used method for the study of the illustrative image'. Additionally, Goldman and Cooke suggest the recognition of 'illustration studies' as a 'discipline in its own right, and not as a subject uneasily positioned in the hinterland between literary criticism, art history, book history, librarianship and cultural studies' (2016, p. 7). Goldman (2016) sets the framework for the illustration studies recognizing several parameters and the background of the field.

In that framework, regarding aesthetics in publishing an interdisciplinary approach has to be used in the basis of book history and art history with methodology also from media studies, marketing, literature, information science and communication studies. As the artistic identity of the book is constantly been developing, especially in the new forms of the book, 'new' or 'older' questions are set. The study of the development of the artistic identity of the printed book and of the aesthetics in publishing is an often 'magnifying glass' and may well explain current trends. The democratization of taste since Renaissance may also interpret issues of our era regarding public taste, bestselling cultures and consumer behaviour further enlightening the aesthetics publishing chain-circle-circuit. The historical explanation of books together with the technological and the communicative ones may offer a privileged point of view for understanding concepts and introducing strategies. Obviously, interdisciplinarity is the order for publishing studies and for the aesthetics in publishing too.

'Print is a medium of images as well as texts, and the study of visual print culture extends into art history and cultural history' (Robertson, 2013, p. 7). Even though, the role of book illustration and decoration and more generally of the aesthetics of the printed book, although significant, is often not studied deeply, and certainly not in all its parameters: 'perhaps because they fall between academic disciplines, illustrated books are rarely the subject of scholarly consideration' (Sillars, 2008, p. 3); thus there is still much to be studied. As Ionescu (2011, p. 13) recognizes regarding the 18th century illustrated book, 'the illustrated book has slowly emerged from the shadows to claim its rightful place herein [book history]' recognizing that 'this recent development, however is definitely not widespread'. Taking into consideration what Roberto Calasso (2015, p. 24) says that what makes the book recognizable is the image, we can wonder for the extent of its study. At the famous communication circuit introduced by Robert Darnton, which offered certainly much to book and media studies, the art of the book is not considered and the author recognizes that 'manuscript books and book illustrations will need to be considered elsewhere' (Darnton, 2009, pp. 179-206).

Additionally, we have to recognize that art historians usually give light to 'exceptional' editions (this is identified by Ionescu, 2011, p. 11), to editions of certain and recognizable artistic value due to the artist or/and to the elaborative incisions. That happens, for example, in the case of *Hypnerotomachia Poliphili*, published in Venice in 1499, a curious edition (Lowry, 1979), a masterpiece but certainly not the average edition of Aldus Manutius and definitely not the one or among the ones that created print culture, consumer behaviour and readers' taste. Whereas, libelli (libri) portatiles (portable little books, pocket-sized books), ornaments (such as initial letters) and typographic fonts (the famous italics existing at all the computers nowadays) that were introduced and established by Aldus Manutius created not only a typographic culture but mainly an everyday culture related to the printed book which in turn developed taste, created reading experiences and defined information behaviour. Obviously, as cultural and market value coexist, the book has to be studied in all its cases: exceptional or not, as a mass medium and as a work of art.

Publishing and book history include and presuppose the study of the art of the book or the artistic identity of the book. Publishing is anyway an interdisciplinary field, as analysed at the introduction, 'a marvelous blend of theories, developed by historians, literary critics, economists, sociologists, marketers, and a small but growing number of individuals interested in the history of the book' (Greco et al., 2013, p. 2). Nowadays marketing implies and uses the artistic identity as a tool, and we will argue in the chapter that this happened since Renaissance: the book as an object had always been a powerful medium, visual and more than visual, for book promotion. Aesthetics served marketing and advertising giving also readers' feedback to the publishers.

Hartley et al. states that (2012, p. 3): 'In the marketplace aesthetics is a component of consumer choice, not a distinctive feature of producer identity. As a result, aesthetics in the creative industries should be seen as a component not of critical philosophy but of social learning'. In the publishing activity, though critical aspects have to be taken into consideration. Undeniably, aesthetics can explain to a certain extent and in turn can be explained as a component of social learning (Halsall et al, 2008) but the producer's (whoever is, from publisher to editor to patron...) strategies and values lead to the creation of taste as well as to consumer and reading cultures. The art of the era has also to be taken into consideration as an important component of the creation of the artistic identity of the book. Nowadays the emerging publishing and business models (such as crowdfunding, self-publishing, personalized publishing services etc.) as well as multimedia technologies have to be considered and in the aesthetic framework.

The identity of the book, whether printed or electronic, is decided and developed according to specific attitudes, values, behaviours and conditions. Deciding, defining and offering the artistic identity of the book has always been complex. In that context, the practical, utilitarian concept cannot be overlooked: the artistic identity of the book serves at the same time different functions, apart from artistic and cultural, such as informative, emotional and functional.

Nowadays, audiences globalized, multilingual, technologically informed, embedded in marketing strategies, integrated in aesthetic and productive procedures are further and deeper encouraged by the publishers so as to be engaged. Reader engagement is among the main challenges for the publishing companies, a step forward than the direct communication between reader and publisher. We will argue that reader engagement in the publishing aesthetics is not new, but going back in time is a strong business model. From this point of view, we shall also focus on 'personalized copies' and personalized publishing services.

Terms such as 'storytelling', 'gamification', 'augmented reality', etc., are more than often used when talking about publishing. Initially, 'the most popular books in the early phase of the ebooks format were those with strong narrative content, and little or no illustration' (Clark and Phillips, 2014). Thereafter, multimedia uses the image in a new framework. Photographs, videos, illustrations, visual material from different sources and with different origins coexist. On the other hand, as the printed book coexists with new forms and even thrives in some cases, printed decoration and illustration continue their more traditional itineraries even though with the influence of new technologies.

It is interesting to note that the French publisher Curmer in 1839, regarding the emergence of publishers and their different role from the printers and booksellers, 'attributed the appearance of the publisher to new techniques for reproducing illustrations' (Haynes, 2010, p. 24). By connecting illustration to the emergence of the publisher, Curmer exhibits not only the role of illustration and of the artistic identity of the book but the importance of new technologies relating with the book as visual object and as a commodity. Furthermore, Curmer referring to the combination of skills and capacities in the framework of new opportunities for the publisher, referred to 'the point toward which converge a crowd of industries' (Haynes, 2010, p. 24). Although being a specific and under question point of view, relating the definition of the role of the publisher with illustration technologies points out the preliminary role of the artistic identity of the book and also the exploitation of the new technologies.

Undeniably, the artistic identity of the book is redefined by new media and by the digital opportunities. Aesthetics in publishing is a concept and a methodological umbrella for explaining, evaluating and using patterns not only of the artistic identity of the book as developed till now but also patterns of production, distribution, promotion, marketing, reader engagement and taste. In the chapter the term 'aesthetic publishing models' will be used so as to explain publishing-business models. Nowadays information and multimedia technologies redefine priorities and policies, aesthetics in publishing form a challenge and the aesthetic capital may be of value.

2.2   The artistic identity of the book. Publishers, readers and the democratization of taste

2.2.1   Towards the democratization of taste

The book led not only to the democratization of knowledge and of information, but also to the democratization of taste. The printed book consisted of text and images, of words and pictures; this twofold was also part of promotion strategies and developed both reading habits and consumer cultures. Additionally, among the features of the printed book that led to its success we may recognize the strong feeling of owning a book. Silent reading that was prevalent during the Renaissance due to several reasons, among which the advent of typography has to be recognized, led to new reading behaviour.

On the one hand, the reader, owner, or user was free to read the book in the place, time and way he/she wanted (Richardson, 1999; Cavallo and Chartier, 1999): he/she could underline, interrupt or repeat reading, being free to decide on the way to read and think of both context and images when existed. Thus, the advent of printing led to new reading and aesthetic experiences providing the freedom of choice.

On the other hand, the printed book was in many cases a to-be 'work of art' influenced by and exhibiting the art of the era, exploiting the opportunities of the new techniques/technologies for mass products. We should though consider that art in Renaissance was very often the expression of the authority – whether of God or of noblemen who in many cases were patrons of art. The printed book instead was a mass product aimed at a large community of readers, although patronage can be found in early editions. Although illustration and decoration in printed books during Renaissance and the Baroque era served sometimes as a symbol of power, we have to recognize the freedom of the new medium, a freedom in the majority of cases beyond patrons, a freedom praised by Aretino in Renaissance Venice when he compared Venice to Rome. 'For Aretino Rome and Venice were symbolic places – the one epitomized by tyranny, sycophancy, and hypocricy of the Papal court and the other by the freedom and the democracy of the printing press – requiring different occupations, courtier and author' (Waddington, 2004, pp. 5–6).

This freedom of the publishing activity was due to

- Decision making: printers–publishers, as well as editors, authors, scholars, even readers (as will be mentioned thereafter) could decide or codecide on the book both as context and object,
- Financing: It did not depend on patrons (except in cases of patron commissioned editions or edition where specific relations between patron and author had been developed). The vast majority of the printing shops/publishing houses were commercial enterprises and publishers were independent to publish; it is indicative of that freedom that censorship and *indexes librorum prohibitorum* (catalogue of forbidden books) tried to control the production and distribution of books (Infelise, 2013).
- Audience: A wide and constantly expanding reading audience was not always easy to be approached and controlled; publishers, based always on innovation, risk and experimentation, aspired to reaching their potential readers. Thus they tried to intervene in the 'word of mouth' and used advertisement and promotion methods, which were far from patronage aspects; they managed to reach and influence, even manipulate audiences, in a broader framework leaving behind patronage aspects coming from the manuscript tradition.
- Innovation: The publishing activity exploited all the opportunities provided each time (ranging from technical developments to opportunities offered by the social, educational, religious and cultural conditions).
- Marketing (in the origins): Instead of waiting for the patrons to give instructions and financial support, the publishers considered the readers' profile (this particular knowledge being named experience or intuition or else), trying to satisfy and in turn influence and codefine their needs and expectations.

Thus, in a time when artists mainly depended on the patronage of the noblemen and/or of the church, the stakeholders in the publishing chain had usually no such restrictions (although patronage cases can be traced, restrictions being probably of another kind related more with the social, religious, economic and political conditions than with patronage in a stricter framework).

Illustration offered to all stakeholders (publishers, authors and readers) a privileged medium that served their needs and expectations; promotion, marketing, enjoyment, desire, advertisement and reading have to be considered. Moreover, illustration introduced and further developed new terms of book production and consumption. From this point of view, the reader gained the satisfaction of owing a work of art, the book being thus the commodity that created to a certain extent the taste of the reading audience related to each kind of text. Furthermore, although used sometimes for propaganda, the printed book meant in many cases the denial of the authority offering, for example, during the Industrial Revolution, to the development and establishment of the identity whether of class or/and of sex.

Certainly, printed books may be recognized as having a strong contribution to the development of taste and we will argue for this. The artistic identity of the printed book inevitably relates to both politics of publishing and politics of reading serving the first and developing the second. Its contribution on list building, production, promotion and marketing will also be explored.

2.2.2   The role and concepts of book illustration and ornamentation

We may wonder what illustration, decoration and generally the artistic identity of the book offered and offers. This may be summarized as follows.

Illustration may (Banou, 2016):

- be explanatory to the text (with straight or looser relationship with it),
- be representational to the text [Saenger (2006, p. 43) writes that: 'the nature of these woodcuts is not iconographic but representational'].
- have artistic–aesthetic value,
- be an information resource,
- promote the publication,
- advertise the book,
- introduce stakeholders (mainly publisher, author, artist – when know),
- remind the topics to the readers,
- divide the text into sections,
- offer information, visual or not (or coded information),
- offer enjoyment (hedonic value),
- relate the edition to a specific iconographic tradition,
- establish/introduce a visual culture,
- develop consumer culture,
- relate with the art of the era,
- compete with other editions,
- introduce the text to the reader,
- comment, interpret,
- enlighten or even obscure,
- regarding specific editions, illustration plays key role and becomes part of the text,
- encourage reader engagement,
- add symbolic capital,
- add value to the edition,
- praise a person or a group of people.

In that framework, illustration may be for the reader:

1. **Expected**, familiar, part of an iconographic tradition, already used in previous editions, expected according to the kind of text and the tradition of the publishing house, etc., or
2. **Innovative**, experimental (introducing new visual, iconographic and decorative patterns), converged with other media.

In both cases, illustration serves the publishers' aims and satisfies readers' needs. It is often a **combination** of both: expected and according to the tradition to an extent and at the same time innovative. The broader framework is that of the print culture and of the art of the period in specific social, political, economic and educational conditions. Expected illustration and ornamentation repeat and exploit the opportunities of the familiar, the already used and commercially tested. That method for a certain period of time will be of success based on an already created and recognizable artistic identity. But tradition goes hand in hand with innovation in the publishing industry. Innovativeness has been proved to be the key for both fame and sales, as well as for the creation of brand name. The one who innovates has his followers and imitators, and inevitably gains sales and success, such as Aldus Manutius in Renaissance Venice.

In terms of marketing and promotion, as developed nowadays, illustration seems to be a strong and significant medium that promotes the title developing and defining consumer behaviour. New multimedia technologies often presuppose reader engagement, being part of successful promotion strategies for reaching new audiences, while they can offer personalized publishing services, something which was not unknown during Renaissance. Certainly new technologies are effectively combined with other media and are adaptable to new forms of the book, such as reading on tablets and mobiles. Depending on the medium and on the reading audience, publishers are adaptable, risky and flexible aspiring not only to satisfy needs but also to develop new ones and redefine the older. For example, reading on mobiles creates a different reading and consuming culture presupposing the use of new technologies based on tested models. Aesthetics of the book nowadays are deeply influenced by these new technologies that offer also new publishing models and opportunities. The printed origins are strong enough and define to a great extent expectations and desires. McWilliam refers to the aesthetics of the device 'to be an important factor behind the reading experience' recognizing that 'the aesthetics of the device have a subconscious effect on the reading experience' (2013, p. 8). Saenger (2006, p. 7) uses the term 'aesthetic and commercial products' for books.

It must also be noted that apart from the above readers gained and had visual literacy from the book as well (Jung, 2015, p. 3). Regarding this, we can distinguish among periods, places, categories of the reading audience (according to the age, sex, education and social status), kinds of text, languages. Certainly, people were used to pictures before learning to read. Printed books for the wide, popular reading audience in Renaissance (tales, almanacs, lives of Saints) were illustrated. Regarding lavishly and heavily decorated and illustrated books, we may recognize that specific editions were famous mainly due to the artist or to the number of illustrations or to their innovative character; innovation consisted in both style-technique and themes. 'Illustration added a dimension of novelty to a test held in high esteem in the public imagination' (Ionescu, 2011, p. 17).

It is noteworthy that this public imagination has been cultivated and developed from the popular texts of the 16th century to the romances of the 18th and 19th centuries. The reading audience of the Industrial Revolution expanded with new dynamic groups (women, children, workers), setting new rules for the production and consumption of books. The publishers identified the existed and potential audiences for offering and promoting their books. In that framework, illustration was a means for the cultivation of taste and a visual as well as cultural commodity highly appreciated in an era when knowledge was conceived as a threshold to success, wealth, social recognition and education.

Having as a starting point that 'we do not explain pictures but remarks about pictures' (Baxandall, 1985, p. 1), we have though to re-consider trends about book illustration and decoration, and the artistic identity as a whole. There is a tradition and a history behind the pictures, as there are needs and desires beyond the pictures. Similar images offer different aspects according to the time and place, to the readers, as well as to the economic, social, political and cultural conditions. Explanations may differ according to the era and the taste/styles/'rules' set; whereas different images that illustrate the same text in the same or different period offer the 'privilege' of choice according to the publishing and promotion policies as well as to commercial channels.

In our hybrid era convergence is a key word (Phillips, 2014), but even since Renaissance convergence can be found: text and image, words and pictures content and illustration/ornamentation, printed and manuscript, mass product and personalized copy, written and oral... Convergence is better exhibited in hand illumination of printed books where different media were combined for the satisfaction of the needs of the readers and for serving other purposes, among which the cultivation of existing networks has to be recognized.

Printed illustration and decoration became part of the printed book since the first decades of printing, cocreating thus a material culture that led to the interpretation and understanding of the text as well as to the promotion of the book. In some cases printed illustrations were combined and converged with other media. This material culture inevitably changed patterns of book production and consumption.

Initially, during the first decades of printing, the place for initials, headings and illustrations was left blank so as the miniaturist could add hand illumination in specific copies; these copies were offered as gifts from the printers to rich and powerful readers or were ordered by book collectors to booksellers of the era (Armstrong, 1991; Marcon, 1986, 1987, Zappella, 2001, 2013). In these cases, illustration and decoration were initially hand painted (book binding and the quality of paper were taken into consideration in the development of a specific identity of the luxury copies). These personalized copies are of high research interest; thereafter their typology will be approached as in this book we consider them as the antecedents of the personalized copies of our digital era. Hand-painted ornamentation and illustration served not only as a medium for the embellishment of the text but also as a visual introduction to the text and as a symbol of the power and taste of the owner. Obviously this iconographic and decorative method to the printed copies derived from the manuscript books. But this model was soon to be abandoned and redeveloped in other framework for redefined audiences.

Since the first decades of printing, woodcuts were used in all copies of the edition for all readers,

1. changing thus patterns of taste,
2. introducing consumer behaviour,
3. further establishing the printed book as a potential work of mass art owned by each reader–owner.

It is true that the printed book initially had no title page, no printed illustration and decoration, even no page numbers. The manuscript had been the model for the first printers–publishers who aimed at the already existing reading audience consisting mainly of scholars, students, noblemen, men of religious and political power (Baldacchini, 2004). This reading audience had certain values, needs, desires, expectations and concepts for the book as tangible material object. Inevitably, printers–publishers tried to imitate the manuscript book and to offer their customers the books they were used to have and expected to acquire. But since the first decades of printing, it became obvious that the printed book was a new mass medium implying different modes for production, distribution and promotion, and having different opportunities. Publishers used tested methods in a new mass medium, making it quickly clear that implied different techniques and strategies offering new opportunities for new needs and expectations. Page numbers, for example, and page headings were by then necessary regarding the reading trends and the needs in the educational process. The first printed book had no title page which started gradually to be developed; the first step was a blank page in front of the text so as to protect the first page (Smith, 2001; Baldacchini, 2004).

The development of the typology – identity of the printed book as material object – is deeply connected with and should be attributed, among others, to technical/technological developments, the aims and values of all stakeholders, the nature of the book as a mass product, the competition with other media, the emergence of the communities of readers and the need for a friendly, economic and desirable product. The above have to be discussed in consideration with the economic, social, cultural and political conditions.

More specifically, ornamentation/decoration in printed books may:

- have artistic–aesthetic value, embellish the text,
- further and more emblematically divide the text into sections, chapters, etc. (initial letters),
- advertise and promote the title (commercial value),
- (when historiated initials) remind the topics to the readers,
- offer enjoyment,
- relate the edition to a specific decorative (or even iconographic) tradition,
- introduces and develops consumption behaviour/culture,
- have heraldic value, using the emblem of the family,
- introduces the text (mainly through the title page and the cover).

Ornaments in most cases were not designed specifically for the edition. Relation with the text and with the illustrative tradition is often more remote because imitation and repetition of the ornaments had been the rule and the way of work for the majority of publishers – printers.

Regarding ornaments, apart from initial letters and head titles, we have also to refer to 'piccoli ferri tipografici', in English: printer's flowers (Fleming, 2011, p. 64) (found in Joseph Moxon's *Mechanick Exercises on the whole art of Printing*, 1684, where 'flowers to set over the Head of a Page at the beginning of the book'). These ornaments have their origins in the book binders' ornaments and can be found at the beginning and/or at the end of the chapters, as well as in other parts of the book decorating and signifying the end or the beginning of content. Ornaments, apart from visual introduction and explanation to the text, have also artistic and promotion value empowering the visual tradition of the kind of text.

Thus, both illustration and book ornamentation/decoration add value to the edition and create not only visual literacy but also consumer and reading behaviour as well as taste. The same happens in our digital era.

2.2.3   Developing the artistic identity of the book

The book apart from being readable had always to be desirable; it has been through the centuries an artistic object and at the same time a mass product creating mass culture. Undeniably, the cultural, political, aesthetic, ideological significance of book illustration and decoration ought to be explored in each era, place, publisher etc. Historical and artistic/aesthetic explanation of publishing in accordance with technological innovation, economic and political conditions, art of the era, bookselling, reading behaviour, consumption culture offers a privileged, multidisciplinary point of view for explaining and introducing policies.

Parameters that strongly influenced, defined and developed the artistic identity of the book include the following:

- Influence from the manuscript during the first decades of printing,
- Influence from the printed book, as a precedent, nowadays,
- Convergence with other media,
- Iconographic tradition of specific texts,
- Typographic–publishing tradition of specific texts (e.g. religious texts),
- The working methods of printers–publishers who often imitated successful illustrations and reproduced them using material from their stock,
- Art of the period,
- Available printing techniques/technologies (printing in red, for example),
- Illustration techniques, innovations in printing and engraving technologies,
- Publishing policy of the publishing house–printing shop (goals, aims, values),
- Guidelines provided by the author,
- Guidelines provided by the editor,
- Needs and expectations of the reading audience (existed and potential),
- Reader engagement,
- Patronage,
- Competition,
- Collaborations,
- Artistic identity of the book series, when existed,
- Commercial factors,
- Market's orientation,
- Artist.

Regarding the aesthetics in publishing, relations often seem to be based on the following:

- Text–image
- Author–publisher
- Author–illustrator/engraver/artist
- Publisher/printer–illustrator/engraver/artist
- Traditional–innovative
- Used (repetitions, imitations)–new illustrations/ornaments

Nowadays, the kind and the nature of relationships in the new forms of the book are dramatically changing. Apart from the relations underlined, multimedia set the framework for convergence and for transformation of the relations between not only the stakeholders but also different media. More specifically, the concept is not only between new and old, traditional and innovative, used and new but mostly between a **variety of choices** which every day are been broadened by new information and communication technologies. The publishing industry has to explore and exploit them. Furthermore, as the role of the reader becomes more dynamic, reader engagement is among the key features and one of the main challenges for the publishing companies. Publishers want reader participation to be encouraged in a given, mostly controlled by them framework in a way that will offer them privileged marketing tools.

Thus, what seems to happen is that on the one hand, the publishing house tries to exploit, influence and in terms set the rules, and on the other the reader takes a more dynamic role having the chance and the 'freedom' to cocreate, participate, make book reviews through social media. The boundaries of this 'freedom' obviously are set and reset every day according to a number of reasons that will be discussed thereafter.

The challenge for the publishers seems to be twofold; on the one hand, they have to combine the knowledge and publishing experience of the past with the new technologies: given that the page must be first of all readable and familiar, new forms of the book have to keep the balance between the old (which has to be there, although not always recognizable) and the innovative which must create expectations and offer satisfaction at the same time. Gamification, the use of multimedia (experimental or not), augmented reality, storytelling create an interactive environment, verbal and visual, that offers opportunities. Inevitably, there seems to be an interactive chain – even better circuit on the basis of these relations and combinations, where the author, the reader, the publisher, the artist, the editor and the marketing department collaborate.

Key words seem to be flexibility, innovation, interpretation, convergence, engagement, collaborations and synergies. Among the key question is who decides, who codecides or who mostly decides. For understanding this, we have to consider that book illustration and decoration may be

- **Publisher–printer centred**: The printer–publisher of Renaissance and the Baroque era decided on the illustration and ornamentation of the printed editions developing thus the artistic identity not only of the book but of the printing shop/publishing house. The publisher often offered a new point of view, a new visual approach to the text. His aim was the satisfaction of the needs of the readers, the augmentation of sales and the creation of a recognizable profile (title pages, printers' marks, illustration and decoration often were privileged means). Even though it must be pointed out that the artistic identity was often developed in terms of imitation and adoption of existing iconographic types according to the art of the era and the iconographic tradition of the text; the economic and cultural conditions, as well as the financial ones of the company, were also of significance. Famous examples exhibit how the decisions and the publishing policy of the publisher–printer developed and influenced the aesthetics of the book of the era being a module for colleagues and competitors even for decades after. Other publishers–printers imitated and often copied illustrations extensively, sometimes using them in editions in which there was little or no relation with the text. Traditionally, the publisher is the one who decides but we shall take into consideration collaborations (with artists, editors, authors) and factors that codeveloped the artistic identity of the book influencing strategies and policies.

- **Author centred**: Author traditionally gives instructions, collaborates with other stakehold-ers (publisher, editor, artist, graphic designer, etc.) and codecides on the illustration and decoration of the edition. The collaboration with other stakeholders, specifically with the publisher/editor is of significance, especially but not only in illustrated books, such as art books and children's books. The author's role has to be discussed and evaluated according to the era, the case and the specific conditions. 'The author, through the press copy decided to a certain extent the type of illustration; the point is that press copies are rarely found, been considered thus the holy grail of book history' (Banou, 2016). The framework is always more complicated. The author as creator of the intellectual capital could propose illustration and decoration related to the text, often of aesthetic value; patterns of marketing were stron-ger and the publisher, editors or other stakeholders were to propose, codecide or even decide.
- **Editor centred**: The role of the editor was emerging and significant since Renaissance (Richardson, 1994). Especially when the editor was a well-known and respected scholar collaborating with a venerable publisher, his role was important in codeciding or mainly deciding on the artistic identity of the book. We cannot be certain for the role of scholars–editors of Renaissance; although introductory texts and epilogues to the editions as well as correspondence bring sometimes light to this aspect, the process of decision making in aesthetics is rarely enlightened.
- **Artist centred**: Especially in the case of famous, well-known and respectable artists, the decision on illustration and/or decoration depended much on the artist himself. Most of the illustrated and decorated editions were made by artists whose names are still unknown, whereas already tested and used motives and iconographic types were exhaustively repeated and imitated. Anonymity of artists is obviously one of the features and the problems (for both book history and art history); it may be attributed to a number of factors among which we can recognize the concept of illustration and decoration from the publishers' point of view, the use of existing motives, the imitations, and trends concerning the contribution of the artist to the edition. Taking into consideration that the fame and reputation of the artists were gradually established into the wider audience via the prints in the 16th century, we must recognize that in the printed book the name of the artist, apart from the famous ones, was exceptionally mentioned, probably considered not of significance so as to refer it in the title page or in the introductory texts (front matter). The role of the artist in the publishing chain-circle-circuit has to be further researched and evaluated according to the place, the time and the priorities of the publisher. The illustration chain, term recently intro-duced (Banou, 2016, pp. 187–188), is part of the publishing chain defining and recogniz-ing concepts and trends that help us to understand and discuss aesthetic issues. We may also distinguish in the illustration chain between the artist–designer and the woodcutter/ block-cutter (Szepe, 1997). 'Historically, artists have frequently employed the assistance of highly skilled craftsmen – specialist block-cutters, expert engravers or professional printers – to help with the technically-complex, time-consuming or labour-intensive stages of print-making processes' (Blocklehurst and Watson, 2015, pp. 13–15). The distinction between manuscript illuminators and designers of printed illustrations is also of importance, exhib-iting issues of convergence. Meanwhile, prints as described by Vasari in the second edition (Giunti, Florence 1568) of the *Vite* (VI, life of Marcantonio Raimondi, Bolognese), offered fame and recognition to artists. Furthermore, the mass production of printed books offered to the establishment and recognition (being part of the culture) of print illustration and dec-oration being part of a mass culture. The name of the artist only in the case of well known, illustrious examples, was referred.
- **Reader centred**: The reading audience's role is significant in many ways ranging from passive to more dynamic. Certainly, readers decide through the demand and the 'word of mouth'. Since Renaissance printers–publishers took into consideration the readers' needs and expectations

trying to satisfy them and augment sales of the printed books. Furthermore, as we will show thereafter, the reader even from the first decades of printing, especially from the 16th century, had a more active, although often not recognized, role. Among the ways of reader participation we may recognize communities of readers – first networks, correspondence between the stakeholders, comments and corrections on already printed texts. For example, correspondence with the publisher or editor or author, as in the case of Lampsonius, secretary to the Bishop of Liege, with Giorgio Vasari (Gregory, 2012, pp. 2, 19, 63), offered feedback from an often privileged and diversified point of view. The role of the reader in corrections will be exhibited thereafter especially in terms of scholar communication. Thus, although we use to think that the reading audience contributed to the edition in a more passive way, we have to consider new aspects and networks developed since Renaissance that offered ways of participation to the reader and a significant tool for the publisher so as to develop the quality of the book and gain feedback from the reading audience. There were specific, even experimental, networks through which the reader could contribute and influence the publishing procedure. Nowadays reader engagement and participation are among the great challenges of the publishing industry as it will be discussed in the third chapter.

- **Patron centred**: As it will be mentioned below regarding the paratext, there are two types of patronage in the books: first, when the patron commissioned the work and financed it; second, what we shall call 'obscure patronage', when the name of the patron is mentioned in the paratext parts (introductions, epilogues, dedicatory letters, etc.) by the publisher or the editor with mainly the aim to advertise their edition and gain fame and trust. From this point of view, we have to consider the patronage in a broader framework, as researched often in art history, bearing in mind social, cultural, artistic, economic, political and religious conditions (Haskell, 1980).

We have to consider that every edition implies different even in case unique ways in the creation of the artistic identity and presupposes different kind of collaboration between stakeholders. The aesthetics publishing chain-circle-circuit thereafter tries to explain this. Choices and decisions have been made in a broader context (art of the era, book market, political and economic conditions, etc.) as well as in a more specific framework defined by the publishing house (aims, values, backlist) and the stakeholders (publisher, editor, artist, graphic designer, patron when existed, etc.). The fame of the artist, for example, and the choices of the author (especially when well known, respected or bestselling) are of significance. But every publication is a work of many, thus the role of each stakeholder has to be examined according to the case.

Usually the artist illustrates the text, the itinerary being from author to the artist, from text to image; but sometimes this can be vice versa as in the case of Aretino and the prints by Giulio Romano. Aretino wrote to Battista Zatti: 'I took a fancy to see the figures… and on seeing them I was inspired by the same feeling that prompted Giulio Romano to draw them… I dashed off the sonnets that you see underneath them' (Waddington, 2004, p. 26).

2.3   The aesthetics publishing chain–circle and its explanations

2.3.1   The aesthetics publishing chain–circle-circuit since Renaissance

The illustration chain (introduced and discussed by Banou, 2016) as part of the publishing chain offers the understanding of the development of the artistic identity of the book and in general of the publishing activity; at the same time it provides a tool for exhibiting the image–text relationship, the publishing values, as well as marketing concepts, decision making and reader–consumer issues.

We will introduce the 'aesthetics publishing chain', which is broader than the illustration one in its concept. Issues as reader engagement, promotion methods, the role of academies, reading culture, scholar communication, convergence of media, concepts of the audience, the book market, patronage, competition, the art of the era are embedded in the chain-circle-circuit. The development of the 'aesthetics publishing chain-circle-circuit', from Renaissance and the Baroque era to the Digital Age can offer a key and a tool not only for the understanding and explanation but also for the development of strategies and policies nowadays. It is broader than the illustration chain as it deals and includes (1) the visual identity of the book as a whole: illustration, decoration/ornamentation in all parts of the book, cover and visual paratext (title-page, frontispiece, colophon, etc.) and (2) the typology and the process of the making of the book and the page as visual object.

Whether text focused (Jung, 2015, p. 16) or image focused (and that is a complex matter), the visual tools (illustration, decoration, cover, title page, frontispiece, etc.) as marketing mediums/devices have been a worthwhile investment. Thus, different functions for different audiences and kinds of text have always been exploited by the publishers.

The first printed books resembled the manuscript ones which were the only known, familiar, used books for the already existing and mainly powerful (politically and religiously) reading audience. But even from the beginning the printed book, as it was a different product implying different organization and structure for its production, promotion and sales, started to gain specific physical identity. 'These conventions were carried over from scribal culture to print culture, virtually from its very beginnings. But printers developed their own strategies that quickly departed from manuscript models' (Sherman, 2007, p. 71). For example, the title page and front matter as well as back matter (Sherman, 2011) are among the main features used for practical, artistic, decorative, advertising and information patterns. In general, the typology of the book as material object provided promotion and advertisement encouraging and inspiring reading and consumer behaviour, developing at the same time taste. As a material object, the book was and could be considered a work of art, a valuable object for different audiences and for bibliophiles who were often forced to be more engaged and dynamic.

Certainly the book had and has to be **marketable, apart from being desirable and readable**. Publishers knew who the target group was each time according to the kind of text, the specific conditions and the competition.

On the one hand, the publisher–author–artist (and in a few cases the patron) decided and introduced; on the other, readers enjoyed, read, imagined, understood, learnt, communicated, were informed, their taste and behaviour being developed in that framework. Even though, things were never such simple, the reading audience, through its needs, expectations and desires had always a central role in demanding, even asking, for specific texts in specific language and with 'proper' images and ornaments. The role of academies and universities as well as other communities and networks is to be further noted. Additionally, libraries (of universities, noblemen, monasteries, papal, etc.), private and the first 'public' ones (such as the Marciana Library in Venice and the Ambrosiana in Milan) often through patronage, acquisitions and their policies,

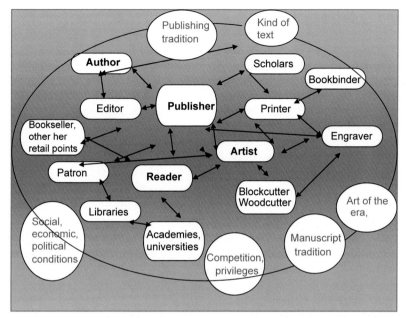

Scheme 2.1 The aesthetics publishing chain-circle-circuit in Renaissance and the Baroque Age.

developed specific synergies and collaborations gaining issues of networking, prestige, access, communication and research.

In the aesthetics publishing chain-circle-circuit (Scheme 2.1), we can recognize a second, smaller one regarding the artist's work in a collaborative network established between block cutters, printers, engravers where the role of the publisher and the author have to be specifically investigated. This 'artist's' chain-circuit included in the aesthetics one may be developed according to the place and time as well as to ways of working, collaborations, commissions. Apart from bookstores and other retail points, libraries and the role of academies, networks, societies have to be noted.

Regarding the reading audience of the first decades and centuries of printing, we could distinguish it in two categories:

1. **Passive** (mainly popular reading audience): through demand and expectations in content, images and price those readers took their role in the publishing process.
2. **Dynamic**, or more dynamic, such as humanist scholars, noblemen, cardinals, bishops, bibliophiles (being patrons often). The role of the patron has to be further discussed concerning the grade and the ways to which they intervened in the publishing process.

From passive to dynamic: The first category becomes more dynamic as its role is emerging due to economic, political, social, educational and cultural reasons. Reader engagement gradually had been encouraged for culminating in the 19th century, during the Industrial Revolution, when new dynamic reading groups emerged (women, workers, children). Furthermore, the role of the reading audience that extended to academies, networks, reading societies is also of value.

Initially, hand illumination was used to decorate a few copies, approximately 10–12 per edition – not of all the editions but of those that interested the specific reading audience of noblemen and of religious power – but since there are no data we cannot be sure of the numbers (Armstrong, 1991). These copies were printed either on parchment (very few) or on paper of better quality or of different colour (Zappella, 2001, p. 133–136) in order to be hand illuminated and specially bound so that they could (1) be offered as gifts from the publishers/printers or (2) be commissioned by the collectors mainly to booksellers of the era.

Since the first decades of printing, woodcuts were adopted for the illustration and ornamentation of the printed books bringing a 'revolution' in the development of taste; the democratization that typography brought about was not only to the text but also extended to the images and to the typology and aesthetics of the book, as referred above. Illustration and ornamentation explored and exploited the opportunities provided by technology of the era so as to develop the quality of the book and augment sales and success. Furthermore, the bedrock of typography seems to be that it provided a democratic, easy to use, cheap to acquire, simple to reproduce, friendly product for the information, education and entertainment of the people. From this point of view, the development of taste to large communities of readers is undoubtable, although difficult for data to be found and studied.

Apart from taste, it is also significant that typography provided the opportunity of owning books and of owning a potential art object. The feeling of owning the book is strong enough and significant for the reader even nowadays. The emotional attachment to the printed copy which apart from being desirable and aesthetically good obtains a personal story (the specific copy that we have read, bought, offered or being offered as a gift, underlined etc.) is a strong factor for the use of the printed material (Janzen-Kooistra, 2011). During Renaissance, for the popular reading audience the printed books were generally valuable objects; probably someone could own a couple of books or a dozen of books. It is noteworthy to mention the Menoccio case as described and studied by Ginzburg (2009). Menocchio, a poor mill worker, having been sentenced to death and executed for reading prohibited books in a small village in Friuli in Northern Italy, possessed approximately a dozen books. Some of them have been bought, some were borrowed by others, some were destroyed when investigation began (Ginzburg, 2009).

Printed books as material objects were developed according, but not only, to the taste and expectations of the readers. The book was a different medium from the manuscript in its production and distribution: it was a mass product, a democratized medium that definitely did not upon patrons, a commodity that also advertized its existence. Printers–publishers were businessmen and managers who started to systemize and protect their activity (the *Universita' dei Librai a dei Stampatori* in Venice is a good example). Although some of them, especially during the first decades of printing, aspired to have financial and other support from wealthy noblemen and from the church, printers–publishers were or tried to be independent. The book was an information medium and as such had its own dynamic role.

What 'public taste' means in those centuries regarding printed books is rather a complex issue under the consideration that consciousness of class and of sex was gradually achieved. During Renaissance and the Baroque, each category of the reading audience had its own treatment from the publishers developed by its own needs, expectations and desires; the printed book was also a mirror of the reader serving to his/her prestige and self-consciousness. We use to think of ours as a complex and unique environment tending to forget that people of Renaissance and the Baroque had great and significant changes in a constantly by then changing world.

Undeniably, the artistic identity of the book explains issues of consumption, aesthetics and taste. Nowadays, aesthetics in the publishing industry, regarding both printed books and new forms of publications (ebooks, virtual publications) that are not tangible, has to do not only with the artistic identity of the book itself and the consideration of beautiful, but also with consumer behaviour, the development of taste, the emergence of tastemakers, the book market, promotion strategies and the impact of best sellers.

Obviously, the publishing aesthetics chain-circle-circuit nowadays, including new and experimental multimedia technologies, has further been broadened and has an augmented role in decisions and policy making. Furthermore, participation/engagement of the reader in the development of the artistic identity is one of the main opportunities and challenges for the publishing companies. The publishing industry has also to consider the following key concepts:

1. Personalized copies that use multimedia and information technology, offering apart from the interactive environment, personalized publishing services to customers/readers.
2. Recommendation technologies. The publisher has to introduce and recommend.
3. Reader engagement/participation in the development of the artistic identity of the book through multimedia technologies, personalized copies and social media/networking. Thus, the book is further being transformed and the publisher obtains a marketing tool so as to communicate with the reader, to get reader feedback, to understand needs and expectations and to satisfy them.
4. Patterns of innovation. Reader feedback and marketing help publishers to offer readers what they need and want. But beyond this, publishing always introduced, discovered and proposed the innovative, shaping thus literary taste and rules. Nowadays, when we are often informed by web pages and social networking, we are recommended and driven to similar titles. That is good, but the element of surprise is underestimated reducing recommendation services to offering similar books. Recommendation and satisfaction of the needs thus should go hand in hand with innovation.
5. Social networking: the role of online communities in the publishing industry,
6. Competition with other media,
7. Convergence of media,

Taking into consideration the above, the aesthetics publishing chain-circle-circuit nowadays is developed as follows (Scheme 2.2).

New stakeholders are to be observed mainly coming from new technologies (multimedia, games, information management, etc.). The publisher maintains a central role, whereas the roles of the agent and of the reader have been upgraded. We have to consider that the artist–graphic designer is still in the middle of the smaller chain related with the design and execution of the artistic identity of the edition; block cutters and engravers have been replaced by game designers, video artists and multimedia experts. It has, however, to be noted once again that changes and new elements have to

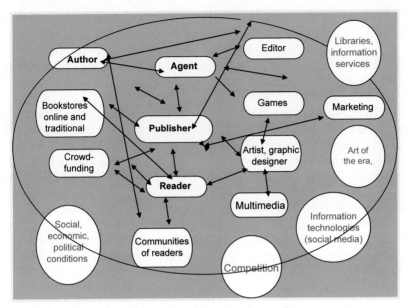

Scheme 2.2 The aesthetics publishing chain-circle-circuit nowadays.

be introduced to and combined with the 'publishing framework'. Words with red are used for factors and conditions set in a wider framework influencing the publishing activity as a whole.

Inevitably, the influence of new information technologies and particularly of social media is of great significance; we should not though underestimate the enhancement of contemporary art, of graphic design, of the development of taste through complex channels and certainly of marketing. Convergence of media takes a key role whereas the competition of media often in the same device (tablet or smartphone) enforces publishers to further compete. In that framework, reader engagement is a major issue discussed in the next chapter.

2.3.2 The book as a visual–valuable–viable object and its historical explanations

Taking into consideration that 'the book was an object which transformed itself into a commodity' (Saenger, 2006, p. 3), we may add that it has always been created, produced, distributed, promoted and consumed as a mass product for the existing and potential reading audience whose needs, expectations and desires were known to publishers or tried to be understood and defined. The printed book had to be friendly, easily accessible, economic, portable, qualitative as text, valuable as material–visual object. The word 'valuable' implies that, although a mass product, whether cheap or not, the book has a specific meaning and a wider concept being transformed for every reader to something potentially unique. Apart from being viable, the book has to be valuable in different frameworks and in different concepts for different people and different needs, often in everyday life.

Art historians usually study editions lavishly illustrated, with elaborative decoration whose artist is famous or ambiguous. *Hypnerotomachia Poliphili* is a good example (Szepe, 1997). But, beyond that edition, Aldus Manutius produced a number of books that changed the publishing policy as a whole and the typographic-visual identity of the book of his era. These editions also changed reading and consumer habits introducing new publishing and business models. His editions were decorated by ornaments that were then used extensively and often repeated, signalling thus a recognizable profile and at the same time developing the audience's taste creating also a decorative and typographic tradition.

Undeniably, *libelli (libri) portatiles*, books of classical texts of smaller size, introduced by Aldus Manutius (Lowry, 1979), developed and established a new publishing, consumer and reading culture; they were claimed to be friendly, cheaper, easily transferred providing to the reader the opportunity of reading it in the time, place, and way he/she wanted. These editions, apart from cocreating new reading and consumption cultures, also developed new aesthetic concepts and public taste through not only decoration and illustration but also through the typology of the book as material object. Familiarity and innovation, tested methods and experiment went hand in hand.

When coming to illustration and decoration/ornamentation, one of the questions raised is how we describe and explain them. The dialogue between book history and art history seems privileged while the interdisciplinary approach is more than challenging. What Baxandall stated, 'we do not describe pictures, but remarks about pictures' (1985, p. 1), seems to be crucial in the description, explanation and interpretation of the artistic identity of the book in all its tangible and intangible forms. Descriptions in bibliographies try to be objective, while stereotypes are sometimes reproduced mainly regarding old books. Additionally, hand illumination in early printed books and the work of the miniaturists has to be studied in a broader framework of art history, book history, history of reading, sociology and marketing. Paratext also offers to us an interpretation of the images and more specifically of the relationship between word and image explaining visual thresholds not only to the text but to the specific edition while it enlightens communication issues between stakeholders.

Thus, apart from the **historical explanation**, we could also use **the technological, the artistic and the communicative explanation** in publishing aesthetics:

- The technological explanation is of high importance especially (but not only) nowadays allowing us to set the framework and to develop strategies exploiting the opportunities provided by the new information technologies, including social networking.
- The artistic explanation offers a privileged point of view for both understanding and introducing strategies having a strong impact on personalized services, encouraging user engagement, and explaining patterns of taste making.
- The historical explanation, as already mentioned, is a necessary tool and a methodological background for understanding trends and issues so as to redevelop them in a hybrid environment proposing models for product development, marketing and promotion.
- The communicative explanation takes into consideration reading and consumer cultures as well as media offering tools for the above.

In this book, all four kinds of explanations are used in an integrated interdisciplinary framework.

2.3.3   Visual information and consumption cultures from Vasari to the digital era

We have also to note that the consumption and culture of prints offered to the artists' fame, whose work was made known and recognizable to the wide audience. On the other hand, prints offered to the publishers profit and fame in a competitive environment. Vasari wrote for Marcantonio Raimondi in the second edition, 1568, of the *Vite*: 'Marc' Antonio, having considered what honour and profit might be acquired by one who should apply himself to that art in Italy, formed the determination to give his attention to it with all possible assiduity and diligence. He thus began to copy those engravings by Albrecht Dürer, studying the manner of each stroke and every other detail of the prints that he had bought, which were held in such estimation on account of their novelty and their beauty, that everyone sought to have some', (VI, p. 96)[1].

Honour and profit are recognized to be twofold of the publishers' values, although later in the same text, a few lines underneath, he blames the publishers for their avarice, interested and focused on profit and not on honour. The publishers as businessmen were often to be blamed for their editions or for the profit they gained; furthermore they were considered to profit by the works of the artists: the latter gained mostly fame and recognition, the former profit and collaborations and other advantages in a competitive environment.

It is though noteworthy that Vasari exhibits the value of the prints as information mediums and devices: 'Many others have occupied themselves with copper-plate engraving, who, although they have not attained to such perfection, have none the less benefited the world with their labours, by bringing many scenes and other works of excellent masters into the light of day, and by thus giving the means of seeing the various inventions and manners of the painters to those who are not able to go to the places where the principal works are, and conveying to the ultramontanes a knowledge of many things that they did not know. And although many plates have been [p 112] badly executed through the avarice of the printers, eager more for gain than for honour, yet in certain others, besides those that have been mentioned, there may be seen something of the good'.[2]

Prints were recognized as mass information mediums offering knowledge and access to artworks in this case.

2.3.4   Information and experience: the old printed book in terms of 'social media'. The case of Peregrinatio in Terram Sanctam

Social and scholar networks were largely based on the printed book which as mass medium, often in a globalized concept, provided, apart from access to knowledge, the framework for experience sharing. The case of the preparation and publication of the *Peregrinatio in Terram Sanctam* by Breydenbach, 1486[3], is indicative.

---

[1] Vasari, Giorgio (1913). *Lives of the Most Eminent Painters, Sculptors and Architects*, v. VI. From Giocondo to Niccolo Soggi, life of Marcantionio Bolognese [and others]. Translated by Gaston Du c. De Vere, available online at Project Gutenberg, http://www.gutenberg.org/files/28422/28422-h/28422-h.htm#Page_89.
[2] Op.cit. http://www.gutenberg.org/files/28422/28422-h/28422-h.htm#Page_89.
[3] GW 5075; BM 15th cent. I, p. 43 (IB.331); Goff B-1189.

It is noteworthy that both the author and the painter (Erhard Rauwich) travelled to the Holy Places so as to write and illustrate text. The creation of the book and its publication has to be considered in terms of almost a diary, a notebook, even an artist's book, of their journey and their experiences; these experiences were regarded as valuable and worthwhile to be shared with the readers. A long time before the web and the social media, before blogs and Facebook, the German clerk (member of the Cathedral chapter in Mainz and then Archcancellarius of the prince electors) Bernhard von Breydenbach had understood, explored and exploited the opportunities of the printed book so as to share and spread ideas and experiences not only by words but also, and equally, by images. The painter Erhard Reuwich of Utrecht who designed the woodcuts travelled with him; the advantage of the edition was that both author and painter had seen and described in words and pictures the places, the animals, the people, the journey so as to benefit the readers.

The edition offers aspects of places and of the experience gained by the two travellers; it must be pointed out that this experience (1) is communicated and shared with the readers and (2) was gained because it was planned to be gained so as to end in the publication of the book. The purpose of the author was to travel, gather, write and publish; that is why he travelled with the artist whose role was to design and prepare the woodcuts. The reader would benefit from the book which was obviously promoted as worthwhile to be bought and read.

The printed book was thus transformed into a medium not simply of communication, information and knowledge but also of gaining and sharing experience. Whether as a substitute of life or as a guide or encouragement to the real journey, the printed book had confirmed its status and power being an ancestor of social media. The edition was thus self-advertised for the lavish illustration executed and created by the artist in the places described.

Every description, of course, presupposes the comments of the author and of the artist. Visual and verbal information is thus offered in defined ideological framework. Ross (2014) writes that 'experience becomes information in the images of the *Peregrinatio* and how the information in turn obscures the complexity and the heterogeneity of the experience and its recording'. The truth of the descriptions and of the pictures is the truth of the author and of the artist who are the intermediaries between the reality and the reading audience. The power of the images tries to ensure the objectivity of the description. 'Through pictorial, textual and material means, the woodcuts are self-consciously constructed as eyewitness views that pronounce their origin in an artist's on site looking and recording', continues Ross who writes about the participation of the viewer 'in the diegesis of the image, when the viewer activates the testimonial force of the view by taking the artist's view as his own' (2014).

In the colophons of all the three editions Erhard Reuwich is named as the printer. Even though, book historians and experts have recognized that the editions were printed with the types of Peter Schoffer, Reuwich's role being thus ambiguous. He could be responsible for the book as material object probably taking care of the printing process – something between editor and artist/graphic designer. No matter the role played by Reuwich, if he used previous prints, he and the author claimed that he was the creator of all pictures.

The book had been a bestseller, translated in Dutch, French and Spanish in the 15th century. The German edition was published 1 year after the *editio princeps* in Latin. It was reprinted 13 times in the next 30 years and it must be noted that the woodcut illustrations were reproduced extensively (Ross, 2014). The success of the vernacular texts demonstrates that the title was intended for a wide reading audience transferring messages and experience. This first travel book was self-advertised in the introduction by the author who proposed the experience of the creators as the advantage of the book and the privilege of the reader.

In 19th century France, the printer–publisher Henri-Leon Curmer produced editions for the wide reading audience; these mass-produced, mass-distributed and promoted books were popular as they satisfied the needs and expectations of the rapidly emerging reading audience. One of the main features of these publications was the illustration. Heavily illustrated literary or historic texts made the book a commodity and a potentially art object for the popular reading audience. Book series, multivolume actually, with a recognizable material profile, helped in Curmer's success. Shelton recognizes that 'thanks to such popularizers and vulgarizers as Curmer, a much broader segment of society was now able to participate in the increasingly commercialized cultural life of the nation' (2005, p. 60).

But going back in time, we can identify Aldus Manutius as the publisher who provided books – both as content and as material object – that were innovative, economic and friendly, considered as valuable by the readers. Numerous other examples led us to the point that the publisher has always been a businessman combining economic, human, social, symbolic and what we call in this chapter 'aesthetic' capital. Although being a printer and a bookseller at the same time during the first centuries of printing, he had the responsibility for all the publishing activity developing the publishing policy of his company and maturing the aesthetics of the book that served also promotion and marketing.

2.4   Reconstructing the book: the value of the paratext

2.4.1   What is paratext?

According to Genette (1997, p. 2): 'The paratext is what enables a text to become a book and to be offered as such to its readers and more generally to the public. More than a boundary or a sealed border, the paratext, is, rather, a threshold or – a word Borges used apropos of a preface – a "vestibule" that offers the world at large the possibility of either stepping inside or rather turning back... The paratext then is empirically made up of a heterogeneous group of practices and discourses of all kinds and dating from all periods which I federate under the term "paratext" in the name of a common interest or a convergence of effects, that seems to me more important than their diversity of aspect'.

By the word paratext we mean both front matter (introductions, prologues, forewords, table of contents, title page, frontispiece, dedicatory letters, table of illustrations, etc.) and back matter of the book (epilogue, indexes, errata, etc.), that is what introduces the text and what comes after it. Paratext has informative, commercial, practical, artistic–aesthetic and advertising value.

Front matter, in particular, epitomizes the contents, declares the value of the text, exhibits the efforts done for the preparation and production (editing, translation, etc.) of the book, promotes the title, points out the difficulties that were overcomed for the edition, enlightens the advantages and value of the edition, encourages the future support from either patrons or subscribers, advertises the future efforts and titles of the publisher. Thus, it defines, and in some way engages, the reading audience and promotes the book. 'The pages of front matter, if viewed in the context of the book market, can be seen as a particularly articulate contemporary sliding edge between the text and the world' (Saenger, 2006, p. 3).

In that framework, Sherman (2007, pp. 68–69) summarizes the term 'paratext' as Genette introduced it and used since then: 'for Genette, the paratext' is a 'group of practices and discourses', mobilized by the 'author and his allies', that 'enables a text to become a book and to be offered as such to its readers and, more generally, to its public'. The paratext is not only distinct from the text but 'always subordinate to it'.

So what is paratext nowadays? Although strongly connected to front matter, it is certainly not reduced to it. The paratext introduces, guides and explains; it also forces readers to participate – being engaged and promotes the book both as content and as material object. Paratext has always presupposed reader engagement, although not clearly outlined. From this point of view, nowadays, it has to be redeveloped and reused in a different environment exploiting the opportunities of new information and communication technologies which provide an advanced framework for empowering its role especially in new digital electronic forms of the book; paratext is the medium for converging technologies, combining opportunities, having a diadrastic impact, enforcing reader engagement. This may be a strong tool for publishers.

2.4.2 Visual and verbal paratext

Initially, we shall focus on the nature, history and development of paratext. It can be distinguished, for methodological reasons, to verbal and visual, both having a strong influence on book promotion and reader participation.

Paratext is:

1. Verbal:
   - Introductions,
   - Forewords,
   - Prologues,
   - Dedicatory letters – epistles,
   - Epilogues,
   - Table of contents,
   - Table of illustrations,
   - Dedications,
   - Half-page,
   - Errata,
   - Index,
   - Comments,
   - Catalogues/lists of books published by the publisher.

2. Visual
  - Title page,
  - Frontispiece,
  - Illustration on both front matter and back matter,
  - Decoration,
  - Book ornaments, borders.

Paratext, according to Genette, consists also of peritext (within the book) and epitext which exists outside the book (p. 5). Thereafter, we will study how the new information technologies can make the epitext, such as book reviews, strongly connected even incorporated into the text so as the reader to have immediate access to it.

Paratext is considered mainly the publisher's responsibility, who decides and organizes it according to the kind of text, the profile of the publishing company, the author, the reading audience, the iconographic and decorative tradition of the text, the promotion that needs collaborating often with the author, the editor, the translator and the artist/graphic designer. During Renaissance and the Baroque era, the role of the patron was of significance in specific editions. In this chapter, the term 'patronage paratext' will be introduced outlining the role of the patron or even better of the mentioning of the name of the patron.

Nowadays, new information and communication technologies have 'revived' the paratext to digital and electronic publications bringing to light new aspects and introducing concepts that often seem new, although deriving from the paratext of the past. Additionally, new multimedia technologies have added value to this, providing new tools for converging and combining different parts of the book as well as parts outside the book. Structural changes may be observed.

In early printed books there is a variety of paratext material both visual and verbal (Smith & Wilson, 2011). As the printed book was its own best advertisement, rich paratextual material demonstrated and further outlined the value and the quality of the book. More specifically, front matter introduced the text, providing information about the author and the content, about its publishing history and the historic conditions related to the creation, pointing out the difficulties of the edition and focusing either on the reading audience and/or on patronage. Thus, front matter, apart from informing and introducing the text to its reader, has also been a promotion and publicity method exhibiting the value of the book both as content and as an object.

Back matter (parts of the book after the text) had a commercial function too. Even though, as it is generally used when the text has been read or during reading (endnotes, bibliography, indexes, etc.), it has a role more focused on the text itself in comparison with the front matter. We can assume, from this point of view, that its commercial value is reduced while the explanatory function is augmented. This balance seems to be changing nowadays as the digital text offers the opportunity of inserting the comments, links, bibliography in the text transforming thus the paratext and updating it so as to meet the needs and expectations of the readers.

Front matter was developed and controlled mainly by publishers/printers and editors. Both visual and verbal paratext has been recognized since the beginning of typography as a privileged area for promotion, advertisement, and building a relationship of trust with the reader. 'Front matter contains intriguing structures which not only introduce a text but also variously epitomize, privatize, publicize, metaphorize, aggrandize, trivialize, and ultimately transform and configure the text, the reader and the patron' (Saenger, 2006, p. 16). We may add that front matter encourages further support (financial support from patrons – distinguished readers, subscriptions from readers) and engagement from readers. Saenger (2006, p. 20) states that 'Information contained in front matter is often unreliable; marketability is the constant, not honesty'. From a different point of view, though, we can add that this information is valuable as it gives us information about the publishing procedure revealing as well, apart from promotion strategies, networks and complicated relationships, ideological concepts and collaborations. Furthermore, it enlightens the book as a commodity and as a commercial object.

In that framework, visual paratext enables promotion of the book by outlining the quality of the book and perhaps the uniqueness of the edition due to a number of reasons, the artistic identity and visual literacy included. Illustrated or decorated title pages, frontispieces and other borders or decorations must be studied not only as supportive to verbal paratext but also of equal and even in cases of augmented significance. From this point of view, the use of multimedia technologies nowadays is continuing this tradition of paratext bringing about new opportunities.

2.4.3 Front matter

It must though be noted that since Renaissance it was not only the title page, but the front matter in general that had a strong commercial, advertising, informative and artistic value being thus one of the main promotion mediums of the era. As the printed book was the medium for access to information as well as for information storage and retrieval, it had to develop its own typology so as to not only disseminate knowledge and information but also organize it.

It is true that the structure and function of the book were rediscovered and redeveloped in regard to the manuscript; title pages, tables of contents, errata, tables of illustrations, forewords, glossary, indexes, tables, headings were part of this organization of knowledge so as to make the text readable and friendly. All the above, being part of both front matter and back matter aimed to offer quick and easy access to information and knowledge. They were tools for the navigation in the text and in the information universe in general. Although some of them have antecedents in manuscripts, there was a systematization and further development of these parts in favour of the opportunities of the new medium and of the needs of the audience. The book had to be readable, useful, marketable, and look good. In that framework, information-seeking behaviour of the first readers was enforced by these verbal and visual tools.

2.4.4 Title page and cover

The title page has to be studied in a broader commercial, artistic, aesthetic, informative framework enlightening current publishing issues in accordance with the art of the period. Much has been written about the title page. Research has been done by Margaret Smith (2001), Lorenzo Baldacchini (2004), and others.

Developed at the printed books, the title page is the child of typography; it did not exist at the manuscript book as there was no need for it. Due to practical, commercial, informative, legal, artistic, advertising reasons, the title page emerged initially as a blank page protecting the first page of the text (Smith, 2001; Baldacchini, 2004). But this blank page obviously was not practical to the printers, booksellers and binders (as they could not distinguish between the editions being thus often confused) neither had any aesthetic value; certainly it did not serve the needs of the reading audience and it did not offer to the promotion of the title. The next step towards the end of the 15th century was for the printers/publishers to print on this blank page the title of the work and the author initially with small, as in the text, typographic characters. And then the title page was enriched and further enriched both verbally and visually, emerging from the blank and being augmented so as to inform (about the edition: author, title, printer, place and time of the edition, editor, translator, illustrator, etc.), to meet the aesthetic needs (through illustration and decoration incorporating ornamental and iconographic types, reminding topics, introducing the theme or the reader), to advertise, to compete with other editions and to reassure the privilege (the copyright of the era).

Thus, the title page (which had the function of the cover by then) had incorporated since its beginning commercial, informative, practical, legal, artistic, promotional and decorative value. Information regarding the edition was emblematically presented outlining the value of the book. The title page is certainly a visual and verbal introduction to the book: apart from the above it had to promise and to reassure on the quality of the edition as content and as material object. The former was achieved mainly by words whereas the latter was obtained by the artistic value of woodcut/engravings that offered visual literacy. Although the title page has to be promising, recognizable, of artistic value, innovative, it should also focus on the tradition; although introducing often new elements and reflecting the art of the era, it has to be useful for the readers. Apart from entry to the text, the cover and the title page are certainly a first guide and a promise having a strong advertising impact. Books are promoted and bought even nowadays to a certain extent by their covers (Matthews and Moody, 2007).

The title page and then the cover were or should be a synthesis and visual representation/synopsis of the ideas and/or the plot of the book. On the one hand, imitation and reproduction of the already used, tested, known and successful iconographic and decorative motives can be observed extensively in Renaissance and Baroque title pages; publishers tended to reproduce the already tested commercially and aesthetically. On the other, innovation and experimentation played a key role; innovation surprises and promises, intrigues the reader and encourages him or her to participate. In a competitive framework the cover has to prevail and often to keep the balance – being recognizable and innovative at the same time, satisfying and surprising.

The cover and cover material in general constitute the external, visual gateway to the book – from this point of view, nowadays publishers have many opportunities and choices so as to introduce and explore. It has to be noted that the transformations of the book and convergence of media mean that the visual introduction to the book is not limited to the cover and title page but expands to the front matter and to material that constitutes the virtual visual paratext.

Illustration incorporates techniques and attitudes. The architectural title page, for example, represents this introduction to the book, as a temple-building of knowledge, information and wisdom: allegorical figures, putti, emblems, books, scrolls, arms, flowers, mythological figures, anthropomorphic motives were largely used so as to be a threshold to the book and to promote it. Publishers/printers did not though commission for every edition a new title page; they used from their stock the existing ones inserting the title and other information. The period, the place and the kind of text were probably the most prevailing parameters for the decision upon the type of the page. Publishers knew from their experience, a kind of "premarketing", what the readers wanted and needed, embedded in the iconographic and decorative tradition.

Questions raised include the following; how much connected to the text were these title pages? Before or after reading the text, readers could understand the meaning of these figures? Obviously, the title page created expectations from the edition in terms of promotion, both for the text and for the artistic identity. The majority of the works, woodcuts or not, are anonymous while even illustrious examples of book illustration such as the *Hypnerotomachia Poliphili* still raise questions both to book historians and art historians.

The privilege of choice for the reader can be also found in Renaissance prints encouraging reader participation. Apart from the point that prints of great artists could be bound together, it is noteworthy that a title page was provided by Lafrery for the edition of the *Speculum Romanae Magnificentiae* 'which could be bound together with prints on Roman subjects, the selection of prints evidently being left to the purchaser' (Gregory, 2012, p. 40).

Nowadays, borders are obviously widened. The cover and jacket, having always been among the factors that determined the success and sales of titles, have been transformed. The cover has to serve the printed, the virtual and the electronic medium. As the majority of people probably come to know the edition initially through electronic bookstores, websites, bookblogs, viewing the book on ebooks, computers, tablets, mobiles, publishers have to face the challenge of creating title pages appropriate for all forms of the publication exploiting the opportunities provided for inserting new elements and developing the aesthetic identity.

2.4.5   Creating celebrities: frontispiece and the author's portrait

The frontispiece as an influence from the manuscript still appears in printed editions during Renaissance, even – although rarely – since now. The inclusion of a woodcut or copper plate engraving at the front of the work had an aesthetic impact, gave authorization to the text, advertised the book, promoted the author. Barchas (2013, p. 22) recognizes that 'for reasons both of custom and cost, the frontispiece portrait quickly evolved into a caste label'.

Coming from the manuscript tradition, the frontispiece in old books is often related to the portrait of the author or of the person to whom the book is focused. The fame and distinction of the person illustrated, the success of previous editions, the relationship with other authors, noblemen, scholars, etc., gave to the reader the reassurance and the confirmation of the quality of the edition. Frontispieces were marketing devices and thresholds for the reader so as to trust, explore and understand text. From this point of view, the visual presentation of the author added value to the edition.

Vasari in the second edition of the *Lives*, Florence 1568, used the portraits of the artists so as to augment their fame, add recognition and embellish the edition having as starting point the traditional frontispiece. Gregory (2012, p. 91) writes that out 'of the 83 portraits for which the resources are known, some 24 (over a quarter) have been altered in a way. Vasari seems, by means of these changes, to have invested some of these woodcuts with visual clues that were intended to convey meaning – meaning related to the content of his biographies'. The comment of Sharon Gregory for the use of portraits by Vasari is revealing for the uses of these images regarding the relation between text and portraits as well as issues of recognition, prestige and fame during Renaissance.

By the printed book the role of the author was certainly upgraded, the work being disseminated to a wider reading audience. Regarding the portrait of the author, Saenger (2006, p. 27) writes: 'are these cases of writers asserting authority, or publishers discovering the writers' names and dignity had become a selling point?', commenting that 'the publisher would not have enshrined any author as an authorial presence unless doing so improved the value of the book, so publishers and book buyers may have had more to do with the widely touted "rise of the author" than authors did themselves' (2006, p. 30). The emerging role of the author was exploited, even developed, by the publishers so as to add value and promote the title whereas communication between the author and the reader was further encouraged.

Publishing was used for creating fame and introducing celebrities; publishers gained both profit and fame. The portrait of the author was multifunctioned; it embellished the page, continued the tradition of the manuscript, reminded the topic, brought fame and recognition to the author, introduced visually the text to the reader, engaged the reader sometimes (especially when from edition to edition this engraving was modified), added value to the edition especially when the author was famous.

The frontispiece in the printed book of the 20th century had almost disappeared surviving and appearing in a few editions that were embellished not such with portraits but with other illustrations. It is though noteworthy that portraits of the authors as appeared in the frontispiece continued in the photos of the authors on covers/jackets of the book. Phillips (2015) says: 'the publishing reality is that readers want to see authors, and authors need to be seen in order to sell their books whether in the media, at literary festivals, or on book jackets'. The photo or the portrait of the author seems to add value and to be connected with the promotion of the book and the relationship built with the reader. It is noteworthy that a new portrait of Jane Austen has been commissioned by a British publisher as the only authenticated portrait of her is too unattractive; Phillips enlightens the case (2015).

2.4.6   The printed page

The aesthetics of the printed page of the paratext material developed so as to be friendly, readable, accessible and desirable in accordance with the technical/technological and artistic framework. Stoicheff and Taylor in their introduction to the *Future of the Page* (2014) referring to the principles of the page's identity and influence distinguish between the page's (1) materials, (2) architecture (the arrangement of information in the page), (3) ideologies (the ways in which the arrangement of information shapes or reflects cultural systems). It is noteworthy that they also refer to information hierarchies: cultures with an ideological investment in information hierarchies produced pages whose organization helped consolidate those hierarchies.

To the above we have to add aesthetics. Certainly, the typology of the page was developed so as to satisfy informative, functional and aesthetic needs and expectations of the readers (Bornstein, 2006). The growth of a specific print and illustrative culture exploited the techniques of the era and implied ideological concepts as well as collaborations between stakeholders. The paratext is a good example; organized mainly by the publishers (and the editors sometimes) for introducing the text to the reader, making information regarding the text accessible, providing a threshold to the context, promoting and advertising the title, bringing fame to the author and other stakeholders, exhibiting in this way patterns of prestige, power, culture and taste.

Bonnie Mak (2011) writes: "the strategies of the page may be simultaneous, overlapping, mutually responsible, complementary, and even contradictory and have been domesticated over a period of centuries, not tied exclusively to one particularly platform or mode of production".

Names of the stakeholders, apart from the title pages, appeared at introductions, prologues, epilogues, forewords, dedicatory letters. For example, the name of the editor (Richardson, 1999) implied the augmented significance of his role which was upgraded, as for example in the editions published by Aldus Manutius. Undeniably the front matter is in the control of the publisher's expressing his values, aims, and publishing policy. There the text is presented and advertised and the intention of making the text accessible and reading easier can be traced among the first editions which also introduced and established parts of the book such as the table of contents.

Taking into consideration that 'western culture has been in many ways crucially determined by the page's materials of information transfer and organization' (Stoicheff and Taylor, 2014), we have to take a look at the typology of the page from an aesthetic point of view. Nowadays the page is constantly being changing. When reading on new mediums, it can be seen that the page has been widened with links, multimedia, audio and visual elements. Its components can be edited, copied, combined, modified influencing thus, apart from the reading behaviour, the emotional and psychological functions of the page and of the book. In that framework, we have also to consider and develop aesthetic policies for the printed book as well which is also influenced.

2.4.7   The printer's mark

The printer/publisher used also the printers' mark so as to visually remind to the reader of the quality and the fame of his editions. Sometimes the printer's mark was the only embellishment and visual element that the title page had, serving thus as an ornament too, often printed with red ink. It is characteristic that printers/publishers reviewed and renewed their typographic marks (Zappella 1988, 1998). The main element – iconographic type was the same having often relationship with the name of the publisher/

printer, but borders or other ornaments were modified. For example, Aldus Manutius had the famous printing mark consisted of the dolphin and the anchor in various ornaments and borders printed differently according to the time, the edition and the size of the book. The printer's mark was a guarantee of the quality that had as well a legal aspect reminding and assuring the privilege/the right to publish the work.

2.4.8   Running titles – page headlines

According to Day (2011, p. 47): 'This space on the page was not deployed mindlessly to reproduce the title of the work or even the chapter headings, but was ingeniously, often wittily and sometimes scurrilously used in a variety of ways in an effort to shape the response of the readers'. Nowadays, in new forms of the book and personalized copies, headlines may serve – in a wider framework – towards the participation of the reader and the redevelopment of the page. During Renaissance, it is true that books shared an economy of forms and of choices combining new technologies with established attitudes; this happens nowadays as well.

2.4.9   Dedicatory letters – epistles

It is noteworthy that paratext tends to create a readership, even communities of readers enabling communication, participation in certain circles and academies, as well as feedback. For example, a scholar could have written after the reading/study of the text to the author or to the publisher for commenting on the edition or suggesting improvements. That was the case of Vasari and Lampsonius. At revised editions often feedback through correspondence was taken into consideration. Scholar networks in Renaissance Europe were emerging and flourishing; the academies offered communication, collaboration and dialogue, as well as reading societies and scientific societies later on. The printed book had been the privileged medium for communication.

Dedicatory letters, epistles were popular in early editions forming a strong and successful promotion medium. Pointing out the quality of the edition (context and image), the work of the printer/publisher and other stakeholders (the editor, for example), the difficulties overcome, they were dedicated often to men of power (political and religious). These dedicatory letters had the advantage of ensuring the quality of the edition, demonstrating the support of noblemen who were further called to continue. In that context, the dedicatory letter was an important promotion tool. Publishers used them so as to reach potential audiences, satisfy the existing ones, augment sales and combat with competition.

Undeniably, dedicatory letters added value to the editions giving a privilege in a highly competitive environment. They were written so as to be printed, to be public; although letters are private, these were intended to be disseminated to all readers. This was not something new in Renaissance culture. Correspondence was published sometimes from the living author so as to gain fame or bring to light several trends or communicate with the audience which expected in turn this publication. The case of Aretino, studied at the third chapter, is of interest. The dedicatory letters, although derive from an older world and reflect the manuscript tradition, served as well the printed book having a strong informative and marketing impact. The private was thus made public and one may wonder for the boundaries between the two; these boundaries seem to be reset and redefined according to the specific cultural and political conditions, by print culture and by the stakeholders.

Nowadays, there is also a convergence of private and public encouraged by new media and social networks. A message or a letter to the author or to the publisher (or to the translator, editor, artist, other reader, etc.) is shared with readers at the social media (such as book blogs) who can intervene as well; from this point of view, we can talk of more interactive mediums where public and private have definitely been redefined and reset their boundaries being ambivalent. Dialogue, collaboration, 'word of mouth', promotion, critic is altered in that framework (Papacharissi, 2015). Thus, apart from the convergence of media we may take as key element the convergence of private and public.

Dedicatory letters had always been oriented to the potential or imagined reader, and social media do so with the already existing readers and the potential ones. In this line of thought, publishers encourage their authors to have blogs, use twitter, be on the Facebook or Instagram etc., so as to communicate with their readers, interact with them, build a relationship of trust and thus promote their books augmenting fame. Furthermore, the authors build a recognizable profile like the one that Aretino wanted to create by publishing his correspondence in Renaissance.

Additionally, the dedicatory letters, as well as introductions, offered to the publisher a medium for creating his profile, developing his publishing policy and be self-presented and self-defined to the audience. The wealth and power of the patron further helped the development and establishment to the public of the profile and of the fame (symbolic capital) of the publisher/printer. In the early years of printing, symbolic capital was been created through various and mainly experimental roads. The erudited ones from the manuscript tradition were not any more sufficient, thus new methods, mediums and ways had to be discovered. The title page, the printer's mark, were among these mediums. Considering also that in the early centuries of printing, the book per se was the best advertisement of itself, the printed dedicatory letters/epistles and the introductions – forewords offered a medium of information and promotion.

2.4.10 Paratext, patronage and book promotion: added value for all

Paratext, apart from introducing the book to the reader, has a more complex and significant role regarding publishing policy, reading and consumer culture. Patronage can be studied as part of promotion strategies but also as a tool for communicating and building communities of readers. Networking was obviously important and complex. We will focus on the impact of patronage in book production, promotion and consumption as presented in the paratext and used by printers and publishers as a means for both promoting books and gaining symbolic capital.

Famous patrons supported editions the number of which was though rather low in regard to the flood of editions and to the abundance of published material. These editions are of significance and of research interest when directly commissioned or produced and used for propaganda or for issues of prestige. But apart from those cases, we will investigate the impact of dedicatory letters, dedicatory poems or just the reference of the patron's name in the paratext (introductions).

We may wonder what patronage exactly means in publishing. Patronage in publishing may be

1. direct financial support,
2. commission for a specific edition with given guidelines,
3. in a wider context, encouragement for the publishing activity,
4. reminding on behalf of the publisher of the previous collaboration and/or of the relationship with the "patron".

Thus, we may wonder on the added value for every stakeholder.

· What did the patron gain?

Fame, respect, promotion, status, aesthetic merit, confirmation for his offer and taste. The book thus was a symbol of status, power, distinction, cultivation and prestige.

· What did the publisher–printer gain?

Promotion, advertisement, publicity of the book and of his printing shop, fame (symbolic capital), recognition, respect, aesthetic merit and distinction.

· What did the author gain?

Promotion, status, fame, respect and recognition.

The reference to the patron, just even the announcement of his/her name (without economic support or other privileges) promoted the title. On building the symbolic capital of the publishing business, the communication or previous collaboration with the patron, even in terms wider than the economic support, offered to the edition a privilege.

Dedicatory letters to patrons had a twofold aim. On the one hand, they aspired to gain material or legal support, and on the other they aimed to gain something more complex, deeper and everlasting: the demonstration of the relationship with a powerful man of politics or religion. This communication reassured the reader for the quality and the high value of the edition as well as for the publisher.

Richardson writes that: 'while the patronage of fine art and of architecture usually depended on an initial commission, in most cases literary patronage involved authors approaching authors speculatively. The author's aspirations to receiving patronage were expressed, above all, in a dedication placed at the start of the work, either in the form of a letter of presentation or woven into the opening lines of the text itself' (1999, p. 51). Relationships revealed between printers–publishers and editors on the one hand and patrons on the other are of research interest and had commercial, ethical and cultural merit. Obviously, typography implied differentiated patronage patterns, and as Finkelstein and McCleery (2012, pp. 73–74) recognize: 'the role of the patron shifted as the rise of mechanical print production encouraged the development of financially viable printed works in the 16th and 17th centuries' referring to the shift in patronage from that of commissioning and controlling to that of promoting, consuming, and distributing.

Later on, during the Enlightenment and the Industrial Revolution, the list of subscribers transformed 'patronage' patterns; the above-mentioned demonstration of communication and support was between different stakeholders in a more democratic framework where rich merchants and middle class bourgeois had their place in the production of book mainly through subscriptions.

As nowadays publishers try to have direct communication with their audiences, their colleagues in Renaissance and the Baroque age, especially in Italy that we often use as case study, had the same aim and strategy. One of their methods was the paratext in which they presented the features, the parameters, history and difficulties of the publishing process with emphasis to the book both as content and object. Translation, the work of the editor, difficulties in obtaining the appropriate manuscripts, the publishing series (when existed or when tried to be created), as well as the printing types, the quality of the paper, the illustration or/and decoration (when existed) were among the topics on which the authors of these texts focused with the aim to promote the title persuading the reader for how useful and nice was. The editor, the translator or the printer/publisher were the ones who usually wrote those texts introducing often not only the book but also the work of the publishing house as a whole.

The book has been – among others – a symbol of power, wealth, cultivation, taste. 'Elites felt the need to communicate their status to others in their own elite group, to other elites, and to ordinary citizens', (Nelson and Zeckhauser, 2008, p. xiv). In that context, the printed book was certainly an effective medium, although not so 'glorious' as monumental art and certainly more difficult to be controlled. Noblemen of Renaissance were often portrayed with a book in their hands so as to outline their cultivation and taste. Some of them had famous, glorious libraries not only due to their bibliophily but also due to status, family tradition, prestige, competition with other noble families. Politics of publishing and complex relationships among stakeholders are among the issues that deserve to be studied.

Additionally, antecedents of reading communities may be traced during Renaissance: attempts in paratext were made so as to develop an often 'between the lines' communication, in which sometimes the anonymous reader was a stakeholder of augmenting importance. The anonymous reader not only through the text but also through the artistic identity of the book became part of the publishing procedure. This 'distant' communication, as time passed, became more specific. We know about communication and letters of readers–scholars to the author, editor or publisher. Furthermore, readers, especially scholars had the opportunity to talk about the edition, review it, debate on it and propose it to their audiences or students or their academies. Later on, the press provided an influential medium for book reviews and dialogue between readers and, between readers and authors in which publishers–printers sometimes intervened.

Moreover, reading societies and reading rooms during the Enlightenment and the Industrial Revolution offered to readers the way to communicate and share. Reading rooms were organized by booksellers or publishers where readers with a rather modest monthly fee could have access to printed material: books, newspapers and periodicals. They usually appealed to the working class and the less wealthy members of society, whereas the reading societies were an expression and institution of the rich merchants and bourgeois whose role was constantly upgraded (Lyons, 1999, 2008). It is though significant that reading rooms in the 18th and 19th centuries apart from access gave membership to the readers who were not just customers, just readers but members of a community that in the late 19th century would be transformed or incorporated to book clubs. We must certainly point out the role of public libraries, as developed initially in Great Britain and the United States, in which 'free to all, open to all' gave not only access to information and to knowledge and also to the society.

Nowadays, the word member regarding the reader is of major significance. He/she is not only a customer but also the member of the community and this is established and demonstrated much due to social media and new information and communication technologies with publishers taking advantage of it in terms of marketing and promotion.

Antecedents of the above, as mentioned, can be traced in the paratext of the Renaissance printed books. Although patronage in publishing had a few things in common with patronage in art, we may point out the differences due to the nature of the medium. The publisher produced a commercial product for the reading audience that tended gradually to be widened. The reader paid for his copy owing thus an information medium with aesthetic merit. Although printing was used for propaganda and promotion of men of politics and religion, the printed book even since the first decades had been an independent, democratized medium that led to dialogue, changes in knowledge dissemination, controversies (Reformation and Counter Reformation), revolutions. It was not easy to be controlled although attempts had been made and censorship can be identified as a parameter of the publishing activity for certain periods (Infelise, 2013). On the other hand, the printed book developed public taste and helped towards what we have called 'democratization of taste'.

A crucial question is if the patron in book publishing had the choice of deciding upon the edition (both as text and context) or if the decision was the printers'. Usually printers offered to the patrons a luxury copy (or more than one), a copy different from the others, printed on vellum or on better quality of paper, hand illuminated and bound properly. The patron received the copy as a gift. Thus the added aesthetic and ideological value of the edition for the patron was decided in a way that went back to hand illumination of manuscripts – a copy different from the tirage. The added value as content depended on the dedicatory letter/poem or on the reference of his name and offer. And this was probably more than enough for gaining fame and distinction between equals, at the elite of the time.

The second issue we must look at is that (apart from the times that the edition had been financed by the patron), his name was mentioned so as to recognize his contribution to the edition not in economic or legal terms but mainly in a more general intellectual, cultural and social context. This served the promotion needs of the publishers and the gaining of the symbolic capital. For example, we are not sure if the Medici had financed every Greek edition of Janus Lascaris in Renaissance Florence – what we do know is the existing relationship between Janus Lascaris and the Medici family that is demonstrated in the paratext of the editions giving information to the readers, reassuring the quality and promoting the books. This relationship between patrons and printers/authors/editors in specific places for specific texts was outlined in the paratext. There was, in the majority of cases, as far as we are concerned, no direct commission from the patron as happened in painting or sculpture or architecture. In printing culture, the patron did not wait for a unique glorious monumental work of art; the best he aspired to was (1) a luxury copy/copies that will embellish his book collection, (2) the mentioning of his name in the paratext being thus identified as a patron of Letters (reminding that the Republic of Letters is indeed powerful).

We should thus consider 'patronage' in publishing in a wider framework that is related with the kind of relationship between the stakeholders and with the benefits acquired. A more specific framework implies the economic support of the patron. A wider concept of patronage implies the information offered to the reader regarding the relationship with the patron. We can name it "obscure patronage". 'In Renaissance Italy many patrons employed both words and actions to communicate self-serving messages. They created an image of themselves that corresponded to, and in turn helped define, the norms of behaviour and appearance in their society. For the affluent and noble, a key aspect of that image was the display of magnificence' (Nelson and Zeckhauser, 2008, p. 5). The printed book was not another work of art but a mass medium which transmitted knowledge and could demonstrated the offer and the 'magnificence', although not always clearly defined, of the patron. 'The system also coexisted alongside a *market economy*: securing a dedication to an important sponsor would guarantee a popular success for an author's composition and work, a significant consideration, particularly from the 16th century onward...' (Finkelstein and McCleery, 2012, p. 72). The message is that of the printer–publisher or of the author and is sent to the reader; in that message the name and the fame of the patron are of particular use. The benefits of the patronage for all stakeholders can thus be traced between the lines.

The message of these 'patronage paratext', beyond recognition and respect to the patron, lies in the communication between the stakeholders and the demonstration of the quality of the edition. Furthermore, through repetition of specific words and phrases, the text created the sense of a community. Multiple networks imply different ways of communicating depended and developed in specific economic, political, social, technological and cultural conditions; the printed books encouraged communication serving also promotion strategies and developing consumer behaviour.

2.4.11   Visual paratext, digital paratext and a comment

The visual paratext must be studied not only in close relation to the text but also as an often autonomous element combined with others and used so as to explain and promote. Apart from artistic and commercial value, the visual paratext has informative, both explanatory and introductory, value. Illustrations can certainly be studied as agents of 'paratextual inscription' (Jung, 2015, p. 3).

Nowadays, the paratext faces many and great challenges due to new technologies. More specifically, multimedia technologies offer new tools and new perspectives so as to redevelop and reconstruct both verbal and visual paratext. Convergence of media and the opportunity of combining and inserting material in the body of the book so as to provide personalized copies, gamified content, etc., lead to new policies. For example, book reviews, context from book blogs, promos, advertisements, photos, games, other texts can be added to virtual publications and to the electronic books. Naturally, major questions emerge regarding convergence, the role of the publisher and of the reader, the permanence or not of these new forms of the book, cocreation, reader engagement, the nature of reading and consumer cultures.

Reading books is certainly not as it was – at least in most of the cases. What has changed is on the one hand the form of the book (being often intangible); even when we read on printed material, reading and aesthetic experiences are redeveloped due to the converged framework in which information and recommendation technologies serve the book. Bhaskar (2015) writes, regarding paracontent, that 'both practitioners and those studying media and publishing need a new language to describe forms of content that exist between content and marketing (276)… By turning paratexts into paracontent, we broaden the range of the paratext and reflect the marketer centricity of the new paratexts…Paracontent is also related to the idea of transmedia, and more generally of "vast narratives"' (278). The body of content is definitely enriched with videos, audios, photos, advertisements, reviews etc. links that form a substantial part of the content as appears to the readers.

The paratext is thus augmented and widened being in the core of both product development and marketing strategies, whereas the influence of contemporary art is of research interest. Jonathan Gray stated that 'Because paratexts help us decide which texts to consume, we often know many texts only at the paratextual level' (2010, p. 26). Social media, recommendation technologies, services from the online bookstores may lead toward this. Taking into consideration that the best advertisement of the book was the book itself during the first centuries of printing, we can nowadays use this as a starting point. For example, electronic bookstores offer access not only to part of the text (paratext mainly) but also to covers, jackets and to the front matter which may have a strong influence on the reader.

It is also true that many times readers come to know a text through tangible and intangible products related to the book. Films, series, music, objects (cups, pencils, bags, diaries, notebooks, games…) set the framework for understanding and consuming the title especially for bestselling books. This '…mania', encouraged and incorporated by the publishers in their promotion policies, creates consumer and reading behaviour. Harry Potter is a good example (Striphas, 2009, p. 2).

Another point is that personalized services and recommendation technologies provide information and recommendation to the reader according to his/her needs, desires and expectations. Thus, the crucial question concerns the element of surprise that will also be discussed in the next chapters. How can the reader explore and discover something new, something that he or she probably did not expect or think? But when he/she comes across, it is recognized as important, introducing something of interest. If we are offered and recommended the expected, do we tend to discover what we expect to discover? The publisher's role is traditionally to innovate, to change, to develop taste, to introduce and 'discover the book whose music is heard when everything is silent' (Feltrinelli, 2013). It is though noteworthy that young people, millennials, insist on reading on more traditional ways (the printed book) and communicating by using new technologies (Cox, 2015).

The uses of text and of the paratext are thus redeveloped and widened implying a range of choices as for example the advanced roles of readers including personalized copies.

2.5 Reader participation and personalized copies: new aesthetic and business models

2.5.1 Personalized copies then and now

The origins of the personalized copies can be traced in Renaissance, when hand decorated/illuminated copies, printed often on paper of better quality or coloured or on parchment, with unique binding, were offered as gifts or commissioned by book collectors (men of political and religious power, noblemen, humanists). Apart from the book as a symbol of power, prestige and influence, the book as luxurious commodity was also prevailing in that hybrid form. Hand illumination derived from the manuscript tradition and expressed complex relationships between stakeholders and different trends regarding taste.

Case study in Renaissance Florence: Eight editions (Legrand, BH, I, 13, 14, 15, 16, 18, 19, 20, 58) of classic ancient Greek texts were published in Florence by the Greek scholar Janus Lascaris and the printer Lorenzo de Alopa during the last decade of the 15th century (Banou, 2000). These classic texts were intended to the humanistic audience of Renaissance (scholars, noblemen, students) and we may distinguish the following:

1. An innovative typology of the page; the comments were printed in the same page, around the text. Text and paratext were thus combined in the same page; although this typology of the page was not reproduced, it introduced though a new type.
2. The dedicatory letters to the Medici. The use of paratext is extensive and strong in terms of promotion, prestige and symbolic capital. More specifically, Janus Lascaris dedicates an epistle to Pietro Medici in the *Anthology*, published in 1494 (Legrand, BH, I, p. 29–38); in that epistle, which was omitted from the copies when the French took over Florence, Lascaris praises the interest and patronage of the Medici family for these editions, as well as for books and letters in general. There is a strong laudation to Pietro, son of Lorenzo the Magnificent. We have to remind that Janus Lascaris was in the court of the Medici as a teacher and scholar; he had also travelled for Lorenzo of Medici to the former Byzantine areas, under the Turkish dominion by then, to discover manuscripts for the famous library of the Medici. The dedicatory letter to Pietro Medici, obviously in the lines of the printing tradition, added value to the edition gaining fame and trust by the readers, whereas the patronage role and interest of the Medici in culture is exhibited.
3. The absence of illustration and book decoration. The aesthetics of these editions have to be explained in the framework of the early printed books in which the initial letters were left blank so as the miniaturist/artist could intervene.
4. Luxury, unique, printed on vellum, hand illuminated, often lavishly, and decorated copies of each edition, appropriately bound, were offered to the Medici family as privileged, unique gifts.

During Renaissance, the printer/publisher offered personalized copies to satisfy the needs and meet the expectations of powerful readers. This was to be abandoned gradually although luxury editions, often with numbered copies, always met the expectations of specific audiences. Woodcuts and engravings were used so as to illustrate and decorate printed books for all readers. But, different title pages serving different needs and audiences may remind of the privilege of options and of the promotion strategies. Additionally, numbered copies or engravings were and are used for specific editions aiming to particular audiences. Special illustration and ornamentation have always been used in terms of embellishment, promotion, marketing, innovation and competition developing the aesthetic identity of the book in the social and cultural context of the era.

Actually, aesthetic/promotion strategies for the printed book can be distinguished in three categories (Banou, 2006):

1. Methods used in unique copies (also called luxury copies):
   - Hand illumination (decoration, illustration)
   - Binding
   - Painted emblems
   - Hand dedications
2. Methods used in a certain number of copies of the same edition:
   - Printing on parchment
   - Printing on a better quality of paper
   - Printing on coloured paper
   - Different title-pages and covers
3. Methods used in all the tirage:
   - Dedicatory letters, introductions, prologues, etc.
   - Title page and later cover
   - Portrait of the author
   - Engraved illustration – decoration
   - Catalogue of subscribers

At the first and second categories personalized copies are strongly related to patronage in all its concepts, whereas at the third category the printer–publisher uses these methods in terms of promotion and advertisement: in that framework, through the name of the patron or of the person who encouraged the publishing activity, the edition gained fame, privilege and seriousness. Furthermore, the printer–publisher called the patron to continue his offer and encouragement.

Nowadays, personalized publishing services have been rediscovered and can be reused so as:

1. to insert personal motives in specific number of copies (personalized copies),
2. to participate and cocreate a certain aesthetic identity,
3. combined with colouring books may encourage readers to continue, finish, redesign, complete the already designed and offered borders/patterns/ornaments,
4. to insert recognizable and tested illustrations, ornaments, frameworks and motifs.

2.5.2 From dedicatory letters of Renaissance to dedicatory copies and editions of the digital Age

Some publishing companies offer nowadays specific publishing services. Usually, readers are informed that they have to take three steps for personalizing the book; for example, these three steps in 'Put me in the story' require the child's name and photo as well as dedication.[4] Thus, both visual and verbal material is required. Personalized services are offered according to the kind of text, the age, the sex, the occasion for offering or creating this book.

Furthermore, platforms and publishing services of that kind provide the opportunity of crowdsourcing and cocreating not only copies but stories, even biographies, dedicated to a friend, college or relative.[5] *StoryTerrace*, for example, provides a '*story making* platform aimed at those wishing to "crowd" create a biography of a friend, a colleague…' (Tagholm, 2015). Gifts are thus no longer offered to the noblemen as in Renaissance but to members of the family or friends, through personalized copies and/or biographies (ghostwritten or not) enriched with visual material provided by the reader who commissions the publication.This continues in a democratized framework the dedicatory paratext and dedicatory editions of previous centuries. These personalized publishing services create a new framework for collaboration and competition widening user engagement and marketing tools. The personalized copies regard both the artistic identity and the content.

It is more than interesting to note that printed books are still and always of value. Practical, emotional, psychological, functional and other parameters explain the coexistence of the printed publications with the electronic and digital ones. Even in younger ages, the printed book is of certain use and value (Cox, 2015). As already mentioned at the introduction, printed sales were augmented in the UK in 2015. 'Nearly twice as many respondents had read a print book (79%) than an ebook on any device – the closest being a tablet (46%). Showing no strong allegiance, young Americans also reported reading ebooks on personal computers (37%), mobile phones (36%) and dedicated ereaders (31%). And, 36% of those polled even spent more money on print books in 2014 than they had the previous year' (Cox, 2015, p. 3). Furthermore, 'millennials mostly discover print and ebooks by word of mouth referrals (45%) and social media (34%), and a quarter of those polled reported finding books through browsing in public libraries and brick-and-mortar bookstores' (Cox, 2015, p. 4).

The opportunity for creating an edition that has the function of a family memoir and of a dedicatory edition brings to light the emotional and psychological attachment of readers as well as the cultural and ideological concepts of the book. By combining storytelling, ghost writing, crowdsourcing with editorial services and multimedia technologies, these specific publishing services revive the interest of the readers. By combining crowdfunding and personalized editions, new technologies offer the opportunity to the publishers to provide unique, specific services to their readers–customers; by enabling them to decide and create or cocreate a novel, short text, memoir, poem for a friend or a relative they engage them in the publishing process. Readers–customers–users decide on the content and the artistic identity too and pay for them (services such as editing, proofreading, graphic design, etc., are required). Continuing thus the tradition of the luxury editions that praised important people or their coronations,

---

[4] This is the case of Source Books providing 'bestselling personalized books for children', http://www.sourcebooks.com/spotlight/put-me-in-the-story-personalized-books-for-children.html.

[5] For example StoryTerrace, v. https://storyterrace.com/and http://publishingperspectives.com/2015/11/storyterrace-crowdfund-private-biographies/.

weddings and other 'important' facts of powerful families, these platforms democratize the old method of dedicatory letters under the magnifying glass of new technologies. It must though be noted that these copies are produced in the quantity decided by the customers for their use only. In that framework, questions regarding aesthetics, multimedia, storytelling emerge.

This is certainly an era of many and various challenges, with pros and cons inevitably. Boundaries seem to be reset influencing the publishing activity and the publishing chain-circle-circuit as a whole. 'New' publishing and business models actually derive from older and tested ones while opportunities and challenges provide the framework for innovation, risk and experiment by old and new publishers. Additionally, the book, whether printed or not, seems to confirm its status and prestige. Being a powerful information and communication medium is still an artistic object of desire bringing about prestige and recognition. Continuing thus its complex aesthetic and ideological roads and meanings since its origins, the book not only survives and coexists in all its forms with other competitive media but also tends to rediscover new roads thriving even in hard times. And according to Calasso (2015, p. 13) times are always hard in publishing.

2.5.3   Reader engagement in the artistic identity of the book

Nowadays book illustration and decoration can be reader focused implying the participation of the reader through appropriate tools, specific strategies, and publishing policies. Apart from reader participation in the text ('Lean Publishing', for example, presupposes the participation of the reader in the creation of content), the chapter will focus on reader engagement in the artistic identity of the book. New information and communication technologies can provide tools so as to offer a successful method for product development, promotion and marketing as well as for gaining feedback from the readers. Among the questions raised we may recognize those concerning the role of the artist and of the graphic design department, the boundaries of reader participation, the enhancement of multimedia and storytelling, the role of the author and of the editor. The aesthetics publishing chain-circle-circuit as developed nowadays (Scheme 2.2) will be further modified in the sense of the upgraded role of the reader; we may also wonder if that is really an active role or a marketing strategy developed by the publisher.

Initially, we may distinguish between:

1. personalized copies from personalized publishing services as mentioned above,
2. the reader's influence on the development of the artistic identity of the edition.

It is true that publishers do have the control of the whole procedure in accordance with the desires and guidelines of the author, the marketing department, the graphic designer, etc., and the publishing policy of the company. Thus, when readers will be called to propose and introduce, instructions have to be given to them so as to cope with problems, use successfully the tools, decide on the options and choices provided, and offer their proposals in a set framework/platform.

One option may be that the reader gives feedback on proposals already made; he/she has options on which to decide but at the same time new proposals are also welcome. That implies an interactive procedure matured through not only tools but also through communication with other stakeholders (authors, publishing company, artist, department of graphic design); this communication can be achieved through specific platforms and social networks. The extent to which these suggestions and proposals would or could be incorporated is a key question.

'The model of the audience in creative industries has evolved from passive consumer to creative producer' identifying 'technology driven affordances that have enabled consumers to become users' (Hartley et al., 2012, p. 16). So, we may wonder: could we come to a stage where artists, departments and publishers decide on book illustration and ornamentation (as always have done) but in a different way proposing and preparing options at the same time, so as to encourage reader engagement for a few editions? Certainly, through communication and reader participation the publisher as well as artists/design departments and marketing departments can gain feedback and better promote their titles. New parameters may be incorporated in the aesthetics of the book and in the publishing chain in which roles are redefined whereas new ones are introduced. The participation of the reader may be seen as a challenge and a tool.

For further understanding, we have to go back in time at the beginning of mass decoration and illustration of the printed book in Renaissance, focusing on strategies and methods regarding luxury, unique hand-illuminated copies. Through differences and common features, an adaptive model of the book as artistic object with or without tangible features may be proposed in the framework of both marketing and aesthetics.

In a wider framework, we may distinguish between the following:

- The use of older, already used motives and iconographic types that may be changed, revived, rediscovered, combined, coloured and altered. The current success of colouring books is of research interest as it will be discussed,
- The introduction of innovative elements and the freedom of the reader to add new ones,
- The provision of options so as the reader to indicate and choose,

Thus, beyond the taste of the publisher and of the author, the taste of the reader is directly expressed. For example, colouring books could be the first step for this: through platforms the publishers can give options for either colouring or redesigning them.

2.5.4 Proposals regarding the aesthetic identity of the book

The reader can intervene through platforms developed by the publishers with the use of social media and multimedia. More specifically, the reader can participate and introduce elements regarding:

- Interactive visual paratext,
- Title page,
- Frontispiece. (1) For example, different photographs and aspects of the author could be proposed offering to the readers the 'privilege' of choice. (2) Crowdsourcing and personalized books nowadays may use the frontispiece in its traditional position so as to insert the photograph or the portrait of the author or of the person to whom the book is dedicated. (3) Frontispiece also may be embellished with other illustrations.

- Photo or portrait of the author,
- Headings, headlines,
- Decorative framework/decorative border with serial patterns using options either from the known ones or innovative. Flowers, for example, or *piccoli ferri tipografici* were a successful decorative method widespread across Europe in Renaissance and the Baroque age. These 'flowers to set over the head of the page at the beginning of the book', according to Joseph Moxon in the *Mechanic Exercises of Printing*, 1684, have been visual borders that define, divide and decorate text. They were used extensively and repeatedly, often without relationship with the text. 'There are visual orders that show nothing', according to Fleming which 'articulate the composition and identity of the entire printed volume as something more than the sum of its parts', (Fleming, 2011, p. 56).

2.6 Reconsidering the boundaries of the book: convergence

2.6.1 Convergence cultures

Certainly, there is a lot of discussion nowadays about convergence: convergence of media, convergence in creative industries, convergence in the book industry and the new forms of the book. Questions that are raised include the nature and impact of convergence, the combination of media, experimentation and competition in the publishing activity as well as the promotion strategies. Beyond these, the development of the book per se and patterns of taste are to be discussed.

Jenkins (2006, p. 3) argues that 'convergence represents a cultural shift as consumers are encouraged to seek out new information and make connections among dispersed media content'. Convergence in the artistic identity of the book means not only innovation, experimentation and new promotion strategies, but also implies continuity between older and new media and concepts influencing communication and taste. It is though significant to note that convergence refers to trends and practices 'within and beyond technology, which describe how individuals connect with their everyday environments through habits of social, political, economic and cultural texture' (Papacharissi, 2013). The same happens in the publishing industry.

According to Hartley et al. (2012, p. 36): 'convergence has three dimensions: technological (when digitization enables the conversion and distribution of content across multiple formats and platform), industry (industry convergence occurs when media and communication media industries merge and form alliances as media conglomerates), and policy convergence is required by those who seek to regulate these rapidly changing industries'.

Convergence in publishing extends beyond the above regarding:

- The book itself, whether printed or not – new information technologies contribute to the development of content and to the aesthetics as well. Gamification, new multimedia technologies (augmented or not), even augmented reality as well as traditional issues are combined,
- The publishing chain,
- Marketing and promotion strategies,
- The publishing policy,

- Media convergence as almost all the conglomerates and large publishing houses combine different products (films, newspapers, music, journals, etc.).
- Reader engagement,
- Interaction between stakeholders. Different media further encourage readers to participate,
- Aesthetics of the book.

Convergence can be traced in all the publishing chain-circle-circuit. We are used to living in digital, converged environment where information is also globalized and converged, where old and new media, producers–publishers and consumers–readers react. 'Convergence represents a cultural shift as consumers are encouraged to seek out new information and make connections among dispersed media content…Convergence does not occur through media appliances, however sophisticated may become. Convergence occurs within the brains of individual customers and through their social interactions with the others' (Jenkins, 2006, p. 3).

Certainly, convergence means different things in different contexts since Renaissance (Briggs and Burke, 2005, pp. 33–40). For example, the above-mentioned and discussed hand-illuminated copies during Renaissance were based on convergence between the manuscript and printed book, combining a new medium with an older one for satisfying specific needs gaining as well issues of power and prestige. Colouring books nowadays imply in a more traditional way interaction used since the beginning of typography. Inevitably, the use of multimedia and gamification in electronic enhanced editions extends the boundaries of the book in a more innovative way. Old and new media coexist, publishers and readers react, printed and digital material interact.

In that framework, relationships and collaborations are redeveloped. Additionally, the art of the era had diachronically influenced the aesthetics of the printed book. Renaissance art certainly influenced the illustration and ornamentation of the book in a crucial period for typography. Art of the baroque era then had its impact on the book creating as well new consumer cultures. In our era of convergence it is inevitable that technology and art (video art, for example) influence the book in all its forms. The impact of convergence has though not to be underestimated in the printed book.

2.6.2   Gamification and other opportunities…

Gamification and the use of multimedia for reaching certain communities of readers as well as for creating new readers are high in the priorities of the publishers. Questions raised regard patterns of promotion, consumption, communication, reading, creation, competition and promotion.

Gamification is a new term used during the last decade so as to define the integration of game mechanics into traditionally nongame environments (Muntean, 2011). Any application, task, process or context can theoretically be gamified. Gamification's main goal is 'to rise the engagement of users by using game-like techniques…', according to Muntean (2011, p. 323). For better understanding gamification, we have to take into consideration what MacLuhan (1997, pp. 237–238) wrote: 'Games are dramatic models of our psychological lives providing release of particular tensions. They are collective and popular art forms with strict conventions… Art, like games, became a mimetic echo of, and relief from, the old magic of total involvement...Like our vernacular tongues, all games are media of interpersonal communication, and they could have neither existence nor meaning except as extensions of our immediate inner lives'. These extensions of our inner lives may explain the use and the success of gamification in books. User engagement, participation, communication, interaction, recognition, promotion and sales are key words regarding the influence of gamification.

Inevitably, the visual part of gamification is of importance for the aesthetics of the book. But gamification is not such a new feature although its use in the printed material was different from that in digital publications. More specifically, trends of gamification have been already tested and used for a long time in children's books although with other name or no name. The combination of both illustration and text with puzzles, quizzes, toys, exercises, pop-ups, stickers, activities has been considered to further encourage reading and thinking, to teach and entertain at the same time. Apart from paper, other material was and is often used so that the child comes to know and understand the world by touching. Furthermore, the child often discovers and is encouraged to reconstruct or continue the story. Often the story/tale is combined with stickers and colouring pages as well as with music and sounds. Pointification also exists as children are often rewarded by the end of the story.

Moreover, gamification is already applied in education and e-learning (Muntean, 2011) making the content more attractive and thus encouraging the readers/pupils/students to participate. Inevitably, educational and scientific publishing take advantage of gamification applying it to educational platforms, websites, virtual publications, ebooks, etc. Tian and Martin (2013, p. 15) wrote: 'As regards changing perceptions of value creation among educational publishers, these are most significantly reflected in visions of an educational paradigm that involves convergence between a range of technologies, content and pedagogies and that provides the level of interactivity and media diversity that is increasingly demanded both by students (as digital natives) and their professors'.

Manuals and cookbooks may also use gamification so as to not only guide and explain but also to engage readers. In cookbooks, the reader can step by step participate in recipes by achieving goals and having rewards.

Games were used in the printed books for the entertainment and engagement of the reading audience. Innovations that were developed in the printed book brought about to the reader new approaches and uses of the printed material. For example, in the edition of *Tristram Shandy*, Laurence Stern (1759–67) 'uses both graphic design and paratexts to test the boundaries of the emerging genre itself, rearranging the conventional ingredients of an 18th century book to challenge readily expectation' (Barchas, 2013, pp. 15–16). Furthermore, the use of marbled paper and of the dedication along with other features was 'manipulating the conventions of print' (Barchas, 2013, p. 16).

As mentioned above, gamification and multimedia technologies, including augmented and experimental multimedia, have an active, ever emerging role in the new forms of the book. In the ebook the boundaries seem to be extended continuously transforming thus the medium. 'Electronic texts are searchable, easily updated, easily distributed, easily analyzed in a 100 different ways, easily manipulable, easily converted into other iterations of themselves' (Shillingsburg, 2006, pp. 28–29).

In that framework, gamification sets various and significant questions related to reading experiences, consumer behaviour, the boundaries of reading and of playing, and the boundaries of convergence as well. One may wonder if gamification turns readers into winners and losers; beyond this, the key question concerns the uses of gamification and its impact on forming the nature of the book and on developing reading behaviour.

Regarding convergence in the artistic identity of the book, obviously multimedia technologies expand the boundaries encouraging often reader engagement. Undeniably, aesthetic along with practical, emotional, experiential, psychological and historical factors (MacWilliam, 2013, pp. 6–10) can be recognized as key concepts in the development and use of the artistic identity of the book, whether printed or digital. Emotional attachment obtained by the printed book is not easily achieved by the new media devices, so publishers have to reestablish as well an emotional–psychological framework based on opportunities provided mainly by technology but which go back in time to tested methods.

2.7   Recalling Renaissance woodcuts: from painted prints of Renaissance to colouring books of the digital era

Colouring books for adults nowadays are thriving (Flood, 2015). This is a trend that emerged rather recently using a traditional old concept: the colouring of prints. In children's books colouring has always been key concept whereas painted prints during Renaissance and the Baroque age were certainly not rare although we use to think of woodcuts in black and white. Colouring books nowadays form a 'new' kind/category of book that not only seems to bring the readers back to their children's age but also offers and promises them relaxation and creativity; in that context, reader engagement is augmented although strongly based on traditional methods. The success of colouring books is certainly a publishing bestselling phenomenon, a concept of our era that might be explained by emotional, functional, psychological, aesthetic and social issues and conditions; familiarity combined with creativity, which is exhibited, seems to be also the key words. Undoubtedly, bestselling colouring books reveal readers' needs and expectations, which in turn have been developed and influenced by the promotion and advertisement of these texts.

'The practice of coloring prints was common during the Renaissance and Baroque eras, and modern question about the vintage of the coloring are often unfounded' (Primeau, 2002, p. 50). We can also read of 'painted poems' in the Baroque era, 'in which words have the material function of giving body to a poem, and the form in which words are disposed convey a meaning through the appearances of painted object' (Cherchi, 2005, p. 70). 'Giovanni Pozzi has shown how the description of the palace of senses (in cantos v-viii) is as well a grandiose *technopaegnium* in which words play the role of material pieces in a LEGO game' (Cherchi, 2005, p. 70).

Publishers may use colouring books also as a tool, often converged, for gaining reader participation in the aesthetics of the book. Having these popular colouring books as starting point they may encourage further reader participation in specific printed editions and platforms so as to gain feedback. By promising creativity and relaxation, colouring books offer a different aspect of everyday life. The readers who are called to colour have an active role that reminds them of their childhood.

Going back to painted prints of Renaissance and the Baroque era, 'the addition of paint to linear black and white images, although unexpected to the eye and mind of a print curator, seemed like a logical impulse. Most Renaissance and Baroque art forms, after all, are polychromatic' (Dackerman, 2002 p. 1). Other media exploited colour. But that addition of colour was regarded as oppositional to the art of printing/ engraving devaluing the art of the printed material. Erasmus wrote for the addition of colour in Durer's works that 'if you should spread on pigments you will injure the work' (Dackerman, 2002, p. 2). We may also recognize attempts to wash out or scrap the colour.

In bibliographies the colouring of the woodcuts/engravings is referred as a disadvantage, as a problem that does not let the beauty and the original form of the illustration/decoration of the copy to be revealed. We often though have copies of Renaissance editions in which readers have coloured the illustrations/woodcuts. The comments in bibliographies usually are focused on the destruction of the engraving – but on the other hand we can comment that these hand colourings exhibit reader engagement and the need of the reader to participate, intervene, create, comment, point out. We may consider that colouring prints attempted not only to embellish illustration and decoration but also to 'mark' the copy with the reader's sign, being thus a semipersonalized copy often of no aesthetic but of emotional value. Furthermore, hand-coloured prints may exhibit special aspects of the publishing activity and of the art of each period, although it is certainly an underestimated area in both book history and art history.[6]

Undeniably, there was a convergence of media, a hybrid medium and art form of printed and painted material; that combination was not always 'successive', depending on the kind of text, the period, the artist and the commentator's point of view, the reader and the purpose of the addition of colour. For example, Erasmus argued that painting was inappropriate for the works of Durer, whereas for other artists this could be an alternative.

Dackerman writes (2002, pp. 10,15) 'approximately ten thousand fifteenth century Northern European woodcuts survive' most of which are hand-coloured identifying that 'the colorist often was an individual other than the designer, block cutter, or engraver'. Due to the fragility of paper and of the kind of woodcuts and their use in daily rituals it is assumed that those survived represent only a small percentage of the ones produced and hand coloured. In *The Book of Trades* by Hans Sachs and Jost Amman, published in 1568 in Frankfurt, there is a description of the job of the print

---

[6] For the bibliography concerning hand colouring of prints v. Dackerman, 2002: 3–4.

colourist (briefmaler) who along with the illuminator performed similar professional functions, translated in Dackerman (2002, p. 17):

A briefmaler am I.
I make my living with my brush
And add color to pictures
On paper or vellum of various hues
Or heighten them with gold.
I look with disdain on stencilling;
It makes for poor workmanship
Resulting in a lesser reward

Colour probably means freedom, independence and expression. Through colour specific meaning and added value are given to the copy. Furthermore, the book is not a 'sacred' object but the reader feels that can intervene, even change it. Nowadays, it is produced so as to be changed by the reader. Publishers can further be benefited from this since by providing the framework, the patterns, instructions and options to their readers/customers, encourage creativity and reader engagement as well as communication.

We have to point out that sometimes these coloured pictures are exhibited on Facebook and Instagram at personal pages becoming thus a medium of communication, dialogue, even distinction of the reader. Readers exhibit what they consider to be their personal work, their personal mark or offer that may be recognizable and of value. Even competitions are organized online by the publishers; illustration prizes are awarded to the readers offering to them the satisfaction of both creation and recognition. As these books are shared, networks are established based on the colour and aesthetics of that kind of books. The addition of colour can thus be a useful tool for gaining feedback.

The democratization of taste regarding aesthetics in publishing from Renaissance since nowadays has been transformed many times; the digital era undoubtedly offers the opportunity to the reader to participate in book illustration and decoration. Colouring books come to meet what Hartley et al. (2012: 2) has stated: 'in economic terms, aesthetics have become what is called a "public good". Discovering hidden patterns or messages may give a motive for further participation. In that framework, interaction has also to be recognized as the next step'.

2.8 Why aesthetics in publishing is still important. The aesthetic capital

Undoubtedly, aesthetics in publishing is a reoriented field, a privileged area implying issues of production, promotion, marketing, reception of the text, publishing policy, relation between image and text, consumer and reading cultures, print culture, art of the book, communication, interactivity, reader engagement and communication. The aesthetic capital is a challenge and an opportunity forming additionally a methodological framework for the understanding and explanation of current trends in publishing.

Illustration and book decoration, as discussed above, apart from being a powerful marketing and promotion method, encourage reader engagement both visually and verbally. Even though, the role of the publisher is always the important one (Calasso, 2015, p. 9).

In that framework, we have to think critically on the consideration that 'the determina-tion of taste has shifted from producer status to consumer choice …ironically, markets decide' (Hartley, 2012, pp. 1–2). Certainly, the reader has taken an advanced, upgraded role through new information technologies and social networking. But this engagement has to be discussed and evaluated as part of the publishing procedure and the publishing chain/circuit.

The publisher's strategies and policies exploit and take advantage of new informa-tion, communication and recommendation technologies. Publishers have always been adaptable: innovation, experiment and risk have been among the key publishing values. Nowadays, the publishing companies have proven to be more adaptable than ever. In a competitive environment of convergence of media, social media, self-publishing, open access, communities of readers, publishing companies have managed not only to main-tain their power but also to expand and develop publishing and business models so as to penetrate into new environments. Publishers have taken advantage of the new technolo-gies so as to communicate with their reader/consumers/users, to develop marketing and promotion methods and strategies, to cultivate reader engagement as a powerful market-ing tool. Social media is also a challenge for them, whereas the transformations of the book and the coexistence of printed and digital as well as the convergence of media have led to the widening of the borders of the book. In that framework, the publishing chain is further developed into information publishing chain-circle-circuit as we shall discuss in the fifth chapter.

But beyond tools and technologies, in the core of the publishing activity we may discover not only the possible answers to our questions but also the ideology and meaning of the artistic identity of the book. That core consists of both content and aesthetic discovery. The book is not a static conventional object; it never was. Since its beginnings it reflected and in turn influenced the cultural, economic, political, social and educational conditions of the era. As a mirror of the reader, apart from the exploitation of the technology and techniques, the book between the lines and behind the images had been the magnifying glass of the expected and unexpected, of the known and unknown. The latter is being introduced often through visual material where familiarity and surprise took turns in the leading roles.

Publishing has always been a business, a privileged business, a unique business that could and can incorporate different fields and methodologies and strategies.

Nowadays, aesthetics and marketing seem to go hand in hand in a rather competi-tive environment. The artistic identity, the making of the book aims (1) to satisfy the desires and meet the expectation of the readers, (2) to surprise the reader redeveloping his/her needs and desires, (3) to promote the book, (4) to encourage reader partic-ipation, (5) to provide a marketing tool (through reader engagement the publisher gets customer's feedback), (6) to augment symbolic capital, (7) to develop taste. The artistic capital of publishing has be studied in the framework of the policy and values of the publishing company in accordance with backlist and art of the era taking into consideration the aesthetics publishing chain-circle-circuit.

As reader engagement has become one of the key values for the publishing indus-try, the artistic identity of the book is a privileged area that can encourage and develop reader participation per se and on behalf of the publisher. Actually, reader engage-ment is not so new as it will be discussed in the next chapter. Furthermore, traditional concepts and the typology of the book as known till now can be redeveloped and rediscovered in the context of new technologies. Paratext, as discussed above, is also an outgoing challenge. Going back to luxury unique copies and dedicatory letters, personalized publishing services and colouring books provide the framework not only for the direct communication between publishers and readers, but also for the participation of readers in the publishing chain/circuit.

Reader engagement though should not be studied in accordance only with the reader or with the publisher but with the book per se. In a world of abundance, the book in all its traditional and new forms has to compete with the other media calling the user/reader/customer to discover and read even on the same with other media device, such as the mobile.

Thus, surprise will be among the key concepts of our era regarding the artistic identity of the book. In a world of convergence of media, of abundance of information, of social networking, of competition and recommendation technologies, surprise leads to discoverability and creation. We usually focus on the satisfaction of the needs of the author; recommendations are made by publishers, by online and traditional bookstores, book clubs, etc., according to the profile of the reader; that is correct, useful, convenient and certainly successful. But readers want more, want after and beyond the above to be surprised so as to discover the different, the one that they like much but did not know that they would like it. That element of surprise was always significant in publishing. Regarding the Baroque era, 'a culture prone to attach the highest aesthetic value to surprising readers and spectators must have had a hierarchy of values, different degrees of measuring the level of surprise a creative technique could attain, a scale by which a daring metaphor could be considered more or less dazzling than a difficult acrostic, a complex rapportatio, or a painted poem' (Cherchi, 2005, pp. 63–64). As Calasso says (2015, p. 81): 'But the story of publishing, when looked at closely, is a story of endless surprises…'. In our era, the measurement, the evaluation and the offer of visual surprise (along with the content) can be the step forward for the publishers.

Jung states that (2015, p. 2): 'the illustrations added to editions serve both as intra-textual interpretive markers and as referents to an extra textual economic and cultural world that anchors the subjects represented in the visual and material cultures of art, music, fashion and luxury objects, as well as practices of collection and exhibition'. The book as an object, as a potential work of art – apart from promising reading and aesthetic experiences – is still a symbol of beauty, power and taste. From this point of view, special book markets, such as the gift and the luxury books, still declare the power of the artistic identity of the book.

Aesthetics in publishing goes beyond the aesthetics of the book exploring and expanding to aims, values, policy and behaviour of all stakeholders regarding the visual appearance of the book. The book is an ever privileged distinguished long lasting mass product that can at the same time be a work of art. From that point of view, aesthetics and marketing should be rather considered as privileged collaborators than privileged rivals. Book illustration and decoration had always a strong impact on marketing and promotion as well as on the participation of the reader. It is true that the democratization of taste came about by the printed book and the spread of prints; the conception of the valuable and beautiful in each era was decided through complex roads in which the printed book had a strong influence. The publishers decided and the readers could always, as discussed above, participate and propose. Social and scholar networking (academies, reading societies, book clubs, etc.) and scholar communication created communities of readers which could intervene in the publishing process before social media and information technologies; and certainly marketing existed under the name of experience, or taste or intuition or knowledge of the publishers.

The artistic identity of the book introduces, invites, encourages, enforces the reader to view, or review the text, to understand and discover, to develop in a different way. We will repeat what Baxandall wrote that 'we do not describe pictures, but remarks about pictures' (1985, p. 1). The same is to be applied to books. We describe and discuss concepts and remarks about books, because the visual identity and the aesthetic identity have to be understood and discussed in the wider cultural, literary, social, artistic, educational, scholar, economic and political context. Beyond understanding or receiving or transmitting or transforming the messages of the author, the artist, the publisher, the book seems to transmit the meaning that the reader needs to discover and the publisher has already discovered.

Challenges for the aesthetics in publishing have already been recognized and discussed in this chapter. The methodological and theoretical framework for the aesthetics in publishing as introduced may be of value for introducing policies and strategies. Additionally, proposals made concerning new strategies, tools and methods may lead to new models regarding the aesthetics of the book whether printed or digital/electronic. Summarizing the above-mentioned points, we can end to the conclusion that already tested methods and practices enlighten new roads indicating the way in accordance with new information and communication technologies which seem to encourage and empower older strategies. But technology is not always enough, probably because 'publishing, as a game, is nevertheless fundamentally the same as the old one played by Aldus Manutius' (Calasso, 2015, p. 11). A game of art and business, we may actually add.

References

Armstrong, L., 1991. The impact of printing on miniaturists in Venice after 1469. In: Hindman, S. (Ed.), Printing the Written Word. The Social History of Books. Circa 1450–1520. New York – London, pp. 174–202.

Baldacchini, L., 2004. Aspettando Il Frontespizio. Pagine Bianche, Occhietti a Colophon Nel Libro Antico. Edizioni Sylvestre Bonnard, Milano.

Banou, C., 2000. Notes for hand-decoration in the Greek incunables printed in Florence. Tekmirion 2, 87–95 (in Greek).

Banou, C., 2006. Promotion strategies of the Greek printed book as a symbol of authority from Renaissance to Enlightenment. Tekmirion 6, 99–111 (in Greek).

Banou, C., 2016. From illustration to gamification of the book: re-developing aesthetics in publishing, re-inventing taste in the digital era. In: Deliyiannis, I., Kostagiolas, P., Banou, C. (Eds.), Experimental Multimedia Systems for Interactivity and Strategic Innovation. IGI Global, Hershey, PA, USA, pp. 176–194.

Barchas, J., 2013. Graphic Design, Print Culture and the Eighteenth Century Novel. Cambridge University Press, Cambridge.

Baxandall, M., 1985. Patterns of Intention. On the Historic Explanation of Pictures. Yale University Press, New Haven and London.

Baxandall, M., 1972. Painting and Experience in 15th Century Italy. A Primer in the Social History of the Pictorial Style. Republished 1986. Oxford University Press, Oxford.

Bhaskar, M., 2015. Towards paracontent. Marketing, publishing and cultural form in a digital environment. In: Phillips, A. (Ed.), The Cottage by the Highway and Other Essays on Publishing. 25 Years of Logos. Brill, Leiden and Boston, pp. 275–291.

Blocklehurst, H., Watson, K., 2015. The Printmaker's Art. A Guide to the Processes Used by the Artists from the Renaissance to the Present Day. National Galleries of Scotland, Edinburgh.

Bornstein, G., 2006. Material Modernism. The Politics of the Page. Cambridge University Press, Cambridge.

Briggs, A., Burke, P., 2005. A Social History of the Media from Gutenberg to the Internet, second ed. Polity Press, Oxford.

Calasso, R., 2015. The Art of the Publisher (Richard Dixon, Trans.). Penguin, London.

Cavallo, G., Chartier, R. (Eds.), 1999. Storia Della Lettura Nel Mondo Occidentale. Edizioni Laterza, Roma and Bari.

Cherchi, P., 2005. Marino and the Meraviglia. In: Ciavolella, M., Coleman, P. (Eds.), Culture and Authority in the Baroque. Toronto University Press, Toronto, pp. 63–72.

Clark, G., Phillips, A., 2014. Inside Book Publishing, fifth ed. Routledge, London and New York.

Cox, E., 2015. Designing Books for Tomorrow's Readers. How Millennials Consume Content. White Paper From Publishing Perspectives and Publishing Technology. Available at: http://www.ingenta.com/wp-content/uploads/2014/10/White-Paper-How-Millennials-Consume-Content.pdf; http://publishingperspectives.com/wp-content/uploads/2015/04/White-Paper-How-Millennials-Consume-Content.pdf.

Dackermann, S. (Ed.), 2002. Painted Prints. The Revelation of Color in Northern Renaissance and Baroque Engravings, Etchings and Woodcuts. Pennsylvania State University Press, Pennsylvania.

Danet, P., 2014. The future of book publishing: seven technology trends and three industry goals. Publishing Research Quarterly 30, 275–281.

Darnton, R., 2009. What is the history of books? In: The Case for Books. Past, Present and Future. Public Affairs, New York, pp. 175–206.

Day, M., 2011. Intended to Offenders. The running titles of the early printed books. In: Smith, H., Wilson, L. (Eds.), Renaissance Paratexts. Cambridge University Press, Cambridge, pp. 34–46.

Feltrinell, C., 2013. Senior Service: A Story of Riches, Revolution and Violent Death (A. McEwen, Trans.). Granta Books, London (Paperback edition).

Finkelstein, D., McCleery, A., 2012. An Introduction to Book History, second ed. Routledge, New York and London.

Fleming, J., 2011. Changed opinion as to flowers. In: Smith, H., Wilson, L. (Eds.), Renaissance Paratexts. Cambridge University Press, Cambridge, pp. 48–62.

Flood, A., April 5, 2015. Colouring Books for Adults Top Amazon Bestseller List. The Guardian. Available at: http://www.theguardian.com/books/2015/apr/05/colouring-books-for-adults-top-amazon-bestseller-list.

Genette, G., 1997. Paratexts. Thresholds of Interpretation (Jane E. Lewin, trans.). Cambridge University Press, Cambridge. ed. pr. Editions du Seuil, Paris 1987.

Ginzburg, C., 2009. Il formaggio e i vermi. Il cosmo di un mugnaio del '500. ed. pr. 1976. Einaudi, Torino.

Goldman, P., 2016. Defining Illustration Studies: Towards a New Academic Discipline. In: Goldman, P., Cooke, S. (Eds.), Reading Victorian Illustration, 1855–1875: Spoils of the Lumber Room, second edition. Routledge, London & New York. [first edition, 2012, Ashgate Publishing].

Greco, A., Milliot, J., Wharton, R., 2013. The Book Publishing Industry, third ed. Routledge, New York and London.

Gregory, S., 2012. Vasari and the Renaissance Print. Ashgate Publishing, Surrey.

Halsall, F., Jansen, J., O'Connor, T. (Eds.), 2008. Rediscovering Aesthetics: Transdisciplinary Voices from Art History, Philosophy, and Art Practices. Stanford University Press.

Hartley, J., et al., 2012. Key Concepts in Creative Industries. Sage, London.

Haskell, F., 1980. Patrons and Painters: A Study in the Relations between Italian Art and the Society in the Age of the Baroque, second ed. Yale University Press, New Haven and London.

Haynes, C., 2010. Lost Illusions. The Politics of Publishing in Nineteenth Century France. Harvard University Press, Cambridge, Massachusetts, and London.

Infelise, M., 2013. I libri proibiti da Gutenberg all' Encyclopedie, ed.pr. 1999. Laterza, Roma and Bari.

Ionescu, C., 2011. Book Illustration in the Long Eighteenth Century: Reconfiguring the Visual Periphery of the Text. Cambridge Scholars.

Janzen-Kooistra, L., 2011. Poetry, Pictures and Popular Publishing. The Illustrated Gift Book and Victorian Visual Culture. 1855–1873. Ohio University Press, Athens and Ohio.

Jenkins, H., 2006. Convergence Culture. Where Old and New Media Collide. New York University Press, New York and London.

Jung, S., 2015. James Thompson's the Seasons. Print Culture and Visual Interpretation. 1730–1862. Lehigh University Press, Bethlehem.

Lowry, M., 1979. The World of Aldus Manutius. Business and Scholarship in Renaissance Venice. Blackwell's, Oxford.

Lyons, M., 1999. I nuovi lettori del XIX secolo: donne, fanciuli, operai. In: Cavallo, G., Chartier, R. (Eds.), Storia della lettura nel mondo occidentale. Edizioni Laterza, Roma – Bari, pp. 371–410.

Lyons, M., 2008. Reading Culture and Writing Practices in Nineteenth Century France. University of Toronto Press, Toronto.

MacLuhan, M., 1997. Understanding Media. The Extensions of Man, Fifth Printing. MIT Press, Cambridge, Massachusetts, and London. ed. pr. 1964.

Mak, B., 2011. How the Page Matters. University of Toronto Press, Toronto - Buffalo – London.

MacWilliam, A., 2013. The engaged reader. A human centred evaluation of ebook user experience. Publishing Research Quarterly 29, 1–11.

Marcon, S., 1986. Esempi di xilominiatura nella Biblioteca di San Marco. In: Ateneo Veneto. CLXXIII, pp. 173–193.

Marcon, S., 1987. Ornati di penna e di pennelo: appunti su scribi-illuminatori nella Venezia del maturo umanesimo. La Bibliofilia 89, 121–144.

Matthews, N., Moody, N. (Eds.), 2007. Judging a Book by Its Cover. Fans, Publishers, Designers, and the Marketing of Fiction. Ashgate Publications, London.

Muntean, C.I., 2011. Raising engagement in e-learning through gamification. In: Proceedings of the 6th International Conference on Virtual Learning. Bucharest, pp. 323–329.

Nelson, J.K., Zeckhauser, R., 2008. The Patron's Payoff. Conspicuous Commissions in Italian Renaissance Art. Princeton University Press, Princeton and Oxford.

Papacharissi, Z., 2013. A Private Sphere. Democracy in a Digital Age. Polity Press, Cambridge.

Papacharissi, Z., 2015. Affective Publics. Sentiment, Technology and Politics. Oxford University Press, Oxford.

Phillips, A., 2014. Turning the Page. The Evolution of the Book. Routledge, Abington, Oxon, and New York.

Phillips, A. (Ed.), 2015. The Cottage by the Highway and Other Essays on Publishing. 25 Years of Logos. Brill, Leiden and Boston.

Primeau, T., 2002. The technology and materials of renaissance and Baroque Hand-Colored prints. In: Dackermann, S. (Ed.), Painted Prints. The Revelation of Color in Northern Renaissance and Baroque Engravings, Etchings and Woodcuts. Pennsylvania State University Press, Pennsylvania.

Richardson, B., 1994. Print Culture in Renaissance Italy. The Editor and the Vernacular Text, 1470–1600. Cambridge University Press, Cambridge.

Richardson, B., 1999. Typography, Writers and Readers in Renaissance Italy. Cambridge University Press, Cambridge.

Robertson, F., 2013. Print Culture. From Steam Press to Ebook. Routledge, New York and London.

Ross, E., 2014. Picturing Experience in the Early Printed Book. Breydenbach's Peregrinatio from Venice to Jerusalem. The Pennsylvania State University Press, Pennsylvania.

Saenger, M., 2006. The Commodification of Textual Engagements in the English Renaissance. Ashgate, London.

Shelton, C.,A., 2005. Ingres and His Critics. Cambridge University Press, Cambridge.

Sherman, W.H., 2007. On the threshold. Architecture, paretext, and early print culture. In: Alcorn Baron, S., Lindquist, E., Shevlin, E. (Eds.), Agent of Change. Print Culture Studies after Elizabeth Eisenstein. University of Massachusetts Press, Amherst and Boston, pp. 67–80.

Sherman, W.H., 2011. The Beginning of the End. Terminal paratext and the birth of print culture. In: Smith, H., Wilson, L. (Eds.), Renaissance Paratexts. Cambridge University Press, Cambridge, pp. 65–83.

Shillingsburg, P., 2006. From Gutenberg to Google: Electronic Representations of Literary Texts. Cambridge University Press, Cambridge.

Sillars, S., 2008. The Illustrated Shakespeare. 1709–1875. Cambridge University Press, Cambridge.

Smith, H., Wilson, L. (Eds.), 2011. Renaissance Paratexts. Cambridge University Press, Cambridge.

Smith, M.M., 2001. The Title-Page. Its Early Development. 1460–1510. Oak Knoll Press.

Stoicheff, P., Taylor, A. (Eds.), 2014. Introduction: Architectures, Ideologies, and Materials of the Page. The Future of the Page, University of Toronto Press, Toronto.

Striphas, T., 2009. The Late Age of Print. Everyday Book Culture from Consumerism to Control. University of Columbia Press, New York, Chichester, and West Sussex.

Szepe, H., 1997. Artistic identity in the Poliphilo. Papers of the Bibliographical Society of Canada 35 (1), 39–73.

Tagholm, R., November 23, 2015. UK's StoryTerrace Extends Crowdfunding to Private Bios. Publishing Perspectives. Available at: http://publishingperspectives.com/2015/11/storyter-race-crowdfund-private-biographies/#.Vv44k9KLRQI.

Tian, X., Martin, B., 2013. Value Chain Adjustments in Educational Publishing. Publishing Research Quarterly 29 (1), 12–25.

Thompson, J.B., 2010. Merchants of Culture. The Publishing Business in the Twenty-First Century. Polity Press, Cambridge.

Waddington, R.B., 2004. Aretino's Satyr. Sexuality, Satire, and Self-projection in Sixteenth-Century Literature and Art. University of Toronto Press, Toronto.

Zappella, G., 1988. Il ritratto nel libro italiano del Cinquecento, 2 vol.. Editrice Bibliografica, Milano.

Zappella, G., 1998. Le marche dei tipografi e degli editori italiani del '500, 2 vol.. Editrice Bibliografica, Milano.

Zappella, G., 2001. Il Libro Antico a Stampa. Struttura, Techniche, Tipologia, Evoluzione. Editrice Bibliografica, Milano.

Zappella, G., 2013. L' Iniziale. Vecchiarelli, Manziana.

Reengaging readers, rediscovering strategies

3

3.1 Reader engagement and the emergence of publishing strategies

Reader engagement seems to be among the key concepts and challenges for the publishing industry nowadays. It is true that user engagement is a goal and an aim for industries in a changing world where technology requires and presupposes the information and participation of the user. We have though to consider that 'the term *user engagement* is frequently referred to as a desired outcome of people's interactions with information technology, but this means different things to different people; many people use the term without articulating their definition' (Lalmas et al., 2015, p. xiii). User engagement has certainly technological, emotional, social, informative, aesthetic merit and till now it has been studied to a great extent in the field of information science.

Regarding the publishing industry, reader/user engagement has been defined and discussed as the active participation and engagement of the reader in the publishing activity and chain as a whole; this implies interactivity, participation, information, motivation, innovation, communication and requires business strategies, technological opportunities, publishing policies and convergence of media. Thus, the reader engagement can be traced in different parts of the publishing chain such as promotion, marketing, product development, content creation, literary review, etc., implying communication and interaction with different stakeholders, from the author to the publisher and bookseller.

Research interest for user engagement has been during the last years developed and encouraged as noted by Rickinson et al. (2011) who distinguish between practitioners, service users and policy makers exploring thus 'user engagement in terms of knowledge exchange processes that involve different players, are multi-directional and have strong personal and affective dimensions'. The term multidirectional can also be used in the publishing activity concerning the publishing chain and different functions of this engagement. Philip Napoli (2011, p. 99) writes that 'engagement can certainly mean somewhat different things depending upon the priorities and goals of different stakeholders'.

Certainly, reader engagement is a challenge exploited and used by publishers. The reader seems to become more active and dynamic having the opportunity not only to express attitudes, to make reviews and communicate with other readers, but also to intervene in book promotion, advertisement, content creation and product development. Some even talk of cocreation but we will comment on this (Hartley et al., 2012). It is true that online communities of readers, due to social networking, have transformed the traditional and always powerful 'word of mouth'.

In that framework, questions raised include the way that publishers use, encourage, plan and take advantage of reader engagement; the boundaries of reader participation

Re-Inventing the Book. http://dx.doi.org/10.1016/B978-0-08-101278-9.00003-6

in content creation; the relationships between authors, readers, publishers and other stakeholders; cocreation; serialization; the use of short forms; the limitations of reader engagement; promotion and marketing issues in that context; the role of crowdfunding; the role of the publisher and of communities of readers on bestsellers and on the creation of literary taste; feedback from the readers; list building.

Features of reader engagement may include innovation, communication, interaction and endurability as recognized by Lalmas et al. (2015, p. 5): 'Endurability builds upon the idea that engaging experiences are memorable and worth repeating'. That is a key issue for the publishing industry as well where the publisher aspires to create a relationship of trust with the reader based on direct communication and information; in that relationship the reader develops specific information seeking and consumer behaviour. Although reader engagement is certainly not new, information technologies have revived it giving tools, options and opportunities in often complex and different environments. For example, the publisher gets feedback through advanced reading copies as well as from sharing experiences improving thus marketing strategies.

Initially, in the chapter we will try to define reader engagement discussing its nature and features nowadays. As reader engagement though is not new, we will investigate through case studies its development since Renaissance and the Baroque era. Thereafter, the rediscovery and revival nowadays of already used strategies such as preorders and crowdfunding will be discussed with the aim to look at the new opportunities and challenges. In that framework, the role of the publisher is of particular interest while new business models and publishing services will be pointed out. Consumer cultures, reading behaviour and the creation of taste will also be considered. Thereafter, the chapter focuses on short stories and serialization, whereas other business and publishing models are then outlined with the aim to point out the significance of online reading communities in cultivating reader engagement.

Undeniably, new information and communication technologies as well as recent developments in social science and information management research have an impact on user engagement. The chapter focuses on the themes referred with the aim to understand, discuss and introduce publishing strategies and trends derived from the past of the industry and enforced by new information technologies.

The role of information technologies and social media on building communities of readers is significant. From bookstores, scientific academies and reading societies of the past to book clubs, book blogs and online communities, the reader's role has further been enriched and upgraded being not only user neither customer but a member and an active stakeholder. The point on which we shall focus is how publishers, being adaptable and innovative, exploit these online opportunities so as to better market and promote books, launching thus new business models.

Reader engagement is desirable for the readers who actually seek for different and more active reading and consumer experiences. Motivation for the readers may include the following:

- Communication,
- Interaction,
- Satisfaction,
- Cocreation,

- Being an opinion maker,
- Making reviews,
- Innovation,
- Involvement,
- Sharing information,
- Creating self-reputation,
- Intervention in the publishing activity,
- Social intervention,
- Recognition,
- Curiosity,
- Self-esteem,
- Positive effect (Lalmas et al., 2015, p. 4–5),
- Empathy.

We may recognize five main different points of view for reader engagement:

1. The author's (aiming to direct communication with the reader, feedback from the reader, interactivity, gaining fame),
2. The publisher's (having previously identified readers' needs and by exploiting technology, reader engagement is a means of getting feedback, promoting books, developing marketing tools, developing content and the artistic identity of the book, creating direct communication with the reader and thus building a relationship of trust, augmenting sales. The question is: to what extent the publishing house can intervene to the procedure),
3. The reader's (aiming to the issues mentioned above),
4. The bookseller's (aiming to promote and advertise books, create a relationship of trust with the customer–reader, get feedback from the customer, endurability),
5. The information scientist's–librarian's (libraries have to exploit the opportunities provided by the social media and the trends in reader participation so as to better reach new audiences, empower the relationship with the existing ones, satisfy information needs, further build communities of readers and interact with the community).

Each strategy can be developed and used from these different points of view. The measures though of user engagement, although a key point, it is recognized that are 'still in their infancy' (Lalmas et al., 2015, p. 9).

At the direct communication between publisher and reader, the former uses information technologies and social media (webpages, emails, electronic newsletters, platforms, preorders, personalized publishing services, book blogs, Facebook, etc.) so as to:

- Better inform the reader,
- Communicate with the reader,
- Build thus a relationship of trust,
- Give access to the reader,
- Offer discounts (special offers),
- Encourage the reader to participate,
- Help the reader to be a member of a community of readers,
- Reward the reader in various ways,
- Introduce new technologies to the reader,
- Promote books,
- Understand information seeking behaviour.

At the nondirect communication between the publisher and the reader, the intermediaries are mainly:

- Bookstores (brick and mortar/traditional and online),
- Libraries-information services,
- Book clubs,
- Social media (book blogs, Facebook, etc.),
- Book critics/reviews (magazines, newspapers…),
- Book prizes,
- Other mass media.

In that framework, old methods and strategies are rediscovered and reused empowered by technology. A characteristic example is the revival of preorders, an old strategy adopted by publishers since the 18th century. We can also trace and investigate
through crowdfunding the transformation of patronage and the development of the
subscribers into a more active role.

It is true that during the 18th and 19th centuries, the widening of the reading audience with new dynamic groups of readers (women, workers, children) led to augmented reader engagement. Magazines and newspapers as well as reading rooms and
reading societies further encouraged reader intervention and participation altering
reading experiences and their sharing (Lyons, 2008). Emerging book clubs thereafter further offered a democratization of taste (Radway, 1997), whereas 'free to all,
open to all' public libraries changed concepts of reading and information sharing.
Groups of readers according to the age, sex, profile, needs, expectations, and desires
formed communities and developed specific reading and consumer cultures through
their information seeking behaviour; these communities have now been transformed
to their vast majority to online ones.

Undeniably, reader engagement is a challenge for all stakeholders – certainly not a
new one. The emergence of the reading audience during Renaissance and the Baroque
era and its upgraded role set the wider framework of reader participation in a former,
globalized environment. In that framework, Aretino converges the private and public
sphere in the publication of his correspondence and his popular works so as to establish his fame and to gain profit; this convergence has also to be noticed in the augmenting Renaissance globalization.

3.2   Lessons from the past: reader participation in the publishing chain. Case studies from Renaissance and the Baroque

3.2.1   The case of Pietro Aretino in Renaissance Rome and Venice

It is not just the book as content or as material object that counts; the reading, cognitive and aesthetic experiences had always been significant in developing audiences
and strategies. Communities of readers were powerful and influential even from the
beginning of the printing activity. For example, academies that flourished in Italy

during Renaissance and the Baroque era provided to their members the privilege of communicating, sharing, debating, developing and redeveloping theories and works. This kind of scholarly communication was based, among other factors, on the printed book that seemed to be the mature product of dialogue and interactivity in a humanist environment.

Regarding the communication between (1) readers, (2) readers and authors, (3) readers and publishers, (4) readers and editors (scholars), we may recognize ways and networks of communication such as correspondence (epistles), academies and later on reading societies, literary salons and book clubs. Bookstores and printing shops were also appointment places where scholars and readers met and discussed. We may also distinguish between scholarly communication and communication among readers of other kind of texts.

Furthermore, the book as product and commodity implies and presupposes a degree of reader participation and engagement; this was developed during Renaissance. Saenger (2006, p. 3) refers to textual engagements as 'contemporary ways of under-standing and marketing relations between readers and books'. We can add between readers and publishers as well. Saenger also noted that 'recent critics have increas-ingly been aware that when it comes to tracing a text's influence, we should look at its original printed state, rather than to our idea of what the author intended' (2006, p. 22). Thus, the content and the aesthetic identity of the book, including paratext, are of particular value. The book, apart from being the best advertisement of itself during the first centuries of printing, was also a medium of information and potential interaction. Paratext played a key role. At the second chapter we outlined ways of information and interaction with readers regarding both verbal (prefaces, introductions, epistles, epilogues, dedicatory letters, poems) and visual (title pages, frontispieces, decoration, illustration, borders) paratext.

In Baroque Naples, the poet Giambattista Marino recognized as key value the sat-isfaction of the reading audience whose role prevailed. The poet had to develop the readers' taste and *meraviglia* was mentioned as the way for this. Snyder (2005, p. 86) writes: 'Marino argued that the ultimate judge of the success or failure of a given work was the public, whose favour the poet thus needed to cultivate. How? In a word, Marino explained, poetry was invention: for the invention of dazzling metaphors and concepts should produce meraviglia in the reader's mind, and this intensely pleasur-able emotion should in turn make the text and the poet irresistible for the reading public.'

In that framework, we will focus on the case of Pietro Aretino who had developed a specific and rather privileged relationship with his reading audience. Readers became a vivid and significant part not only of his work but also of his self-presentation and of the publicity and fame he aspired and finally achieved to gain. Aretino is considered among the first, or even the first, professional writer and as Eisenstein has pointed out he 'made all his profit out of a compete publicity and in a certain sense may be considered the father of modern journalism' (1983, p. 228). Certainly, Aretino 'took advantage of the new publicity system' so as to gain fame and profit. In his effort and strategy he empowered and enriched his relationship with the reading audience exploring the opportunities provided by the printed book and the publishing activity.

Aretino, in a letter to the humanist scholar Francesco Alunno in 1537, points out to his communication with his readers and name himself 'secretary of the world': 'As a matter of fact, I do not believe that Rome itself even saw such a conglomeration of people of different nationalities as burst into my house... For that reason, I have come to the conclusion that I am an oracle of truth, since everybody hires me to relate the wrong done to him by this prince or that prelate' (Folkerth, 2010, p. 69). The above, among others, highlights the direct communication between Aretino and his readers, and certainly his effort for self-presentation.

Furthermore, Aretino published his correspondence while still alive gaining thus fame by enlightening trends of his work and giving a portrait of himself alongside with the social and cultural issues of his era. We may recognize two addresses to his letters: (1) the original private addressees and (2) the wide reading audience. It is noteworthy that Aretino (Folkerth, 2010, p. 72) reminds in his letters that maybe they will be published one day transforming thus this 'private' way of correspondence and communication into a mass medium existing in a developing public sphere. The transformation of private into public, the relationship with his reading audience, the convergence of private and public and the introduction of a new mass medium which was the printed epistle are among the concepts to be identified. Terms of scholarly communication became thus terms of the popular reading audience and of public taste.

The publication of Aretino's letters has to be studied in terms of transforming and sharing experience with the readers engaging them in the publishing chain and 'patronage' issues. The author is the creator who incorporates and transforms into a literary work the desires and needs of his audience further establishing the fame of himself. The reader is transformed into a member of the publishing community; it is noteworthy that: 'rather, he publishes his private correspondence as a means of leveraging his claim to the support of wealthy patrons. By publishing letters to and about them Aretino gives his audience the opportunity to become complicit in these power relationships. Each reader can become a part of a public...', according to Folkerth, (2010, pp. 70–71). Information sharing and reader engagement in complex environments further introduced new concepts in the publishing activity enabling readers of different kind of texts, not only of classic works or scholar texts, to form audiences and communities.

In that context, Aretino reinvented himself each time and certainly promoted his works. Furthermore, via the publication of his correspondence he exhibited his activity in a kind of storytelling. Beyond that, he introduced himself as a celebrity: celebrity of his time and for his readers. He was a professional writer with a variety of audiences and book markets. The printing activity provided Aretino the framework and the tools for being distinguished and gaining both fame and profit. Collaborating with the printer–publisher Francesco Marcolini in Venice in the first half of the 16th century, he reached in his lifetime a total of 151 editions (Waddington, 2004, p. 33) of different kind of texts. As the first *poligrafo*, published various works, some of which were considered to be pornographic and so to be censured (Waddington, 2004, p. xxii) giving though fame to him through other than the traditional roads. Moreover, 'exposure is what Aretino traffics in; the public he calls into existence in his letters, and in many of his more popular works, is carefully developed to feed human curiosity…' according to Folkerth (2010, p. 71). He was probably among the first to develop the public sphere in a globalized concept and to encourage the participation, emotional and psychological of his readers.

Through this procedure, readers felt that they participated in the publishing process. Aretino used this so as to obtain fame and profit but also to develop specific works. He is an illustrious example of how the private sphere becomes public, of how readers become involved before the web and the electronic platforms, of how networks are developed; this engagement of the readers created broader networks adding value to the traditional ones. In nowadays terms, we could say that Aretino gained feedback from his existing or potential readers adding thus value to his work; furthermore, he measured his audience of patrons so as to ask for specific patronage. He was promoting his work and profile to every category of readers gaining what he wanted: financial support, fame, money and recognizable profile. The publisher then had to exploit the opportunities created by the author. A letter to his publisher Francesco Marcolini refers to concepts of money, taste and fame. Aretino makes clear that he does not want profit from his readers: 'I hope God will grant that the courtesy of princes rewards me for the labor of writing, and not the small change of book buyers; for I would rather endure every hardship than to prostitute me genius by making it a day labourer of the liberal arts' (Folkerth, 2010, p. 70; Richardson, 1999, p. 91).

In that framework, Aretino's letters and his strategies could be thought as an ancestor of blogs: direct communication, interactivity, dialogue and creation of networks are the main features. He used the epistles/letters so as to obtain a recognizable profile spreading his fame in the popular reading audience; he also exhibited the fact that his work was appreciated by wealthy patrons who paid for it. Readers had the privilege of reading his precious and estimated work at the price of a copy; even better, readers had the privilege to communicate with him and feel that they participated in the process. Understanding the categories of the reading audience, Aretino applied to all of them (patrons, scholars, wide-popular reading audience) with different strategies encouraging further support or participation from them.

The above enable us to understand and explain the developing Renaissance networks bringing to light complex aspects and relations: Communication with readers, scholar networks, public taste, patronage, the role of the author, power and expression, patterns of prestige, terms of 'social media', information sharing, developing networks, convergence of private and public space, even convergence of media as shown in Scheme 3.1.

Inevitably, networks of people were created as reading and consumer cultures developed. It is noteworthy that Aretino in his early works (*La cortigiana, Il marescalco*) encouraged the interaction and relationship with the public with the aim to get feedback: 'the audience should ultimately relate more to the author himself, directly, than to the characters who are his puppets' recognized Aretino (Waddington, 2004, p. 49).

Certainly, self-presentation that almost reaches exaggeration and narcissism has to be counted among Aretino's features: 'I have made every Duke, Prince and Monarch that there is pay tribute to my genius. Since my shop is the place where men from

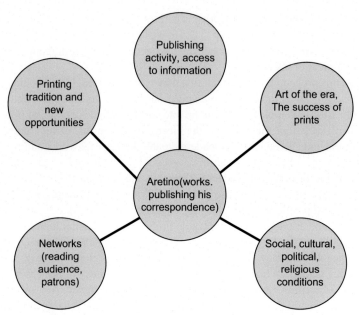

Scheme 3.1 Aretino and his era.

every corner of the globe buy fame.' (Folkerth, 2010, p. 71). But beyond this, he created a culture of convergence and of participation at an early stage. The web nowadays has been considered a public sphere (Papacharissi, 2015) in which convergence plays a key role. This convergence among private and public as well as among localized and globalized was a concept in Aretino's strategies and aims too. New information technologies have changed, even transformed, the media audiences nowadays (Napoli, 2011), but the roots of this transformation may be recognized in the globalized world of Renaissance.

3.2.2   The case of Torquato Accetto in Baroque Naples

It is noteworthy to mention the case of Torquato Accetto, whose treatise *Della dissimulazione onesta* was published in Naples in 1641. The work of Accetto had then been completely forgotten and was rediscovered by Benedetto Croce almost three centuries after his first publication (it was republished in 1928 by Laterza). 'So far no proof positive has been found of any contemporary reaction to the appearance in print of his Treatise entitled *Della Dissimulazione onesta* (1641) and after its publication in Naples with a regular imprimatur, Accetto himself vanished form the view of history' (Snyder, 2005).

Accetto, a member of the Academia degli Oziosi in Baroque Naples, wrote and published his work in a much interesting and challenging place and era. Between the lines of his treatise the social, economic, cultural and political conditions of Baroque Naples in the mid-17th century may be traced and recognized. Under the Spanish dominion, governed by the Viceroy and the Council of Italy, Naples was one of the largest cities in Europe, an economic centre in which convergence of politics and cultures can be counted among the key features.

The author himself recognized that his treatise *Della dissimulazione onesta* was revised and developed years before its publication in the Academia of the Oziosi (Girolamo, 2000): 'ha un anno ch' era questo trattato tre volte piu' che quanto ora si vede, e cio' e noto a molti; e s'io avessi voluto piu differire il darlo alla stampa, sarebbe stata via di ridurlo a nulla' (a year ago this treatise was three times larger than it is now, and many know this; and if I had wanted to differ further its publication, this would have been a way to reduce it to nothing; Snyder, 2005, p. 95). We may wonder if the laconic, even 'minimalistic' style of his work may be attributed to this. At the first edition of 1641, 'nella stampa di Egizio Longo', the 93 paged text was printed in 12° and it is noteworthy that did not have a dedication to any patron.

Accetto admits that the success of his work was not the desirable one. It is also of interest that he names in his text 'public taste': 'Dopo ogni sforzo di *ben servir al gusto pubblico*, io conosco di non aver questo, ne altro valore, e solo ho speranza che sara gradita la volonta' (after [making] every effort to serve well the public's taste, I know I do not have either this or any other value, and I only hope that my intent will be appreciated) (Snyder, 2005, p. 95). The above can be used so as to explain the role and impact that these academies had on scholar works and on research outlining communication and interrelation issues.

Accetto had to face challenges in a complex social, political and cultural environment, in specific and still developing networks (Scheme 3.2): he and the Academy of the Oziosi, he and the reading audience, and in a broader sense he and public taste of Baroque Naples. He also faced challenges regarding his work and position: initially, the creation of his work and then its reception, waiting finally for his audience for centuries. 'In this life one should not have a transparent heart', Accetto admits (Snyder, 2005).

Probably the most important network in the creation of Accetto's work was the Accademia degli Oziosi in terms of scholarly communication (Scheme 3.2); the wider

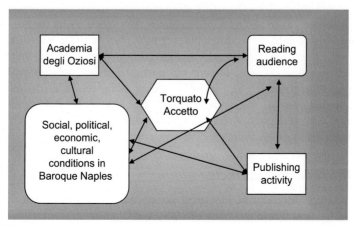

Scheme 3.2 Torquato Accetto: Creation and reception of his work in Baroque Naples.

network was obviously the reading audience of the era whose taste may though be rather difficult to define. Accetto's failure was admitted by himself, although not clearly explained. Snyder argues that Accetto's treatise was written 'in response to a debate that took place within the academia degli Oziosi c.1640' (2005, p. 87). From this point of view, the treatise was targeted to specific audience. 'E percio quantunque a ciascuno sara lecito di favellare di fuore degli ecercitij dell' Accademia, non sera pero convenevole discrovrire [sic] i difetti o gli errori de gli Accademici' ('however legitimate it is for members to speak on the outside of the Academy's proceedings, it is inappropriate to reveal the faults or errors of the academicians').

It is noteworthy that Torquato Accetto decided and proposed as main priority the public taste and the satisfaction of the readers' needs recognizing at the end that he failed to do so. Although he identifies the importance of his reading audience, he does not define it. It is, in that context, of research interest what 'public taste' exactly meant and which was that audience. Considering the kind of text, we understand that public taste was considered by Accetto probably as the taste of scholars, including members of the Academia degli Oziosi and of other academies existing in Italy, noblemen and those who could read a treatise. The popular reading audience, although widening, in a time in which illiteracy was still high, is certainly to be further defined. Public taste, public sphere, reading public: their emergence and development during Renaissance and the Baroque has to be further exhibited. The ways by which public taste was defined and approached by authors and publishers (mostly in paratext material) reveal issues beyond reception related to complex networks between patronage, scholarly communication and mass market.

Regarding the Baroque era, we read that 'a culture prone to attach the highest aesthetic value to surprising readers and spectators must have had a hierarchy of values, different degrees of measuring the level of surprise a creative technique could attain' (Cherchi, 2005, p. 63). This 'surprise', which prevails as a key word (although obviously not the only one or the most significant one), meant rather obviously promotion strategies, list building, and new business models for the publishers. 'To surprise' readers meant innovation, risk and success, meant to introduce new elements regarding both content and object. Books had to be more economic and friendly, combining illustration with content, word and picture, combining the expected with the unexpected.

The transformation of the reading audience took place with the invention of printing and is still continuing. Renaissance and the Baroque are interesting and challenging eras, between mass consumption and manuscript influence, between oral tradition and silent reading, patronage and popular reading audience, hand illumination and woodcuts; in that context, reading habits, consumer behaviour, and printing culture were emerged and established. And reader participation started to prevail altering concepts in the publishing chain–circle.

3.2.3   The reader as corrector

The reader as corrector can be identified among the ancestors of reader participation and engagement. From this point of view, Ann Blair, relating errata lists and the reader as corrector (2007, p. 35) recognizes that in the sixteenth century 'the reader's activity was acknowledged in these instances as producing the final version of the text, which the author tried to direct, although he could never of course control it'. Thus, the participation of the readers was energetic or at least more active of what we usually have in mind; the publisher gained feedback from the reading audience, precious as a marketing tool. This is true in the case of scholarly communication and humanistic - scientific editions where the scholars corrected and shared these corrections-reviews with other readers and publishing stakeholders such as the editor and the publisher.

From this point of view, the errata list was a new part of the book that encouraged readers to participate and offer to the edition. Furthermore, comments on the quality of printing or on the illustration/book decoration helped the publishers and the author to obtain a better result in the next edition. Readers wrote to the publishers and/or to the editors and/or to the authors; in their correspondence they reported, mentioned, indicated, commented, revised, proposed on certain aspects of the edition, of the book as text (quality of the edition or the translation, typographic errors, etc.) and as object (illustration, decoration, printing types, frontispiece, etc.) contributing thus to the development of the edition. Publishers took under consideration the corrections and comments in the revised editions. Thus, readers had a dynamic, active role through

- comments made directly to author/publisher/editor,
- circulation of their annotated copies,
- their teaching activity,
- collaborations with other scholars or communication with other readers.

It is mentioned that 'books annotated by famous scholars were sought out for purchase in learned circles precisely for their annotations and corrections' (Blair, 2007, p. 40). This offers to the history of the book but mainly to trends of scholar communication, and book editing and production.

It must though be noted that 'we have a far greater record of one side of this conversation (what publishers printed) than the other (what readers did to books)'(Saenger, p. 4). Proofreading and corrections in the printing shops were done under pressure and often in difficulties (of time, conditions, noise, collaborations, expertization, competition, etc.). Authors and editors corrected the sheets, whereas correctors proofread the compositors' work before printed.

Nowadays, comments, reviews, corrections, proposals and other 'interventions' to the text are made shortly not only after the publication but even during the publication process. Readers participate to the publishing activity by expressing attitude, deciding, judging, proposing, adding, commenting and intervening. Questions about limitations and boundaries come next.

3.3 Readersourcing

Reader engagement seems to be among the significant challenges and opportunities of nowadays publishing industry. Clark and Phillips write (2014, p. 21): 'Publishers have always published books for people sharing common interests, termed vertical communities…The internet and the development of social media tools have fostered the development of vertical communities, and the connectivity between readers, authors and publishers.'

In this chapter, we introduce the term 'readersourcing' that attempts to attribute and explain the benefits obtained by the publishers through reader engagement. Publishers through readersourcing explore and gain knowledge of the market developing at the same time strategies, tools and policies. More specifically, readersourcing offers the following to publishers:

- Feedback from readers,
- Communication with readers,
- Building relationship of trust with the reader,
- Book promotion,
- Publicity,
- Sales, often direct,
- Effective tool for marketing,
- Discovering new talents and good books,
- Interactivity with other stakeholders (authors etc.),
- Sharing risks.

In that framework, online reading communities, social media and self-publishing platforms owned by the publishers offer to them the privilege of intervention. In a changing publishing world in which new business and publishing models rise, reader engagement adds value to these online business models.

Author – reader communication and interaction (through social media or through traditional ways). The reader participates in the writing process by offering comments, corrections, proposals for the plot (probably among options). The author thus gets feedback and fame, and sets a recognizable profile. This kind of interaction was familiar through correspondence between stakeholders, as mentioned above, or through specific parts of the paratext that had a discrete and privileged role as means of communication and information. In the 19th century, the press provided a new means for communication between readers and authors through published correspondence as well as criticism. Furthermore, concerning novels published in series, in magazines and newspapers, we can also recognize the interaction between readers and authors through the conversations and the dialogue developed especially during the publication and writing process. Charles Dickens and Thomas Hardy are illustrious examples.

Building communities of readers. Free content, recommendation technologies, rewards, serialization, advance reading copies are among the challenging business models for the publishers (Cox, p. 48). Some publishing houses, such as Penguin with the *First to Read* initiative, call selected readers to read advance copies of the publisher's new releases or digital galley proofs. Then, as expected, these readers comment, write reviews and share information for the books on their blogs and other social media. It is important to note that *First to Read* also has a points program in which readers are rewarded with content, discounts or other types of acknowledgement for their participation. Readers can also request a copy; it is important that readers are members of that program. With the motto 'Access the hottest new books – months before they hit the shelves',[1] *First to Read* encourages them, apart from commenting and sharing reviews about the titles, to be members. That is an opportunity for publishers: by offering to the readers the privilege of being members they gain feedback and promote successfully new titles.

Another example is 'Lean Publishing' described as 'the act of publishing an in-progress book using lightweight tools and many iterations to get reader feedback, pivot until you have the right book and build traction once you do' (Armstrong, 2015); the philosophy and the strategy is 'Publish early, publish often'. The word 'early' is of significance since it is combined with reader feedback, with the relationship and communication between readers and authors, and with the revised editions or series published in the future.

In that framework, it seems that nowadays too 'the "eye" of the reader replaces the "I" of the poet affirming the book's human uses and social destinations', as Janzen-Kooistra (2011, pp. 1–2) writes for poetry's materiality in Victorian England, when 'the illustrated book participates in the 19th century process of elevating the image and the reader and detaching the author from his work'. Kooistra focuses on the book as material object which in turn upgraded the role of the reader considering the relationship between the periodical press and the illustrated gift book of the Victorian period (1855–1875). Goldman and Cooke (2016) in their work, after discussing the impact of illustration studies, exhibit aspects of the Victorian illustration.

Building online communities of readers is a key issue for the publishers; through the opportunities provided by information technologies, publishers can further and better develop recommendation technologies taking into consideration not only the needs and expectations of the readers but also the time available, uses of the text, mood and other concepts.[2] By being offered free content, often in mobiles, in serialized form, the reader is engaged and is encouraged to participate not only in the promotion of text but also in its development, both of content and of the artistic identity. The reader is better and further informed receiving alerts and newsletters; in that context, the role of emails should not be underestimated. Membership is significant; apart from being rewarded through advances copies, discounts, competitions etc., the reader has to be identified as an active member in the publishing process outlining the emotional and psychological attachment in a broader social and cultural framework. A step forward, the reader has to be recognized as contributor.

Developing writing communities. Communities of writers are also developed. For example, in *Bookcountry*, a division of Penguin Random House, we read that 'writers find and connect to other writers, workshop their manuscripts, learn about the craft of writing and the business of publishing, and build their audience as they prepare to publish their books'. They can also 'receive comprehensive feedback on their writing from community members'.[3] Publishers thus widen their role extending at the same

---

[1] http://www.firsttoread.com/.

[2] For example, Harvey Ellen (July 20, 2016). Harlequin Dives Deeper into the Reader Behavior With New Mobile App. Book Business. Available at: http://www.bookbusinessmag.com/article/harlequin-reader-behavior-new-mobile-app/.

[3] http://www.bookcountry.com/; About Book Country, and http://www.bookcountry.com/Help/General/About_Book_Country.aspx.

time the boundaries of creation, information sharing and communication between authors.

Reminding vaguely of the academies and scientific communities, these platforms that use the web and social media provide the framework to authors who, apart from communicating and sharing, can gratis get feedback, have editorial advice, review manuscripts, be informed about the publishing process, communicate with readers, develop their work and then publish it 'with a click of the button'. Publishers by creating these communities and offering publishing services engage not only readers but also existing or potential authors altering thus concepts of creation, production, communication, promotion and marketing. By offering self-publishing platforms and intervening in the creation and dissemination of text have advantages. It is noteworthy that self-publishing platforms are not only developed but sometimes acquired by publishers with the aim to intervene, control the process and get access to worthwhile works. Authors on the other hand get feedback from the readers, communicate with them, create a relationship of trust with them.

Discovering talents? Models as the above-mentioned provide the opportunity for discovering talents and books. For example, *Swoon Reads*, a young-adult imprint of Macmillan Publishing, provides the opportunity to users to 'explore manuscript submissions'.[4] In this platform, new talents are discovered, tested already by the reading audience and more specifically by the site's registered users. Decisions are based on comments and ratings (from one to five hearts) from readers who participate in the editorial evaluation process. It is though not clear if these works are published (Alter, 2014).

The question set is if the readers' choices lead to publishable and successful books or if they are a marketing tool; obviously, list-building is not in the hands of the readers but we have to recognize that communities of readers develop and add value to reading and consumer experiences, satisfy the need for communication, interaction, intervention, and at the same time provide a successful tool to the publishers.

Interactivity with other stakeholders. The above-described opportunities lead to interaction between authors, readers, publishers, agents, editors, marketers, etc.

Providing the framework for scholar communication such as *ResearchGate, Mendeley, Academia.edu* ....Researchers, academics can communicate, connect themselves and share papers through these platforms (Chi, 2014). Apart from communication and access, they self-present themselves (as Aretino did in Renaissance). These platforms also, apart from communication, provide access to material often copyrighted. Chi mentioned (2014, p. 348) that 'only 20% of scholars do not use social media professionally, while over 40% of scholars use social media to discover peers, over 45% use it to post their work, and nearly 50% use it to follow online discussions' ending to 'we as publishers are beginning to better understand how users interact with these platforms, which means we can improve our products...'.

Concerning the academia though we can talk for a different and already existing reader engagement. The reader is at the same time or can be a potential

- author,
- editor,

---

[4] https://www.swoonreads.com/read/.

- peer reviewer,
- member of the scientific committee,
- member of the editorial board,
- responsible for series.

Thus, the researcher/academic is among those who decide, recommend, share risks, create, cocreate, intervene, participate, suggest and participate. From this point of view, reader engagement in scholarly publishing is different from other publishing sectors as the role of the reader has already been upgraded. It though seems that publishers push forward the academics into multiple roles, obtaining thus services of high quality (peer review, editing, etc.) usually at low economic cost.

This online connection probably was the dream of scientists and scholars since the Scientific Revolution in the middle of the 16th century. Nowadays, researchers use these platforms interacting with them with the aim to reach their academic audience and promote their work through a developed scholar network. The economy of knowledge presupposes these networks.

'Prior to the internet, but particularly prior to social networks, this kind of network was limited to those with whom you interacted regularly', as Weller writes (2011, p. 7) recognizing that 'whether these are different in nature or are complementary to existing networks is still unknown'. Building networks is identified as of significant value.

Promoting books. Via the above an existing audience is created for certain titles often before they are released, even during their creation. Thus, promotion and publicity strategies use selected readers so as to market books and redevelop word of mouth in a digital environment. We can also add preorders. 'Given the relationship social media enables between publishing companies and their readers there is the opportunity to spread word of mouth (WOM) and identify key individuals who might help promote a title online. By letting interested readers feel engaged and involved with the publishing process of a title, they are more likely to spread their excitement to other users' (Criswell and Canty, 2014, p. 353).

Thus, publishers, authors and readers are further empowered. Online platforms and social media allow readers to create communities, to link to each other, to contribute and share content so as to facilitate and encourage collaboration, conversation, communication, interactivity, even empathy. The key point is that they offer to the reader new reading and sharing experiences defining thus new consumer behaviour and new communication cultures. Recommendation technologies that are constantly redeveloped play a key role.

In that framework, convergence and cocreation have also to be identified. Social media marketing is an opportunity for publishers. As Criswell and Canty (2014, pp. 352–353) write: 'Social media marketing is changing the relationship between publishers and readers. This connection need no longer be dominated by sales, but by mutually beneficial conversation and debate. It allows publishers the platform from which to build the trust of their readers directly, and tailor their output to specific readerships. This new situation also allows publishers to build their brands, because through social media readers use the publishers' pages to access information on titles and authors.'

Thus readersourcing is developed by the publishing companies mainly through a combination of information and communication technologies that converge media and transform recommendation technologies. It enables them to exploit challenges, develop tools and marketing strategies, promoting their books and creating a steady reading audience.

It seems that the publishing process tends to become more open, exposed and immediate. Obviously connected with the public sphere created by new information technologies, the emergence of reading and writing communities derives from the desire and need of authors and readers to unlock, understand, intervene, participate, demonstrate and redevelop. This desire goes back in time and originates in emotional and psychological concepts. But we have to identify that in our digital age borders between the public and the private are reconfined. In that framework, the publishing activity is often exposed and opened to social media where personal taste, opinions, attitudes, experiences are made public creating a culture of sharing. The publishing industry certainly can be no exception in a world of openness and abundance; publishers exploit the borders of accessibility and openness so as to penetrate into new audiences and promote their titles; gaining feedback from their readers is essential. Readers are encouraged to participate and express opinion, intervene and judge, share and write, review and recommend. This public expression and commitment leads to techniques and methods that often, although innovative, derive from the past.

3.4   Rediscovering preorders

A book has to be known before it is launched; it is a matter of competition and of struggling with the time, especially in fiction, as the '6-weeks rule' for the book to stay at the bookstores more than often sets the boundaries (Thompson, 2010, pp. 266–270). In a highly competitive environment characterized by the abundance of information, discoverability is high in the priorities and values. Publishers aim to inform their audiences and promote their books before they are launched. Promotion strategies take into consideration information seeking behaviour of the readers as well as consumer behaviour.

In that framework, preorders have been revived and used extensively during the last years by publishing companies and online bookstores. The reader is informed for a book to be published so as to preorder in order to have it immediately after it will be released.

What does the reader gain?

- Information (valuable in a world of abundance of information),
- Discoverability,
- Immediate access to the publication,
- Probably discount (or other bonus),
- Communication and information in the future for similar titles,
- Recommendation (in the future),
- Gift, offer for other titles,
- Probably being a member of a community.

What does the publisher gain?

- Information for the market,
- Feedback from the reader,
- Sharing risks,
- Sharing cost,
- Direct sales,
- An advantage for the negotiations with the bookstores,
- Communication with the reader,
- Knowledge of the reader profile,
- A marketing tool.

Preorders, otherwise the subscription model, are though not new. They were developed and used in Britain since the 17th century. More specifically, during the crisis that the publishing industry faced in the decades 1640–1660, the publishing companies discovered and exploited new opportunities for the widening reading audience. Barnard (2001, p. 9) dates the development of subscription publication to the 1650a as a model for 'producing large learned books that were commercially unviable... This provided a model that the trade itself was to take up in the later 17th century and that became common practice in the following century.' In a period of riots, religious wars and significant changes in the economic and social life, new opportunities were provided: 'this period saw the development of new genres and audiences. Some of these innovations, such as subscription publication and the serial publication of literary texts, were to be later taken up as trade practices' (Barnard, 2001, p. 11).

During the 18th century, subscriptions were successfully used in Britain (Sher, 2006, pp. 224–235) combining the older patronage concepts with the systemization and commercialization of the publishing process. Sher (2006, p. 225) describes them as traditional or elitist: 'such books were normally published in quarto or even folio, often at inflated prices, and they nearly always contained lists of subscribers, which were headed by prominent members of the aristocracy. The purpose of these books was typically to patronize a worthy (and often needy) author, who received the profits from the subscription as well as a conspicuous display of support in the form of the subscription of the list itself.'

Multivolumed and expensive books were among, but not the only, books published by subscription. As patronage was changing by engaging the 'new' readers, subscription models were developed and flourished in the 17th century. According to Brewer (2013, pp. 139, 135) 'the object of subscription was to secure down-payments on and promises to purchase a book before its publication', whereas 'numerous publishers advanced authors loans, helped to organize subscription editions of their work, and tried to put their financial affairs in order'. The readers paid in advance part of the price of the book (usually the half) and the balance when the book was published, on delivery.

Although their origins go back to the 17th century, subscriptions flourished and became, in Britain and elsewhere, an established method during the 18th century due to a number of reasons including economic, social, competitive and cultural parameters. Lockwood (2001) provides the numbers of subscribed editions: 'by 1701 fewer than a hundred books had been issued in this way. Between 1701 and 1801 the total reached at least 2000 and probably more like 3000' stating that 'subscription published books never made more than a fraction of the total published: perhaps five percent of all new books each year even during the flourishing subscription-book years between 1720 and 1750'. In other publishing industries, as well, such as the Greek (Banou, 2013), subscriptions became a popular method exhibiting aspects of social, educational, cultural and economic issues of the Enlightenment. In that context, emerging methods and strategies were developed so as to adapt to the changing environment.

The reader's–subscriber's name, together with the profession and city of residence, were referred to the catalogue of the subscribers that appeared in the edition, offering thus to the subscriber respect, fame, recognition and social status. In a changing environment characterized by the emergence of specific social classes, subscription was a medium for demonstrating, apart from their offer, taste and cultivation. From this point of view, subscription was a systemized way of patronage provided to those who could financially afford it. During the Enlightenment book subscriptions were used as a popular strategy across Europe engaging the uprising classes of merchants and bourgeois as developed after the French Revolution.

In that framework, the publishing industry further enforced the democratization of patronage by providing systemized ways of financing editions. Rewards were offered according to the opportunities provided, the competition and the available techniques of the era. The reference of the subscriber's name was among the rewards which also included copies gratis, discounts and gifts (such as prints). Subscription lists provide valuable information to the researcher about books and their audiences, reading and consumer behaviour, patterns of production, promotion and distribution.

What did the reader gain in the past in a different way than nowadays? Additionally to what mentioned above, the reader had the following privileges deriving from the reference of his name and the gifts received:

- Fame, recognition,
- Social status, respect, prestige,
- Social influence,
- Discount especially when the copies were many,
- Other gifts, especially prints, maps,
- A mass produced, though probably to a limited number, print–illustration

What did the author gain?

- Fame,
- Recognizable profile,
- An advantage to be used when in the future negotiating with publishers,
- Social recognition, as among the subscribers well-known members of the society were to be found.

Apart from the commercial and business background, emotional, social, cultural and ideological factors have to be identified. But the most significant point and key concept for the emerging classes was probably not information neither access to the text; it was the reader's/subscriber's recognition and fame, the gaining of respect and of social status as his name was referred to the edition at the printed list of the subscribers probably among well-known members of the society. So the subscriber, the one who preordered was not just a customer–reader waiting for his/her copy, but a supporter, a kind of micropatron, and a cultivated reader active in the production and publication whose participation and support were acknowledged.

Furthermore, the copies ordered, for example, from merchants were often offered to members of specific communities. Thus, the reader's role was upgraded in the publishing chain-circle-circuit. Lockwood refers to subscription publishing 'as an intensively nostalgic replication of personal patronage within a publishing system long since operating on market motives – a commercialization of patronage, or even a democratization of it, but in the sense only of a commercially expanded opportunity for lots of people to pay cheaply at being patrons as the old' (2001, stated also in Downie, 2013, pp. 65–66).

Another aspect of the subscription model (or preorders) is the profit/reward of the author. Downie (2013, p. 65) states for the 18th century that 'subscription schemes remained an option both for authors who wish to make as much money as possible out of their work, or for authors who were not in a position to subsidise publication of their works entirely out of their own pockets'. More specifically, women writers used this model in an attempt to reach their audience and publish their books 'in order to generate whatever income they could'.

The reader was informed for the books to be published for which the publisher asked to preorder by

1. the introductions or other paratext material appearing in recent editions,
2. printed catalogues of the printing shop,
3. the press (newspapers and magazines).

These announcements provided information for the book both as content and as material object.

Regarding the book as content among the information and the features exhibited were

- Text (theme, plot) outlining often that it was a useful text, a work of great value from which the reader would benefit,
- Author (famous, recognized),
- Quality of the translation,
- Quality of the edition (scholars, editors named),
- Manuscripts used for the edition,
- Success at other publishing markets, in other languages,
- Reviewed edition (why it is better from previous editions),
- Competition with other titles

Regarding the book as object among the information exhibited we may recognize:

- Illustration,
- Decoration,
- Additional material offered to subscribers, for example, prints,
- Quality of paper,
- Typographic fonts,

- Cover,
- Title page,
- Fame of the illustrator, artist,
- Size of the book,
- The making of the book/edition as a whole, its artistic identity.

The value was thus both in the use of the book and in the book as material object. The quality of the work was outlined often in detail providing information about the stakeholders (publisher, editor, translator …) and the process, referring also to competitive works or to previous editions with the aim to point out the innovation and the value added to this specific edition. Advantages for the readers are also exhibited including both utilitarian (book as content, social recognition by the subscription as stated in the subscription lists) and hedonic concepts (book as material object and probably gifts related to the aesthetics of the book such as prints/illustrations).

Nowadays, the privilege of recognition has been replaced by other privileges focused more on the information needs of the readers, on access and recommendation technologies. Having preordered the book means that the reader will not consume time for this anymore; on the contrary he/she will be benefited by keeping informed and by recommendations done for other similar titles. In a broader concept, the reader – although anonymous – feels engaged to the process enforced often to be a member of a larger online community. Undeniably, the publishing companies get feedback and a marketing tool through preorders. All stakeholders are thus benefited. Furthermore, preorders is an aspect of readersourcing.

3.5   From patronage to crowdfunding

3.5.1   Crowdfunding and the evolution of patronage

Aesthetic, reading, economic and ideological concepts are related to crowdfunding which may be defined and synopsized as 'the collective operation by people who pool their funds, usually via the Internet, to support efforts initiated by other people or organizations' (Dresner, 2014). And, 'it is the idea of people pooling their resources in order to realize a common goal, sharing tasks and responsibilities' (Bruntje and Gadja, 2015, pp. 1–2). Crowdfunding presupposes support and decision, certainly exceeding family and friends by engaging a large number of people who 'pool relatively small individual contributions in order to support a specific goal' (Micic, 2015, p. 13). Micic provides literature review upon definitions of the term (2015, p. 13) recognizing though that 'substantial academic knowledge in this field is yet to be developed in order for consensus to emerge' while Moritz and Block (2015) apart from literature review provide research directions. Obviously, crowdfunding is a transformation and a democratized evolution of subscription and patronage in the digital environment.

The crowdfunding market is still growing and experimenting. More specifically, in crowdfunding in publishing people pool their resources, via the Internet (specific platforms), so as to support the publication of a work. In that framework, though, questions are set regarding the role and relationships between stakeholders and changes in the publishing chain, the quality of the book both as text and as artistic object, reader participation and engagement, the role of social media and online communities, as well as marketing and promotion trends. Crowdfunding is an alternative way mainly for supporting financially the edition, but it goes beyond that. Reader engagement and participation is strong: people may interact, share, offer, propose, intervene and influence. They are informed for every step of the publishing process being active members of an online community that, apart from offering, can also promote, discuss, communicate and intervene. From this point of view, it is a democratized patronage medium deriving from the past.

The origins of crowdfunding in publishing have to be remotely recognized on the one hand in preorders and subscriptions mentioned above, and on the other in current publishing models such as self-publishing. From this point of view, crowdfunding and self-publishing may be assumed to go hand in hand, when it is difficult for the author to publish his work at a traditional publishing company. Storytelling has also to be taken into consideration as well as personalized copies and personalized publishing services. In that framework, the publishing chain-circle-circuit has to be reconsidered.

'Crowdfunding typically contains three participating stakeholders: the project initiators who seek funding for their projects, the backers who are willing to back a specific project, and the matchmaking crowdfunding platforms acting as intermediaries' (Bruntje and Gadja, 2015, p. 10). It is noteworthy that all definitions recognize Internet as the basic tool and medium. Besides, social media influence the decision and behaviour of supporters/backers/capital givers/readers (Gierczack et al., 2015, p. 10). In the past, the basic medium for subscriptions was the printed text, the printed word in introductions and other paratextual parts of books, as well as in advertisements and announcements at the Press. Nowadays, the medium has been changed; it is faster and gives immediate access bringing together authors and readers–supporters. The printed word of the past has been transformed into the virtual word, but it is always a word, a message, a text aiming to gain support and engagement. Aims and values are the same in the digital environment that further and better encourages participation and provides information, managing also small-scale economic transactions.

Regarding crowd we may distinguish between (1) the wide reading audience of supporters–contributors of the edition, (2) friends, relatives, and colleagues of the author. Certainly, communication between the author and the reader is further encouraged, whereas the reader is fluently informed about the publishing process. In that context, information seeking behaviour in crowdfunding is a challenging topic for further research.

Crowdfunding may offer, apart from financial support, feedback to the author and an active community of readers who expect and promote through social media the book even before it is published. Furthermore, it can be proved to be a good marketing tool. Under discussion are certainly the boundaries of reader participation and the degree of innovation of such titles. As Micic states (2015, p. 11): 'crowdfunding can be viewed as more than just a form of financing; it is an important point of reference when estimating the market for future products or services, a source of collective wisdom and feedback during venture development and a foundation for future community of lead users.' Obviously, readers engaged in the edition through crowdfunding have already decided (or think they have decided) on the quality of the publication which share with others. Thus, online reading communities will probably be deeper influenced by this taking into consideration the 'experience' and the choice of the already engaged financially readers.

Pros and cons of crowdfunding should further be outlined and examined according to a number of trends including the expectations created, the quality of the produced book, the participation and communication between stakeholders, the role of editing and the artistic identity of the book. Regarding reader/user engagement, we have to distinguish between the two options that the author has: (1) platform providing direct communication with the reader and (2) publishers that use crowdfunding. If the book is not published, the funds are returned to supporters. But what about if the book was not the one that the reader expected?

Return types vary (Gierczack et al., 2015, pp. 12–13), and can be distinguished in hedonism, altruistic and for profit. The profit-oriented type is difficult to be found in publishing till now. On the contrary, return types and 'profit' of the readers are more connected with preordered products and rewards that range from personalized information, signed or advanced copies to membership. In that framework, hedonism as 'a type where backers pledge for innovative and creative projects… and receive a non monetary return in form of preordered products or rewards' is the most popular (Gierczack et al., 2015, p. 13). Readers are not so much interested in monetary returns but in rewards connected with the value of the book and from membership deriving from concepts of prestige, access and taste.

Crowdfunding encourages the publishing of works which would be difficult to be published otherwise covering the expenses for publishing services, such as editing, proofreading and design of the edition. It is actually noteworthy that these 'traditional' publishing services are high in the priorities of the authors. These alternative publishing models though further add value to services provided by the publishing houses. It has also to be pointed out that the vast majority of self-publishing authors sign contracts with a publisher when discovered and been offered this.

Questions raised regarding the boundaries and limitations of crowdfunding include the following: Why readers crowdfund and what do they expect? Why they cannot find it in the already published works? Are there emotional and psychological concepts or a matter of intervention of deciding in a process and activity in which traditionally the publisher and the editor decided? Is it a matter of prestige for the reader? Thus, crowdfunding as well as personalized copies go deeper to trends related to the relations developed, decision-making, reader engagement, prestige and power, taste and pleasure, reward and recognition.

In that framework, concepts of crowdfunding can be exploited and used in reader engagement regarding social media, platforms and communities controlled by publishers and booksellers. Key point is obviously the recognition of the support of the reader that in turn encourages him/her to be more active and further promote the book. This recognition can be achieved through rewards beyond discounts and gifts that are exploring engagement such as intervention in the plot.

What does the reader gain?

- Participation
- Information
- Engagement
- Rewards: material (copies, discounts etc.), fame
- Access
- Membership to a community

What does the author gain?

- Financial support
- Reader participation
- Feedback from the reader
- Marketing tool. Knowledge of the reader's needs and expectations
- Promotion
- Recognition
- Online community

In the case of crowdfunded personalized copies the production of books is restricted and limited to a specific number of copies for informed and already engaged readers/users (MacWilliam, 2013) who are rewarded not just from the copy, or the participation to the publishing procedure but also from the recognition by the author or of the author who is often a friend and relative. This goes certainly back in time at patronage times, although references nowadays to the reader–subscriber–supporter are not as illustrious as in the past.

Crowdfunding, apart from financial support, presupposes participation and probably emotional attachment especially in cases of friends; rewards are related to psychological and social factors bringing about a new kind of communities of readers. In this way aspects of 'patronage behaviour' survive in a more democratized framework supported by new information technologies, whereas the support of the readers may be used as a promotion method indicating the receipt of the edition and proclaiming this book as viable and worth published. 'Public taste', or even better an aspect of it, is thus exhibited and developed serving thus marketing methods and satisfying stakeholders.

3.5.2 *Personalized copies, crowdfunding and storytelling*

The restricted number of copies of personalized editions, often crowdfunded by friends and relatives as gifts, reminds us of the luxury copies in Renaissance. It has to be noted that with the current publishing models, including self-publishing and crowdfunding, from personalized copies (such as in the case of children's books) we pass to personalized editions. Both content and the artistic identity will be decided by the commissioners.

In that context, storytelling has also to be discussed. Nowadays, there is the opportunity of creating an edition that has the function of a family or a friend memoir: such a dedicatory edition/gift may use ghost writing as advertised (Tagholm, 2015). Like patrons in the past, readers or friends nowadays offer financial support and information, provide the memories and the material for these stories and editions, and sometimes collaborate and even cocreate. Personalized editions financed and developed by the authors or by their friends, relatives, supporters set questions regarding not only the publishing activity and the literary and aesthetic quality of the edition, but also creation, consumer behaviour, reading habits, prestige and cultural concepts. It seems that everyone thus can be – if not a writer – a hero in the story or a 'patron' for his family and himself/herself. Is there just a matter of prestige? Finally, regarding publishing, which is the value of that procedure? Does it create readers and further encourage reading, or is it limited to the value of a unique and expensive gift?

These business and publishing models obviously are successful by satisfying the readers' needs and desires offering at the same time new perspectives and cultivating new expectations. From the point that 'everyone has a story to tell' new models have proposed that everyone can publish his/her story in which he/she can be the author, the hero/heroine, the supporter, the patron. The combination of storytelling, crowdfunding and ghost writing may develop a successful model for applying to the wide reading audience. 'Tradition of storytelling', according to Papacharissi (2015, p. 4) existed and 'newer media follow, amplify, and remediate that tradition of storytelling'. New forms of the book may further encourage this tradition.

Going back in time we can trace storytelling not only during the Industrial Revolution in the Press, but also in the first decades of printing. The 'Peregrinatio in terram sanctam…' discussed in the previous chapter can be an example. Also, memoirs, autobiographies and epistles were a kind of storytelling as in the case of Aretino who published his correspondence as mentioned above. Nowadays, new media provide new opportunities in storytelling further encouraging the dynamic role of the reader who is rewarded in various ways among which we have to recognize the social and aesthetic concept. Beyond these, every book is a battle with time or a struggle against time: the story or the person will thus not be forgotten; and this is probably the greatest reward.

At the second chapter we focused on personalized copies during the first decades of printing; unique hand-decorated and hand-illustrated copies, specifically bound and often printed on parchment or on better quality paper added value not only to the copy but to the edition as well. These personalized copies were offered as a gift or commissioned mainly by collectors–noblemen who often served as patrons, reminding to the reader not only and not mainly of the previous form of the book (the manuscript) but also of the new medium that could be transformed into something unique. According to the kind of text and its readership, printers/publishers and editors tried to engage readers at introductions, dedicatory letters, epistles, epilogues and other parts of the paratext, whereas the emergence of the Press brought about a new medium for this dialogue. In that framework, reading communities were raised and built.

'Not unlike other media preceding it, the internet reorganizes the flows of time and space in ways that promise greater autonomy but also conform to the habitus of practices, hierarchies and structures that form its historical context' (Papacharissi, 2015, p. 7)'. This happens today and obviously happened in the past; it can be recognized in print culture as well. Publishing promised and provided greater autonomy to all stakeholders leading to the democratization of taste and of knowledge, as mentioned earlier. At the same time, though, to certain publishers–printers and editions it conformed to the hierarchies; innovation and tradition coexisted and different publishers served different aims and purposes according to the place, date, strategies and values.

3.6 Short forms, serialization, series and bestsellers from Renaissance to the digital age

3.6.1 Short forms

Short forms from the time of *Tales*, *Lives of saints* or *Almanacs* at the beginning of typography till the modern ones constitute a special book category. They encouraged readers to further read developing at the same time their reading skills; often accompanied by illustrations that mainly intended to explain text, they helped reading capacity and embellished the edition. Directed to mainly – but not only – the popular reading audience, short forms offered entertainment and satisfied at the same time educational, religious, cultural and social needs. Printed on more economic quality of paper, often with greater printing types and with illustrations (woodcuts) repeated extensively so that it is often obvious in prints that the wood was almost destroyed, these texts create a long tradition of developing on the one hand consumer – reading habits and on the other promotion strategies and publishing policy.

Regarding reading, a short text presupposes an economy of time and specific management of place; the text can be read and be finished shortly and everywhere being usually portable and friendly (small sized). Furthermore, a culture of series may be created so that the reader is getting used and engaged by knowing the heroes, the plot, the historic background, etc., as well as being familiar with the artistic identity of the book. These short forms may be economic (although special editions have sometimes collective and bibliophilic interest), and, if in series, they develop consumer as well as collective cultures: the reader wants to acquire all the titles so as to complete the series which probably can exhibit and share. Readers, including children, recognize and trust series which have the same recognizable artistic identity and texts are of the same quality. The publisher through the production and success of short forms often expands audience penetrating in groups not easily accessible. Nowadays, new information technologies and the devices on which we read seem to further encourage short forms, which are recognized as a feature of our era (Phillips, 2014).

During the industrial 19th century, when the new dynamic reading groups (women, working class) read mainly novels, the French publisher Louis Hachette 'created seven special series for the railway bookshops. Each one was cheap, relatively short, in the portable in 16o format, contained inoffensive material for a wide public, and was colour-coded, including his "bibliotheque rose" for the schoolchildren' (Lyons, 2008, p. 57). These series were popular and successfully establishing consumer and reading habits. Hachette's bookstores everywhere (in the railway stations across France) also sold books published by other publishers but at Hachette's prices. Thus, Louis Hachette exploited two opportunities: (1) he opened at every railway station in France a bookstore and he came to own as much as 750 bookstores in the second half of the 19th century (Barbier, 2000) creating thus a publishing "empire" that still prevails; (2) he developed a series of friendly books exploring as well, but not only, short forms. It is noteworthy that in an era of novels and multivolumed literature Hachette systematically proposed to the public the opportunities of shorter works. These short texts though have to be examined and discussed in a wider framework considering social, educational, economic and cultural conditions.

It seems that short forms and multipaged, even multivolumed novels went hand in hand during the 19th century when the 'revolution of reading' took place. Publishers had the privilege of a wide and constantly widening reading audience with augmented needs, expectations and desires that were influenced by their publishing strategies and the press. Accessibility was a key point; readers wanted access to many texts: this was obtained by libraries, reading societies, reading groups, subscription libraries, but also by cheap books easy to be found, bought and been circulated/lent between readers. Publishers developed and established works and series of such editions satisfying the readers' needs and creating in turn new ones, whereas magazines and newspaper were also used for publishing on series, as in the case of the works by Charles Dickens and Thomas Hardy.

Nowadays, short forms seem to be an emerging trend for the publishing industry. 'Already we can see a return to shorter forms of writing, such as short stories and novellas, and serialized fiction which responds almost in real time to the market' (Phillips, 2014, p. xiv). One explanation and motive may be the medium on which we read. Reading on mobiles and tablets often presupposes a short or relatively shorter text according to the concerns and needs of the reader. Obviously questions set include the following: Do readers really need something shorter? And how is this shorter defined considering the profile of each reading group? How does technology redefine short forms?

Probably emotional and psychological motives can initially be traced; readers, especially the potential ones or those who do not read much, feel convenient with content that they think they can manage to read (and finish) in their (often spare) free time (especially when reading in public transport or as waiting or in small breaks between other activities). Practical, functional issues may also be recognized: some readers admit that they are tired of reading large texts on the screen; short forms give them the satisfaction of having finished the text on time. Furthermore, short forms are more convenient for the creation of series that keep readers engaged; concepts of taste, specifically literary taste, have to be identified as well. Creating taste and developing a kind of tradition regarding content and artistic identity are a strong motive for both readers and publishers. Readers can easily make reviews, share opinions or even content in online communities/social media, introduce authors, discuss with other readers. Publishers create a culture of endurability: readers return to the publishing series of short texts identifying the quality of text and of aesthetics, feeling thus satisfied.

Reading on mobiles–smartphones or on tablets has certainly changed the artistic identity of the book/publication: how should the fonts – typographic types, the cover and the typology of the page be developed so as to be readable, friendly and convenient for the reader? Illustration, decoration, cover and the making of the page continue to have to satisfy readers' needs. We shall focus on these immediately after.

Thus, nowadays the desirable number of pages is influenced by both the medium and the kind of text as well as of the already developed and still developing needs and expectations of the readers. It has to be considered that over the last 15 years the average number of pages has grown by 25%, according to a survey recently carried out. More specifically, 'a *relatively consistent pattern of growth year on year* has added approximately 80 pages to the average size of the books surveyed since 1999'

(Lea, 2015). Thus, two 'opposite', conflicting trends can be recognized in the publishing industry nowadays. But, the question that inevitably arises is if they are really conflicting or if they are rather combined according to the needs and expectations of the readers.

In that framework, we may wonder what 'short' means in a broader context; for example, readers in the industrial 19th century read quickly and consumed novels that had a considerable size extending to a certain number of pages. In that context, relatively short texts or serialized content were also introduced. 'Relatively' has to be underlined demonstrating that the definition of 'short' ranges according to the era and to the kind of text.

Although these attitudes and trends seem probably conflicting, they are not as they cope with different groups or with the same group but at different periods and for different purposes (information, education, entertainment...). And obviously they are not new as in the past novels and multivolumed books coexisted with short forms. Striphas analyses (2009, pp. 119–120) the core of the choices made by Oprah Winfrey explaining thus the success of these book proposals in defining trends and issues in both publishing and reading. The number of pages seems to be a strong factor in association with the time available for reading. Striphas (2009, p. 119) writes for the books proposed by Oprah Winfrey: 'that she repeatedly referred to specific selections as summer books, holiday books, and so forth, indicates that both time and page length are criteria she carefully considers. Longer books have tended to coincide with the summer months, when Oprah viewers presumably have more time to devote to reading. Shorter books have tended to coincide with occasions (e.g., the winter holidays) when women are assumed to have more responsibilities and thus less time to read'. Thus, the same reading group has different needs, expectations and desires according to the period of the year and the available time for reading. In accordance with them, recommendations have been made creating and further establishing at the same time consumer and reading culture.

Furthermore, we can observe that nowadays bestsellers are mostly novels of a considerable size. Practical factors though (due to the new devices the reader does not have to carry a heavy book) do not play the most significant role. Most important seem to be the psychological factors related to the book itself and to its printed origins. In our digital age, we download and collect a lot but we just read what is of interest or useful to us: we often do not finish the text and mostly we do not read it from the first to the last page. In that context, reading multipaged books, whether printed or not, creates a concept of what we can call the 'luxury' of reading, thus the luxury of having the book, the time, the convenience, the 'equipment' (whether ebook device or armchair) to concentrate on reading as a threshold to research, relax, learning or enjoyment. Taking this a step forward, the book is also a threshold to communication, to be a member of a community of readers, to discuss and intervene (mainly through social media), to be better informed and evolved. Then, the reader waits for the next title of the author or of the series or of the tetralogy, trilogy, etc.

Two can be identified in the above as the strongest issues. The 'luxury' of the book means mainly the 'luxury of time'. The reader will choose something worthwhile, valuable, tested; regarding fiction, bestsellers are often being intended for this. The valuable time is the key point; the time for reading as an ever winning time. The book had been a commodity, being often sometimes connected with specific reading patterns and book collection. Macchiavelli, for example, had described the way he was reading during his walks with small in size, 'pocket' books and the way he studied at his office when he returned home (Grafton, 1999, pp. 199–211). He then wore other clothes, he sat at his desk with his books (of another size) and with these 'adequate' clothes and furniture had his threshold in the world of ancient glorious writers where he felt no fear neither of poverty neither of death. Grafton, starting from this letter by Machiavelli, enlightens the uses, trends and concepts of reading and studying of the humanist readers during Renaissance.

George Steiner (1996), taking as starting point the work of the French painter Chardin *Le Philosophe lisant*, further recognizes and discusses this management of time, place and other conditions in accordance with the typology of the book as well as with reading practices related to social, economic, educational, psychological and cognitive issues. Nowadays, in a highly competitive environment, publishers have to persuade for the promoted book that it deserves the valuable, available time of the reader.

3.6.2 Serialization

Serialization is turning into a key point of the publishing industry. Publishers seem to aspire to continuity with which engagement is strongly connected. The reader may return again and again to a familiar and successful hero, author, story, style and certainly is waiting for the continuity of the story with anxiety. Marketing and promotion are thus much easier. This is certainly not new. Publishing in series had been especially in the Victorian Age familiar and successful (Turner, 2014); novels were published in newspapers and magazines in series for the widened reading audience of the Industrial Revolution creating thus new reading and consumer cultures. Works by Dickens, T. Hardy, W. Collins and other famous, or less famous, novelists were published in this way developing a framework of anxiety and emotional engagement of the readers, further encouraging in this way new concepts of the 'word of mouth'. Furthermore, communication between publishers and readers as well as between authors and readers was redeveloped. Apart from the readers' letters to authors or to publishers, the author was certainly concerned with discussions, arguments, even bets on the plot. Readers' feedback existed, certainly not systemized as nowadays, but in a rather innovative context bringing about changes in collaborations and communication between stakeholders.

Author Anthony Trollope, in one of his lectures in Edinburgh in 1870 said: 'the web of complex interactions uniting the writer, the reader and his publisher will have inevitable effects on the finished product, repercussions which must be considered in any complete evaluation of the work' (quoted in Delafield, 2016, p. 4). It is noteworthy the word 'web', before the web we all know, referred to 'complex interactions' between stakeholders. Trollope recognizes the influence on the 'finished product' considering probably the book both as content and as material object. Going a step forward, he comments on the evaluation of the work. Undeniably, serialization altered the creation, consumption, reception and evaluation of literary texts creating also a consumer and reading culture. Furthermore, the role of the reader was upgraded further democratizing the publishing activity.

Serialization, apart from engagement, means endurability in a competitive environment. The illustrous, but certainly not the only, example of Harry Potter exhibits the readers' need for continuing the story, for enjoying the familiar and tested that still seduces and surprises in a known framework. Moreover, serialized works published online offer to the publishers the opportunities for specific strategies for both content developing and promoting. If text is delivered weekly or daily, the reader is engaged. Even in bestsellers the reader waits for the next title to be published; anxiety for the plot is the one aspect; the other derives from emotional, psychological and practical factors as readers are used to reading certain works, are familiar with the characters and create their own options of the fictional world.

Serialization has undoubtedly been a used method that has revived nowadays and provides to publishers:

- Sales,
- Promotion,
- Marketing tools,
- Feedback from the reader,
- Communication with the reader,
- Loyalty of the reader,
- Participation, engagement of the reader that is further encouraged nowadays by social media,
- Sharing experience.

Serialization in the digital environment may encourage further engagement of the reader who can (1) communicate directly with the author, publisher and other stakeholders, (2) participate, (3) review, (4) share content and (5) be a member of reading online communities.

It is though noteworthy what Delafield (2016, pp. 3–4) writes regarding the serialized novels in mid-Victorian magazines: 'the boundaries of the novel text were redrawn with the volume edition of the novel and were also restated in a new context by the volume edition of the periodical in which the reprinted serial then appeared' recognizing that 'the novel in its revised volume format still bears the imprint of its serialized original'. These boundaries related to literary taste, consumer behaviour, participation, communication, reading cultures and intertextuality should be traced and highlighted nowadays. A study on how and to which extent the works after their serialization are published as independent works is of further research interest.

Furthermore, Frost (2015, pp. 12–15) in discussing the coordination of economic and aesthetic practices, refers to serialization and the viability of periodical publication taking into consideration reading and consumer patterns in the emergence of new publishing forms.

Thus, serialization can be developed into a strong marketing tool and promotion method converging media and mostly converging needs and desires of the reader. As a used method, having been accepted after criticism in the Victorian Age (Delafield,

2016), it can be applied to all publishing sectors, mostly fiction and children books. Serialized content may be implied to smartphones: short forms can be read easily without tiring the reader, whereas the development of series by creating anxiety and engagement can be a competitive advantage for publishing.

3.6.3   Series and the publisher's judgment

The creation of publishing series with a recognizable profile regarding content and the materiality of the book was extremely popular in the 19th and the early decades of the 20th century. For example, Hachette's 'bibliotheque rose' was famous. Actually, series have never stopped to be famous; readers, including children, recognize and trust them. Additionally, there is a concept and a motive of continuity even if not directly expressed. Familiarity regarding content is exceeded in

- Plot,
- Characters,
- Theme,
- Writing style,
- Literary taste.

Familiarity regarding the artistic identity of the book is connected with the design of the edition, whether printed or digital:

- Cover,
- Jacket,
- Size,
- Illustration,
- Typographic fonts,
- Decoration.

The size and the cover/jacket make books recognizable.

Regarding series, the reader (Scheme 3.3) recognizes the title which respects and trusts due to previous titles of the series. Then he reads and recommends it. This seems simple but a series should be recognizable and respectable both as content and artistic identity; and this has to be obtained in a competitive environment in which, as Thompson (2010, p. 11) has written, the publishers 'must compete both in the *market for content* and in the *market for customers.*'

Meanwhile, during the 19th century we have to recognize strong factors behind the spread of these series: the development of literary and artistic taste, new reading habits, the rise in book consumption, the spread of mass education, the use of lithography and stereography, as well as changes in book production (mechanization of printing and papermaking) and distribution. Furthermore, the impact of the press was strong, whereas the bookstores in the centre of the cities and the development of the 'free to all, open to all' libraries led to the development of new reading behaviour and new ways for accessing books. As the social, political and economic conditions were changing, the printed material (books and newspapers) was still the medium for education, entertainment, social improvement, communication, access to information

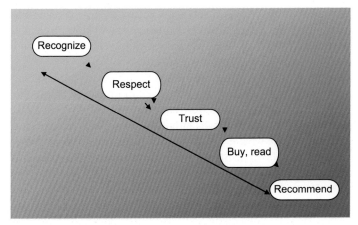

Scheme 3.3 The (consumer) behaviour of the reader in series.

and knowledge. Series, as recognizable and trusted, created tradition and a consumer habit that empowered experience sharing.

'When Kurt Wolff, a century ago, published young prose writers and poets such as Franz Kafka, Robert Walser, Georg Trakl, and Gottfried Benn in his "Judgment Day" series, those writers immediately found their first few readers because there was already something attractive about the appearance of those books, which looked like slim black exercise books with labels and came with no program announcements or publicity launches. But they suggested something that could be already sensed in the name of the series: they suggested a *judgment*, which is the real acid test for a publisher' (Calasso, 2015, p. 131). Judgment by the publisher is obviously behind and beyond the decisions, strategies and motives in the scheme above. The creation of series, introducing authors and works in a preset framework, creates a threshold to certain kind of texts and to literary as well as aesthetic experiences.

3.7 Other business and publishing models

Most business models in publishing require reader engagement. Beyond these models, we have to understand the expectations of the readers and examine parameters that define consumer as well as reading behaviour. These business models apart from promotion and sales have an impact on cultural, educational and communication aspects as well.

For example, pay per use models offer to the reader the option to pay for the pages he/she has read and not for the entire book. Fragmented content is a rather more accurate definition as the reader has access and reads the pages just needed or those that can be acquired. So, there is a wider concern and question mark regarding reading culture and research: when we read/use what we are just (or think we are) interested in, do we miss the discovery of the whole text and the unexpected? In that framework, the word 'use', and not 'read', is probably more accurate? If we know in advance what is useful to us and ask for that, how we can explore the new? How do economic factors develop the reader's behaviour? Do recommendation technologies recommend only the expected?

Furthermore, it is suggested that the reader can create his/her anthology of texts that serves current reader's needs. That goes back in time even before the advent of typography when students and pupils were encouraged and instructed by their professors/teachers so as to compile their own anthologies in order to remember, choose and study. The readers choose what they like, need, expect, can combine and think it will serve their aims. Probably, these digital personalized anthologies may serve as a next step for personalized publishing services.

In the core of these business models the word 'member' is outlined for the reader. He/she is not a subscriber, a user, a customer but a member of a community (whether book club, book blog, research community, etc.). 'For members, the subscription fee is secondary because the Website or the platform itself is their ultimate goal, it is the place where they want to be.' (New Business Models, 2015, p. 24). Business models not only take into consideration the engagement of the reader but mainly and most precisely aspire to that. Stability, loyalty and desire of belonging are strongly connected to reading communities.

In electronic bookstores and publishers' webpages embedded advertisements are personalized according to the information seeking behaviour of the reader recommending titles similar to the ones searched.

Whereas, we may consider **giveaways** in the framework of the reading communities; readers, more specifically active readers, may receive complementary copies. In the past these copies were intended only to critics and scholars, who would review and suggest the title. Nowadays, readers receive complimentary copies being thus among the upgraded stakeholders of the publishing chain-circle-circuit. Complimentary copies mean that the reader then will write about them, review the work and share comments with other readers in social networks. Publishers know this valuable tool incorporating complimentary copies or advanced reading copies to specific readers, mostly those who take an active role in social media and in influencing 'word of mouth'.

It must also be considered that complimentary copies, especially in fiction, have also a psychological and high emotional impact – they often serve as a recognition and reward to the reader. This emotional and psychological motive, difficult to be measured, is high and will be expressed in the promotion and content sharing. The upgraded role of the reader offers to the publisher a new opportunity. In that framework, limited edition prizes have to be explored as a promotion method of sharing and rewarding. From this point of view, complimentary copies have to be studied in the reader engagement strategies.

Bundling, selling books together or selling the ebook with the printed version or vice versa is also used taking into consideration needs, expectations and taste of the readers.

Nowadays there is much concern and discussion regarding **big data**. The keyword seems to be 'know your audience', both potential and existing. But this is what traditionally publishers have done whether they named it experience, taste, intuition, research, data etc. Publishers had not only to satisfy the needs of their readers but also to widen these audiences penetrating into new ones. They had to discover and approach potential readers, or to develop them. Furthermore, they had to discover new business methods as 'the number of potential patrons stayed the same while the number of books increased dramatically' identifying in that framework that 'advertising became particularly prominent in the later 16th century, as printing became more efficient and patronage more scarce' (Saenger, 2006, p. 9). The reading audience was transformed thus from a specific, limited according to education and class, well known to publishers (scholars, students, noblemen) to a gradually augmenting audience, as described thereafter. Relationships and collaborations were cultivated in that framework. Nowadays big data is an opportunity and an effective tool.

The pleasures and privileges of the backlist. New information and communication technologies offer to the publishers the opportunity of promoting, marketing and reviving a classic or older title combining often the success of the author, a book prize, a film made and the current needs and expectations of the readers. Revised editions – with introductions and other paratextual material – give a 'second chance' to these texts, whereas new technologies are used for further and better promoting the titles. Backlist can also be used so as to better engage readers through discovering and demonstrating the symbolic capital of the publishing house. A matter of concern is also the artistic identity of these books. New covers and jackets as well as the typographic design that may offer on the one hand a revival and a new option to the edition, whereas the old, used cover, jacket, frontispiece and making of the page can be used so as to reassure the quality of the edition and to continue the tradition. Thus, publishers have to experience both options according to the kind of text, the author and the reading audience.

On the other hand, with printing on demand the reader can have access to works out of print. Additionally, social media have a role in reviving and further making known the title.

Advance reading copies through specific technologies and services offer to the publishers the opportunity of measuring reactions and reading behaviour getting thus significant feedback. Reading history of each book and of each reader can also be studied and be available as technology provides through specific tools the opportunity of tracing and measuring it. For example, they may provide information about finishing or not the book, about the ways of reading (fast, slow, on specific days of the week, or specific hours), about the pages in which they gave up, or pages and chapters that were re-read, etc. This is undoubtedly precious feedback for the publishers when used before but even after the publication of the book. Questions raised include the boundaries of these methods (how free feels someone if knowing that inside the device information is gathered about the way he/she reads, enjoys, understands…) and the limitations regarding the number and the profile of the readers (age, sex, educational and cultural background, information literacy, etc.). Obviously, this is precious data for publishers who develop specific marketing strategies.

Gamification, as outlined in the previous chapter, aims for strong reader engagement and participation. Games in publishing and in new forms of the book are used so as to make readers participate, be more active and intervene. Especially, gamification is used in educational publishing. Even though it is not widely used, being thus till now a trend and an issue for the upcoming challenges and strategies. Aimed mostly to young readers, gamification is an opportunity that will be mostly explored. Undeniably, points, levels, competitions, achievements lead readers to revisiting websites, sharing content, shopping, being members of online communities, fan clubs and online book clubs. Endurability may be developed to a key point through defining behaviour and redefining concepts of everyday life.

3.8   Redefining online communities of readers

The reading audience of the first printed books was, as expected, the same with that of the manuscript book. Printers aimed to satisfy the needs and meet the expectations of an established, developed and known reading audience by using tested and thus successful methods. The reading audience during Renaissance was reduced mainly to humanist scholars, students, noblemen and clergy. Due to a number of reasons, typography included, new reading groups were gradually developing.

The printed book as mass information medium and as commodity, the Reformation, the use of vernacular languages and the influence of the art of the era are among the factors that brought about changes in the reading audience. Popular texts penetrated into new reading groups in which reading silently coexisted with reading loudly to those who could not read. Undoubtedly, the printed book helped towards the expansion of literacy; through intensive reading (reading the same texts again and again) of texts intended for those audiences (illustrated and with bigger typographic fonts often) potential readers developed their ability of reading. Thus, there was a reading audience popular, that could hardly read or could read with difficulty or enjoyed loud reading. Publishers–printers of Renaissance and the Baroque era aspired to satisfy the existing readers through their publishing policy regarding the book both as content and as object.

Data from these centuries regarding literacy and reading behaviour may be, according to the historians of reading, problematic and complex, ranging according to the region and the era (Cavallo and Chartier, 1999; Chartier, 1994). What nowadays we call communities of readers existed too during Renaissance. Apart from the academies noted above in the case of Torquato Accetto, communities of readers were created in everyday life; Menocchio, for example, tried to comment and share his feelings and concepts regarding his readings so as to create a reading company which failed even before the Sacra Congregatio condemned him (Ginzburg, 2009).

Nowadays, new information technologies and social networking offer the reader more such as:

- Personalization,
- Participation,
- Enjoyment,
- Intervention,
- Creation, cocreation,

- Rewards,
- Convergence,
- Emotional attachment,
- Psychological commitment.

Furthermore, it is interesting to take into consideration how readers define themselves. Do they consider themselves readers or members nowadays? Online communities undeniably play a key role in reader engagement; membership implies participation, direct communication, feeling of belonging, emotional and practical attachment. It is an investment of both time and resources. Sometimes this membership is advanced and upgraded as in the case of advanced reading copies or of premium customers.

It is noteworthy that many of the online communities have been acquired by publishers and booksellers. For example, Amazon in 2013 purchased the popular online community Goodreads for 150 million dollars (Cox, 2015). In a 2013 study it was reported that the number of publisher-owned online communities was set to more than double over the next 2 years with '64% of respondents convinced that their investment is already paying off and [will] continue to do so by providing good marketing support to sales channels.' (Cox, 2015, p. 5).

Online communities run by publishers focus on the promotion of their books and sales (direct sales been the desired). For that purpose among their strategies may be recognized:

- Interaction between readers and the publishing house's authors,
- Interaction with readers,
- Access to information for the readers,
- Information sharing,
- Offers, discounts (bundling),
- Preorders,
- Newsletters (magazines),
- Storytelling. Sharing stories,
- Encourage reader participation, engagement.

These communities go back in time to reading societies, reading groups and book clubs. Online opportunities provide them the framework for further, better and deeper engaging readers. This brings about changes in the roles of the stakeholders and in the publishing chain which has been developed as circle-circuit. Beyond these changes, concepts of satisfaction and of completion from each stakeholder's point of view are implied and presupposed. Publishers undeniably through online reading communities and reader engagement have great opportunities to develop strategies and publishing policies ranging from acquisition to promotion and recommendation.

3.9 Epilogue: the unexpected in publishing

Apart from 'user generated content', we may suggest the term 'user generated aesthetics' in publishing. Reader engagement, apart from content, should be extended to the aesthetics of the book. As things are changing every day, the printed book still coexists with other forms of publications. In ebooks the main attempt is the page to look like the printed one; in that framework, the vanilla ebook (looking like the printed page, such as pdf) has been thriving (Phillips, 2014); most readers expect to find the printed, familiar page, or even better, the typology of the page as used for centuries. On the other hand, they expect from technology better access and better services; according to their age and background readers are familiar and use multimedia and games in the book they read and buy. Thus, a constant challenge for publishers is to imply technologies in the new forms of the book redeveloping a product useful, easy to be used, friendly and desirable.

In that framework, readers have a more active role; they can feel to be opinion makers and taste makers. Through online reading communities and social networking, they certainly push forward the traditional 'word of mouth'. Making reviews, sharing content, communicating, ranking, recommending, collaborating, intervening, expressing attitudes upgrade their role and position. On the other hand, publishers use these opportunities for their aims, as addressed above.

Questions raised include the boundaries and limitations of reader engagement such as the extent to which reader engagement, as highlighted and discussed above, can decide and develop publishing patterns and strategies. Is the publisher the one who decides and has the last word? That seems to happen in most of the cases. How can we measure the impact of reader engagement in book promotion and sales? Which is the value of big data? How these strategies can penetrate in the already set behaviour, change established attitudes and influence potential readers?

Obviously, this is a world of abundance, not only of information but of opportunities as well, in which publishers have to

- Know the audience: this is as old as the publishing activity. New technologies provide new tools and promising strategies for engaging and approaching readers, existing and potential.
- Provide membership. In a world of no free meals, to be a member seems to be the magic word. Reader engagement is partly related to this. Emotional and psychological attachment and the feeling of belonging form strong connections and relationships.
- Take advantage of big data
- Take into consideration qualitative and quantitative research through surveys conducted, etc., regarding specific publishing sectors and audiences (students, children…)
- Provide recommendation technologies which though have to be more inspiring in the future.

But in that framework, there are questions that go deeper concerning the following:

- Reading is an action and not only interaction. No matter how interactive and successful new technologies may be, the nature of reading in its function and nature has not changed (readers want to read) and is developed and defined in broader concepts related to social, cultural, educational and economic conditions.
- Knowing not only the current but also the consuming history or information history of particular reading groups.
- Apart from content, there is engagement in the artistic identity and typology of the book. There is always the aesthetic merit to be considered.
- Short forms prevail regarding specific audiences and devices.
- **The unexpected in publishing**. The publisher has been traditionally the one who introduces, proposes, gives to the reader the option and the vision of something different, something innovative and certainly unexpected.

There is certainly much concern about the needs and expectations of the reader. Publishers get feedback from the reader, use big data and develop social media marketing so as to satisfy the readers' needs and meet their expectations. Recommendation technologies recommend to the reader titles similar to the ones that has read, searched, browsed, etc. Personalized publishing services certainly apply to the reader's profile. It seems that everything aims to offer the reader what he/she needs. But what about the unexpected? If we have only what we expect and need, or think we expect and need, or the others expect from us to have, is this finally a boring world? Discoverability mostly focuses on discovering what the reader needs and wants. But the significant question is how the reader can discover something different.

In that line of thought we are reminded of what Giangiacomo Feltrinelli said that the publisher 'can publish certain books that come to be a part of the world of books and change it with their presence. This statement may seem formal and does not fully correspond with my thinking: my mirage, the thing that I hold to be the major factor behind that 'Fortune' I mentioned earlier, is the book that lays hold of you, that book that throws things out of kilter, the book that 'does something' to the people who read it, the book that is a 'good listener' and picks up and transmits messages that may well be mysterious but not sacrosanct, the book that amid the hotchpotch of everyday history listens to the final note, the one that will still ring out when the nonessential sounds have died away' (Feltrinelli, 2013).

To read something different, something that is a step forward from what the reader is used to is connected on the one hand with *reader development* in terms of reading policy, and on the other regarding publishing with list building, the editors' choice, the publishing policy as well as social and cultural concepts related to literary taste, reading and book sharing. We may think that if the only concern is the reader's needs, then list building and criteria relating to it will be reduced probably to satisfying these needs reproducing thus the same kind of texts and aspiring to bestsellers. But will this be a boring world even for publishers?

Certainly, data play a key role and market needs guide list building; but decisions obviously should not be limited to this. Tradition of the publishing house, backlist potential, existing collaborations, quality of the text, suitability for the list have to go hand in hand with market needs, frontlist potential, promotion and sales. Even competition has to be based on innovation as the reproduction of the same kind of text and of certain style will not have success after a, whether short or not, period of time. In that context, the element of surprise emerges regarding both text and the artistic identity of the book.

Kurt Wolff stated that (1991, p. 9): 'By taste I mean not only judgment and a feeling for quality and literary values. Taste should also include a sure sense for the form – format, type area, type face, binding, dust jacket – in which a specific book should be represented. Literary taste, on the other hand, must be combined with an instinct for whether a particular book will interest only a small group of readers, or whether the subject and form make it suitable for a larger audience. This will have a decisive influence on the size of the edition and advertising, and care must be taken that personal enthusiasm does not entice us into false and over-optimistic expectations.' Meanwhile, among the essential tools of a publisher, 'intuition for the meaningful currents of the times, those that will shape the future' (Wolff, 1991, p. 8) is recognized.

Publishing is an innovative business that takes risks; publishers have been the ones who introduced and proposed, inserting in the game, new players: new texts, new trends, new authors (such as Franz Kafka and James Joyce) and new aesthetics. They redefine taste and rules, literary and others, redeveloping also the lines of thought. So in a world of information abundance and of updated publishing opportunities, it is not always enough to recommend what someone really needs, expects and already knows. This would be a rather boring world.

The question that goes deeper is how the expected and the unexpected, known needs and unknown desires can be converged. Does the reader want and wait to be surprised and how and when? Probably not every day and this is a challenge for the publishing houses to cope with. They have to define and measure the extent to which readers want to be surprised taking into consideration that on the other hand they use to repeat things and on the other to explore new ones. So, the real concern may be: 'the expected versus the unexpected, the expected hand in hand with the unexpected'. Thus, which strategies have to be developed and how all the above-mentioned tools and methods can be implied to this? Or in other words the statement and the challenge may be: the expected surprise, the book that makes the difference (for a short, for a long time or for a lifetime).

In that framework, the role of the publisher prevails. Information, discoverability and reader engagement play a key role and, as discussed in the next chapter, the publishing chain-circle-circuit can also be called 'information publishing chain-circle-circuit'.

References

Alter, A., August 11, 2014. Publishers Turn to the Crowd to Find the Next Best Seller. New York Times. Available at: http://www.nytimes.com/2014/08/12/business/media/publishers-turn-to-the-crowd-to-find-the-next-best-seller.html?_r=0.

Armstrong, P., 2015. Lean Publishing. Available at: https://leanpub.com/lean/read.

Banou, C., 2013. Reviving and Re-using book promotion strategies: the case of pre-orders. Thesaurismata (Venice) 43, 511–526 (in Greek).

Barbier, F., 2000. Histoire du livre. Armand Colin, Paris.

Barnard, J., 2001. London publishing, 1640–1660: crisis, continuity and innovation. Book History 4, 1–16.

Blair, A., 2007. Errata lists and the reader as corrector. In: Alcorn Baron, S., et al. (Ed.), Agent of Change. Print Culture Studies after Elizabeth Eisenstein. University of Massachusetts Press, pp. 21–41.

Brewer, J., 2013. The Pleasures of the Imagination. English Culture in the 18th Century. Routledge, London and New York.

Bruntje, D., Gadja, O. (Eds.), 2015. Crowdfunding in Europe. State of the Art in Theory and Practice. Springer.

Calasso, R., 2015. The Art of the Publisher (Richard Dixon, Trans.). Penguin, London.

Cavallo, G., Chartier, R. (Eds.), 1999. Storia Della Lettura Nel Mondo Occidentale. Edizioni Laterza, Roma and Bari.

Chartier, R., 1994. The Order of Books. Readers, Authors and Libraries in Europe between the 15th and 18th centuries. Trans. Lydia Cochrane. Polity Press, Cambridge, (first edition in French: 1992).

Cherchi, P., 2005. Marino and the Meraviglia. In: Ciavolella, M., Coleman, P. (Eds.), Culture and Authority in the Baroque. Toronto University Press, Toronto, pp. 63–72.

Chi, Y., 2014. The E-volution of Publishing: Challenges and Opportunities in the Digital Age. Publishing Research Quarterly 30 (4), 344–351.

Clark, G., Phillips, A., 2014. Inside Book Publishing, fifth ed. Routledge, London and New York.

Cox, E., 2015. Designing Books for Tomorrow's Readers. How Millennials Consume Content. White Paper from Publishing Perspectives and Publishing Technology. Available at: http://www.ingenta.com/wp-content/uploads/2014/10/White-Paper-How-Millennials-Consume-Content.pdf;http://publishingperspectives.com/wp-content/uploads/2015/04/White-Paper-How-Millennials-Consume-Content.pdf.

Criswell, J., Canty, N., 2014. Deconstructing social media: An analysis of Twitter and Facebook use in the publishing industry. Publishing Research Quarterly 30, 352–376.

Delafield, C., 2016. Serialization and the Novel in Mid-victorian Novels. Routledge, London and New York.

Downie, J.A., 2013. Printing for the author in the long eighteenth century. In: Jung, S. (Ed.), British Literature and Print Culture. D. S. Brewer Publishing, Cambridge, pp. 58–76.

Dresner, S., 2014. Crowdfunding. A Guide to Raising Capital on the Internet. Wiley.

Eisenstein, E., 1983. The Printing Revolution in Early Modern Europe. Cambridge University Press, Cambridge.

Feltrinelli, C., 2013. Senior Service. A Story of Riches, Revolution and Violent Death (A. McEwen, Trans.). Granta Books, London, (Paperback edition).

Folkerth, W., 2010. Pietro Aretino, Thomas Nashe, and early modern rhetorics of public address. In: Wilson, B., Yavhnin, P. (Eds.), Making Publics in Early Modern Europe. People, Things, Forms of Knowledge. Routledge, New York and London, pp. 68–78.

Frost, S., 2015. The Business of the Novel: Economics, Aesthetics and the Case of Middlemarch. Routledge, London and New York.

Gierczack, M., et al., 2015. Crowdfunding: outlining the new era of fundraising. In: Bruntje, D., Gadja, O. (Eds.), Crowdfunding in Europe. State of the Art in Theory and Practice. Springer, pp. 7–23.

Ginzburg, C., 2009. Il formaggio e i vermi. Il cosmo di un mugnaio del '500. Einaudi, Torino. [ed. pr. 1976].

de Girolamo, M., 2000. Una quiete operosa: forma e pratiche della Accademia napoletana degli Oziosi, 1611–1645. Fredericiana Editrice Universitaria, Napoli.

Goldman, P., Cooke, S., 2016. Reading Victorian Illustration, 1855–1875: Spoils of the Lumber Room, second ed. Routledge, London and New York.

Grafton, A., 1999. L' umanista come lettore. In: Cavallo, G., Chartier, R. (Eds.), Storia Della Lettura Nel Mondo Occidentale. Edizioni Laterza, Roma and Bari, pp. 199–242.

Hartley, J., et al., 2012. Key Concepts in Creative Industries. Sage, London.

Janzen-Kooistra, L., 2011. Poetry, Pictures and Popular Publishing. The Illustrated Gift Book and Victorian Visual Culture. 1855–1873. Ohio University Press, Athens and Ohio.

Lalmas, M., et al., 2015. Measuring User Engagement. Morgan & Claypool Publishers.

Lea, R., December 10, 2015. The Big Question: Are Books Getting Longer? The Guardian. Available at: http://www.theguardian.com/books/2015/dec/10/are-books-getting-longer-survey-marlon-james-hanya-yanagihara?CMP=twt_books_b-gdnbooks.

Lockwood, T., 2001. Subscription Hunters and Their Prey. Studies in the Literary Imagination, pp. 121–135.

Lyons, M., 2008. Reading Culture and Writing Practices in Nineteenth Century France. University of Toronto Press, Toronto.

MacWilliam, A., 2013. The engaged reader. A human centred evaluation of ebook user experience. Publishing Research Quarterly 29, 1–11.

Micic, I., 2015. Crowdfunding, Overview of the Industry, Regulation and Role of Crowdfunding in the Venture Startup. Anchor Academic Publishing, Hamburg.

Moritz, A., Block, H., 2015. Crowdfunding. A literature review and research directions. In: Bruntje, D., Gadja, O. (Eds.), Crowdfunding in Europe. State of the Art in Theory and Practice. Springer, pp. 25–53. Also available at SSRN, https://papers.ssrn.com/sol3/Papers.cfm?abstract_id=2554444.

Napoli, P., 2011. Audience Evolution. New Technologies and the Transformation of Media Audiences. Columbia University Press, New York.

New Business models in the Digital Age, 2015. A Dosdoce.Com Study. Available at: http://www.dosdoce.com/2015/04/07/new-business-models-in-the-digital-age/.

Papacharissi, Z., 2015. Affective Publics. Sentiment, Technology and Politics. Oxford University Press, Oxford.

Phillips, A., 2014. Turning the Page. The Evolution of the Book. Routledge, Abington, Oxon, and New York.

Radway, J.A., 1997. A Feeling for Books. The Book-of-the-Month Club, Literary Taste, and Middle-Class Desire. The University of North Carolina Press, Chapel Hill and London.

Richardson, B., 1999. Typography, Writers and Readers in Renaissance Italy. Cambridge University Press, Cambridge.

Rickinson, M., Sebba, J., Edwards, A., 2011. Improving Research through User Engagement. Rouledge.

Saenger, M., 2006. The Commodification of Textual Engagements in the English Renaissance. Ashgate, London.

Sher, R.B., 2006. The Enlightenment and the Book. Scottish Authors and Their Publishers in Eighteenth Century Britain, Ireland & America. The University of Chicago Press, Chicago and London.

Snyder, J., 2005. Truth and wonder in Naples circa 1640. In: Ciavolella, M., Coleman, P. (Eds.), Culture and Authority in the Baroque. Toronto University Press, Toronto, pp. 85–104.

Steiner, G., 1996. The uncommon reader. In: No Passion Spent. Essays 1978–1996. Faber & Faber, London, pp. 1–27.

Striphas, T., 2009. The Late Age of Print. Everyday Book Culture from Consumerism to Control. University of Columbia Press, New York, Chichester, and West Sussex.

Tagholm, R., November 23, 2015. UK's StoryTerrace Extends Crowdfunding to Private Bios. Publishing Perspectives. Available at: http://publishingperspectives.com/2015/11/storyterrace-crowdfund-private-biographies/#.Vv44k9KLRQI.

Thompson, J.B., 2010. Merchants of Culture. The Publishing Business in the Twenty-First Century. Polity Press, Cambridge.

Turner, M.W., 2014. The unruliness of serials in the nineteenth century (and in the digital Age). In: Allen, R., Van der Berg, T. (Eds.), Serialization in Popular Culture. Routledge, New York and London, pp. 11–31.

Waddington, R.B., 2004. Aretino's Satyr. Sexuality, Satire, and Self-projection in Sixteenth-Century Literature and Art. University of Toronto Press, Toronto.

Weller, M., 2011. The Digital Scholar. How Technology Is Transforming Scholarly Practice. Bloomsbury Academic, London and New York.

Wolff, K., 1991. Kurt Wolff. A Portrait in Essays & Letters. The University of Chicago Press, Chicago & London.

Re-discussing the publishing chain as information value chain-circle

4

4.1 Information as an agent of change in the publishing industry

Information is asset, key value, product, opportunity, challenge in our Information Age in which information technologies have defined and are constantly defining our behaviour, communication, research and everyday life. More specifically, access to information is an aim, whereas information management and information seeking behaviour enlighten and reveal aspects of our era including the way we think and act. We live actually in the economies of information, and information science looks at the above.

Publishing is part of the information industry. Furthermore, publishing is an industry that not only offers information but also offers access to it and evaluation of it. There is information in books, and information about books and the publishing activity. The printed book was not the first (neither the last) medium that provided information (before it, the manuscript book had this role) but it was the first mass medium that revolutionized knowledge dissemination and democratized access to information. It is also true that the publishing industry during the last three decades has been transformed due to a number of reasons, among which the role of information and communication technologies prevails (Phillips, 2014). In this chapter, the role of information as an agent of change in the publishing activity and the publishing chain is discussed.

Actually, information technologies have transformed the publishing industry through not only innovative tools but also through the systemization and standardization of existing practices and methods widening thus the borders of the book and of the publishing activity. Undeniably, there is abundance of information in publishing that requires

1. New strategies for the publishers so as to further and better inform the reading audience, to get feedback from it, to develop strategies based on data and to promote and develop their products. Marketing is based on information.
2. New tools and media for the readers so as to be better and fully informed according to their information needs and have access to information.
3. New strategies and collaborations for the booksellers.
4. Exploitation of the new opportunities by the libraries – information services.
5. Collaborations and synergies between stakeholders.

We have to consider that new information technologies have changed the publishing activity as a whole, regarding more specifically:

- Text acquisition,
- Editing,

Re-Inventing the Book. http://dx.doi.org/10.1016/B978-0-08-101278-9.00004-8

- Publishing services,
- Book design, aesthetics of the book,
- Book production,
- New publishing models (printing on demand, self-publishing),
- Distribution,
- Marketing,
- Promotion,
- Advertisement,
- Reading,
- Criticism,
- Communities or readers,
- Library/information services,
- The creation of the text,

Thus, new information technologies set the framework and provide the tools for the emergence of new publishing and business models. In that context, the information seeking behaviour of all stakeholders has to be studied whereas there is concern about the use of big data. In that framework, information seeking and consumer behaviour as well as information needs and literacy are studied through surveys, statistics and researches. As expected, in a highly competitive industry the information's role is augmenting as a tool for developing strategies.

In a world of abundance, discoverability as a value is strongly connected with access to information and evaluation of it. Readers discover titles according to the information they have, related with their information seeking behaviour and information literacy. 'Every book is a new product. Readers discover their preferences and spread information, both positive and negative, via the "information cascade"' (Greco, et al., 2013, p. 3). Social media related to the book industry provide access to information encouraging information sharing and communication; online communities of readers are based to a great extent on information sharing.

Regarding information in publishing, we have to set and consider the following questions. Information is offered, provided, exploited and studied:

- To whom?
- By whom?
- Why?
- When?
- How?

The above have to be discussed from the stakeholders' point of view:

1. the publisher's,
2. the author's,
3. the bookseller's,
4. the reader's,
5. the information scientist's – librarian's,
6. the agent's.

Readers are seeking information, whereas publishers are seeking customers/readers. More specifically, we can recognize the following regarding readers: on the one hand, they are seeking for information per se, on the other hand, the information is a tool for discovering new titles of interest (that in turn, of course, may provide information).

Publishers not only provide information and knowledge but also access to information and curation. It is noteworthy that the role of the publisher goes deeper. 'In a world of abundance, the publishers offer a vital service in selecting authors and developing their content to meet readers' needs. They manage the author's brands and focus readers on the books they have selected. That service is worth paying for when time is scarce. To attempt another definition: the publishing process may be described as managing the scarcity of good authors and content to drive profitability' (Clark and Phillips, 2014, p. 21). Publishers, beyond information, have to provide content, and then to provide editions valuable both as content and as aesthetic objects. Thus, they have to introduce, offer options, propose, and even lead to the way of getting answers. As Chi (2014, p. 346) writes: 'This makes our role as publishers even harder – it's no longer enough to provide information, we need to help our users find the right information in the right context at the right time. Now, we need to provide answers, not just information'.

Obviously, information adds value to the publishing activity; that is the start point. It helps publishers to have direct and successful communication between stakeholders, to develop promotion and marketing methods, gain feedback from the readers, develop innovative and creative collaborations; information also encourages risk and innovation, provides the background for the development of policies and strategies.

Since Gutenberg publishers aspired to gather information by various ways that nowadays may seem simple or have been transformed into something that seems more complex. Nowadays, publishers take into consideration the information seeking behaviour and information literacy of their reading groups according to the kind of text. We may distinguish between existing and potential readers, the first characterized by book devotion, passion, desire for book discovering while the second ones have to be approached in different ways and probably through different media. Existing and systematic readers are frequent visitors of publishing and bookselling websites and users of social media such as book blogs, members of online reading communities and book clubs, whereas potential readers are not. Publishers come to know their audiences; but this is not enough. They have to satisfy and engage that audience through various ways including social media as well as other more traditional methods. Key point is reader engagement used from the publishers' point of view.

Turner (2014, p. 395) writes that 'in addition to innovation, re-examining the overall processes of the publishing cycle and introducing an integrated approach to using data to drive the business brings new insights in the overall operations and can help publishers gain an edge'. Obviously, information in publishing is a tool, a value, a requirement, part of the strategy, an aim, a privilege and a step forward. Access to information is an asset for both authors and readers. Publishers develop information services through their special departments so as to satisfy the information needs of the readers getting feedback from them. Data help publishers to develop strategies, to identify and exploit opportunities, to know deeper the market, to create policies and encourage collaborations. The connection between information and inspiration–creativity is undeniably a challenging theme for further research. Even what was used to be called 'experience' or 'intuition' or 'taste' of the publisher is systemized and measured.

Undeniably, new information environments are constantly changing the way people seek and use information in the publishing value chain. What we call engagement of the reader is to a great extent engagement with the information and the use of information technologies from different and often privileged points of view, as described in the previous chapter. As innovation, experiment and risk have been through the centuries among the main characteristics of the publishing industry, the use on new information technologies and the access to information are assets and strategies exploited by publishers. In that framework, new reading experiences lead to new information behaviour and vice versa. Obviously, information is an agent of change in the publishing activity bringing about changes in the publishing chain in which specific roles have been altered or upgraded, such as the reader's, the literary agent's, the librarian/information scientist's and certainly the publisher's, or introduced such as the audience development director.

4.2   Inside the page: information mechanisms of the page

The information revolution undeniably begins with Gutenberg. As discussed in the previous chapters, the printed book was the first mass information medium that revolutionized knowledge dissemination, access to information, scholar communication, educational process, etc., whereas the book as a product and a commodity was gradually and constantly developed having acquired its typology mainly during the first decades of printing.

Mechanisms were developed in the printed book so as to provide better access to information, to make the book readable and friendly, to help readers in their research, to create new reading and aesthetic experiences. In that context, page numbers and headings appeared in the first printed books so as to improve the reading experience, to reduce the time of searching and provide the reader with tools in order to better use the book and communicate with other readers exchanging often information. Thus, new aspects in educational process, scholarly communication and the building of communities of readers were developed. The printed page was transformed into a friendly, readable and adaptable form so as to satisfy the needs of the reader. So headings, number pages, subtitles, markers in the margin of the text, paragraph breaks, notes were used and established. 'The printed page, with its system of sections and subsections, footnotes, marginal notes and paragraph divisions developed a standardized spatial display; different typefaces might denote hierarchies of information' (Rhodes and Sawday, 2000, p. 7).

Furthermore, introductions and other paratext material as discussed in the second chapter, both of front matter (forewords, introductions, dedicatory letters, poems/epigrams,…) and of back matter (epilogues, indexes,…) constitute what we could also call information mechanisms of the edition aiming to help readers to better study, read, search and share content. Accordingly, indexes, errata, tables of contents, tables of illustrations, tables of abbreviations, epilogues, etc., further systemized the information behaviour and enhanced the reading habits. The text, apart from readable and desirable, had to be easy to use, easy to search, easy to find what the reader was seeking and easy – a step forward – to discover the unexpected.

In the title page of the old printed books, long titles served both as a kind of summary and of advertisement. Often accompanied by epigrams, these long titles exhibited verbally the value of the text, whereas the decoration–illustration of the title page demonstrated the aesthetic value of the edition. Beyond this, the visual message was strong enough through not only the decoration but also through the printer's mark. We have also to consider that the title page's typology was developed and defined in the framework of the art of the era expressing at the same time the social, cultural, religious, political conditions and reflecting the printing tradition (Smith, 2001; Baldacchini, 2004). The visual information of the page and of the edition was as strong as the verbal, even stronger in terms of subconscious reaction and memory, while we cannot overlook that it helped potential readers to develop their reading ability pushing thus forward literacy.

The art of the era was the starting point for illustration and decoration. As the printed book was a mass medium, the images, as discussed in the second chapter, were the means of visual information bringing about simultaneously a democratization of taste. The typographic and iconographic tradition of the text, previous editions, the reading audience, the book market and the opportunities of the printing shop/publishing house have to be recognized among the parameters that defined illustration and decoration. Furthermore, the artist–designer had often to collaborate with woodcutters and other artists (Szepe, 1997, p. 43). 'Historically, artists have frequently employed the assistance of highly skilled craftsmen –specialist block-cutters, expert engravers or professional printers – to help with the technically-complex, time-consuming or labour-intensive stages of printmaking processes' (Blocklehurst and Watson, 2015, pp. 13–15). The role of the publisher or of the editor in that process has to be further investigated. The publisher–printer used often woodcuts or engravings from his stock according to the kind of text and of audience; sometimes the illustration had no relationship with the text.

Information had been even from the beginning of printing the backbone of printing enabling research, dissemination and complicated projects in comparison with the world of manuscript. 'Vasari's was the first systematic investigation, based on interviews, correspondence and field trips, of the procedures used and the objects produced by generations of European artists. The *Lives* also reflects the given opportunity offered by print to extend the scope of a given work from one edition to another' (Eisenstein, 1983, p. 132). Eisenstein, apart from identifying how printing enhanced Vasari's work, especially the second edition of 1568 also points out the importance of the portraits of the second edition. Gregory examines Vasari's use of prints as a resource for information. She uses the term 'visual reference', (2012, p. 134) pointing out cases in which Vasari certainly or probably used prints as primary resources or as a supplement to his own memory.

The printed book also established and introduced 'celebrities'. Authors and publishers, but also editors and artists gained fame though the printed book. The portrait of the author at the frontispiece or of the person described in the book offered fame and recognition. Even if they were already well known, the printed book helped them to establish and further spread their fame.

The Information Revolution goes beyond the printed book. The above-mentioned mechanisms are developed or even transformed nowadays due to the new materials and forms of the book. Information technologies provide the tools and opportunities for a page 'widened', more friendly to specific audiences that provides better and faster access to information; apart from links, the use of multimedia technologies and the convergence of media are constantly redefining the boundaries and the typology of the electronic page. In accordance to these technologies, storytelling and personalized publishing services are developed.

The book always had and still has its own systems of information storage and exhibition as well as of access to information. During Renaissance, these systems were 'strong' enough for a number of reasons; first, due to the experimental nature of the book in a time when its identity was developing; second, because the book was the best advertisement of itself that had to be autonomous in the provision of knowledge and information promoting itself as well. Additionally, the absence of reference works implied autonomous and often self-developed systems for finding and evaluating information. Things changed, of course, when Conrad Gesner, the father of bibliography, compiled and published his bibliography *De biblioteca universalis*[1]; from then on other bibliographies were published as well as printed catalogues of libraries that facilitated the research and work of scholars and students. Gesner and bibliographers after him provided reference works for offering information resources to researchers, students, scholars and readers.

Moreover, during Renaissance, the publication and success of 'mirrors', 'theatres', 'anatomies', 'compendia' and other compilations, together with dictionaries and maps that served as reference works, set the information framework. Access to information was easier and faster than in the world of manuscript. As Rhodes and Sawday (2000, p. 9) comment 'these collections became far more than mere repositories of knowledge. In the seemingly limitless world of production, distribution and retrieval spawned by print culture, a new model of the human mind itself began to emerge'.

Thus, during Renaissance the public sphere of books and of information emerged. This public sphere nowadays is often mentioned when talking about the Internet, the social media, the technology or globalization, the boundaries between public and private (Papacharissi, 2013).

The limitless, as it seems, world of information nowadays has much in common with what people of Renaissance or of the Industrial Revolution thought of themselves. People tend to think that solutions and answers are in the technology. It is true that digital opportunities provide access to material and information that was difficult to be reached so quickly some decades ago. But because 'there are more things in heaven and earth, Horatio, that are dreamt of in your philosophy',[2] not everything

---

[1] For bibliography concerning Conrad Gesner, v. Chartier, 1984, p. 110.
[2] Shakespeare, *Hamlet*, act 1, scene 5, 167–168.

can be into the digital sphere. Information mechanisms as developed nowadays in the multiformed page may push forward the satisfaction of the information needs extending the boundaries of the book into new converged media and penetrating into new audiences.

4.3 Renaming experience: from the publisher's intuition to data

From the past centuries' experience, taste and 'intuition' of the publisher we have moved towards marketing and data. On the basis of all these, we can though identify information: information about authors, readers, sales, editions, previous editions, publicity, competition, publishers, libraries, bookstores, royalties, bestsellers, needs, expectations, etc. It seems that everything can be measured and that for every aspect of the publishing activity there is data, information available deriving from surveys, interviews, statistics, marketing tools, numbers and researches. For example, among the criteria recognized for deciding on publishing a book, especially in trade publishing, sales of the previous book/books as well as the fame of the author are taken into consideration.

Feedback from the readers is information. Publishers always got feedback from their readers and identified their audiences, existing and potential. 'Complicity with unknown people can be created only on the basis of their repeated experiences of not being disappointed', Calasso wrote for the reading audience (2015, p. 69). This can be, to an extent, obtained by the studying of information needs and information seeking behaviour; it is not though enough just not to be disappointed. The readers must be beyond satisfied; they have to be surprised, engaged, involved and inspired. The key word in what Calasso says is 'repeated experiences': communication with readers is based on this. Readers tend to repeat what they do every day, they visit the same webpages, buy from the same bookstores (electronic or brick and mortar), write to the same blogs, buy the works of the same author or of the same series, identify and buy the editions of the same publisher, visit the book club of which they are members. Probably data means to investigate these 'repeated experiences', to satisfy them and then go beyond this.

Nowadays there are tools for explaining, studying, measuring the information needs and behaviour of all stakeholders:

- Authors,
- Agents,
- Publishers,
- Editors,
- Marketing department,
- Booksellers,
- Librarians–information scientists,
- Readers,
- Book reviewers, book bloggers,
- Critics,
- Book clubs

Information is the basis for decision making. For example, how authors select publishers? How do they get information about publishers and agents? How do they decide on the future of their finished work? Canty's research (2012) based on a survey carried out in 2011 on the novelists who published their first novel in Britain enlightens the above. The upgraded role of the agent is demonstrated and it is noteworthy to mention the various ways through which the author discovered his/her agent (being approached, recommendation, through research, introduced, already new). Although these answers ranged to the same question regarding how the publisher of the first published novel was selected: 'in over 60% of the cases the decision on which publisher to approach was made by the agent' (Canty, 2012, p. 225). The research made by Canty highlights aspects of information from the author's point of view that is often overlooked.

So, information and data in publishing mean to:

- know what has been done,
- know what happens today,
- know what can be done today,
- know what can be done in the future,
- have data,
- understand the opportunities beyond the numbers,
- innovate based on data,
- invest based on other criteria (qualitative),
- explore the role of taste.

Thus, apart from data and statistics, publishing history is important. In that framework, publishing studies and research done, as discussed above, empower the understanding of current trends and lead to the development of strategies.

4.4   Books everywhere: from *libelli portatiles* to mobiles

People tend to use the device they have with them; it is a matter of convenience, access and familiarity. From that point of view, reading on mobiles and tablets undeniably consists a great challenge for publishers who are called to create books (not just content) aimed to be read not only on ebooks' specific devices but also on tablets and mobiles. In a highly competitive environment – in which the user at the same device, apart from reading, can listen to music, answer to emails, play games, read newspapers, be connected to online communities, visit a blog and share opinions, tweet, chat, download content – the book has to be more than promising and desirable combining the expected and the unexpected, satisfying needs and at the same time surprising, converging tradition and innovation.

We have though to recognize that these books, created for tablets and mobiles, go beyond content since it is also their aesthetics that matter. The artistic identity of these new editions forms an experimental and challenging field in which traditional and innovative concepts will coexist in a converged and promising amalgam. Thus, content is not the only, as it is often appeared to be, and neither in some cases the most significant feature and aim. The artistic identity of the edition/book, as discussed in the second chapter, is important and exploits the use of new technologies, thus exceeding the borders of the book as known for centuries combining text, image, narration, text magnification, embedded multimedia, interactive opportunities, background music and animations. Thus, we should not talk for content but for editions of books.

McIlroy (2015) provides data for the upgraded use of mobiles and tablets arguing that 'the challenge for book publishers is to align their content and business models with mobile's vast opportunities'. He points out that book buyers are online, referring to 'a surprising phenomenon: time spent on mobile does not appear to be taking away from PC use, and certainly not from TV watching. The time spent with mobile devices is incremental to other screen interactions' (McIlroy, 2015).

Undeniably, the use of mobile phones for reading is among the current challenges for the publishing industry. '...the percentage of e-book buyers who read primarily on tablets was 41% in the first quarter of 2015, compared with 30% in 2012. But in a Nielsen survey of 2000 people this past December, about 54% of e-book buyers said they used smartphones to read their books at least some of the time. That's up from 24% in 2012' (Maloney, 2015). Judith Curr, publisher of Simon & Schuster's imprint Atria Books, has said: 'The future of digital reading is on the phone. It's going to be on the phone and it's going to be on paper' (Abrams, 2015).

In that framework, we have to remind ourselves that the printed book, as statistics demonstrate, still not only coexists with other forms of publications but even thrives. Sales of printed books have augmented in the UK. According to the Publishers Association's Statistics Yearbook 2015, 'A. Sales of physical books from publishers increased for the first time in four years while digital sales fell for the first time since the PA started collecting figures, B. There was particularly strong growth in sales of physical non-fiction/reference books which saw sales increase by 9% to £759m, C. Academic journal publishing also continued strongly up by 5% to £1.1bn with digital revenues accounting for 95% of this, D. School books sales were up overall by 9% to £319m with growth in physical and digital both home and abroad, E. Audiobook downloads had another good year with 29% growth in 2015' (Anderson, 2016).

According to data provided by the Pew Research Centre Internet & American Life Project (published in McIlroy, 2015), printed material prevails when the book is to be shared or used with children; when sharing books with others, the use of printed book reaches the 69%, whereas when reading with a child the percentage goes up to 81%. It is interesting though to note that reading in bed is shared almost equally between printed and electronic books. Electronic books prevail for reading while travelling (73%), or for having a selection of books to choose from (53%), or for being able to get a book quickly (83%). Obviously, the readers pass from one medium to the other converging them in everyday life according to their needs, expectations, kind of text, accessibility, price and purpose.

Research has shown that 63% of American adults read at least one book in print in 2015 (the percentage has fallen from 69% in the previous year and 71% in 2011), 27% read an ebook (from 28% in 2014 and 17% in 2011) and 12% an audio book (14% in 2014 and 11% in 2011). It has also to be noted that in the USA half of newspapers readers rely on printed editions (Barthel, 2016).

Obviously, printed and digital/electronic books coexist in a hybrid environment, estimations for the death of the printed book having obviously failed. We read on all forms of the book, passing from one to the other, from paper to the screen of the computer or of the mobile, according to the time available, the circumstances, the kind of text, the availability, the access, the information literacy, the aim of the study, the need for sharing, as well as other educational, scientific, social, economic and cultural conditions related also to emotional and psychological factors that in turn define reading and consumer behaviour.

It seems that it will be a rather long period of coexistence of media: the printed book will probably exist in the years to come as a friendly, used, well-known, established object related to personal and social prestige. This can be attributed to strong practical, psychological, social, emotional, aesthetic and cultural assets of the printed book that define consumer behaviour and ideologies. But electronic-digital reading increases as well. We read on the screen, on various type of screens, we are used to and convenient with it.

In that framework, the use of mobiles and tablets for reading is upgraded day by day. For better understanding this, we have to consider the opportunities provided by mobiles/smartphones in accordance with the available time for reading and with other social, financial and cultural factors. Friendly, convenient, readable, economic, easily accessible and portable books have been desired and demanded for centuries. These 'libelli/libri portatiles' since the time of Aldus Manutius are a constant aim and value for readers and publishers as well as for other stakeholders who better promote, advertise, distribute and offer access to them. The small-sized books launched by Aldus Manutius in Renaissance Venice brought about a steady value and concept revolutionizing the publishing activity according to the technology and opportunities of each era. Nowadays, new forms of the book try to reach the same goals. Ebooks try to be friendly, even personalized, easy to use, easy to carry (of no weight), convenient, providing a variety of choices for reading, information sharing, access and enjoyment. They often remind of the printed page, which is the module; but ebooks will go beyond it by combining and converging media, multimedia, social media, art of the era, etc. The aesthetics of publishing, as discussed in the second chapter, have to be applied to the new forms of the book adapted for tablets and mobiles.

Usually lack of time is recognized among the main factors that prevent people from reading. Reading in a more 'traditional' concept implies and presupposes, according to the common sense (or stereotypes), specific management of time and place: a common picture is that of reading in an armchair or at an office where there is space and time for everything, for the book, the reader, the pencil, the bookmark, the library and also the other books around. The revolution brought about by the portable books introduced by Aldus Manutius meant that the reader could read at the time, place and in the way chosen. Nowadays, we all have a device on which we can read, anytime, everywhere from news to literary works with access to libraries and databases, with no extra weight and most significantly no extra care of bringing with us the book: it is already on the device that we have with us for communicating and be informed. Mobile phones and tablets provide the opportunity to get immediate access to information and to knowledge regarding our readings. Furthermore, we can have the books we want, need, like with us; from this point of view, the devices try to resemble to a potential personal 'Alexandrina' library available everywhere.

Taking into consideration the competition with other media and information resources even on the same device, we may recognize the features and the opportunities of the editions that the publishers can provide for mobiles and tablets regarding the book as both content and object so as to be readable, friendly, competitive and desirable.

1. **The edition as content**: Short forms and serialization, as discussed at the previous chapter, are of value since they engage readers and satisfy practical and emotional–psychological concepts. Furthermore, the access to out of print material is exploited. Content needs to be easily read on mobiles and tablets often converged by using multimedia, links, music, photographs and games. In that framework, the element of surprise should not be underestimated. Readers and potential readers want and may try something experimental and new as they are convinced that technology runs fast providing opportunities that they have to know and explore. But what the publishers should offer goes beyond content and access to it: it is the edition that matters; content and information are everywhere in the cyber space but the edition, the book provided by the publisher is content judged, evaluated, reviewed, edited, proofread, with added value and the reader will trust it.

2. **The aesthetic identity of the editions** developed and designed for tablets and mobiles has to take into consideration the nature of the medium, art of the era as well as the factors described in the second chapter, including the needs, desires and taste of the reading audience both existing and potential. 'To engage readers, publishers are now experimenting with ways to make the mobile–reading experience better. They are designing book jackets with smartphone screens in mind. (Handwritten scripts or small fonts may not be legible.).... Amazon and Google recently introduced custom e-book fonts, both designed to be more legible on smartphone screens' (Maloney, 2015). Obviously, although not in a tangible form, the artistic identity of the book still and always matters, as discussed in the second chapter. The typology of the page and of the edition is to be deeply and further considered and planned by the publishers.

More specifically, the illustration and decoration of the book by exploring the new opportunities (links, multimedia, gamification, photographs, music, interactive tools, etc.) may provide new aesthetic experiences, focused and personalized to specific groups of readers. The page always has to be readable and desirable, and certainly to be adapted to new needs and widened by the new opportunities. From covers and jackets of the printed book the publishing companies have to develop the threshold, the introductory visual parts of the book whether they are named 'jackets', 'covers', or not. Among the challenges to be exploited is also the combination, even convergence, of tested, well-known, recognizable aesthetics with the opportunities provided by technologies.

In that framework, publishers have to consider for their publishing policy the following:

1. The 'second life' of books: older, revised editions have to be properly designed and launched on tablets and mobiles,
2. Gamification and other multimedia technologies,
3. Serialization: among the advantages is that it keeps readers engaged,

4. Short forms,
5. Cocreation,
6. Books out of print that can be available,
7. Convergence,
8. Reader engagement.

Questions raised include, apart from the consumer and reading behaviour, the quality and nature of reading, the information literacy and information seeking behaviour of readers, the typology of the book, the boundaries of convergence; and certainly, much has to be surveyed and studied regarding the above.

Undeniably, mobiles offer to the publishers an emerging market of people who probably do not read systematically; services provided by mobiles introduce these groups of readers or of potential readers to the reading galaxy. Most adults own a smartphone, the size and clarity of which further encourages readers to read. That 'read anywhere' issue reminds of the reading 'mania' at the end of the 18th and during the 19th century when readers, especially the 'new' readers (women, workers) were reading constantly (Wittmann, 1999, pp. 337–369; Lyons, 1999, p. 371–410, Lyons, 2013). Nowadays, readers take advantage of the time available for discovering favourite readings that are on their mobiles. Like the pupils and students of late Medieval and Renaissance that were encouraged to create their personal anthologies of classic authors choosing text, modern readers can create their personal library stored in the devices portable everywhere. In that context, reading and aesthetic experiences change, even dramatically.

4.5   Rediscussing the information publishing chain–circle

Changes in the publishing activity and in the roles of the stakeholders are expressed in the publishing chain to which information adds value. In that framework, the publishing chain can also be described as information chain/circuit (for the term circuit, v. Darnton, 2009, p. 182). The upgraded role of the reader (and of communities of readers), of the literary agent and of the marketing department can be identified among its main features. We may also consider that the stakeholders' roles depend on the publishing sector and the kind of text. For example, the academic publishing chain/circuit is different from other publishing sector. "Books belong to circuits of communication that operate in consistent patterns, however complex they may be" (Darnton, 2009, p. 206)

The role of the reader (and of the author) has been upgraded due mainly to new technologies; but changes have to be explained in a broader framework considering marketing issues, the demand for innovation, psychological and emotional factors, aesthetic needs.

The publishing chain-circle-circuit nowadays may be developed as in Scheme 4.1:
According to the above scheme, we can point out the following:

1. **The upgraded and emerging role of the reader** who traditionally was found at the end of the publishing chain, as the last stakeholder (but certainly not the least) or among the last stakeholders of the chain. Although his/her role was never underestimated, as discussed in the third chapter, it is, and is further encouraged to be, more active, energetic and interactive. Reader engagement, empowered by new information technologies and social media,

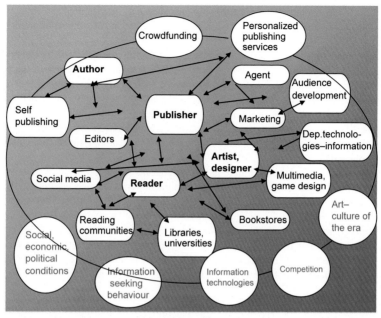

Scheme 4.1 The information publishing chain-circle-circuit.

has redefined the reader's position in the publishing chain altering the chain per se. In that framework, publishers develop strategies, policies and marketing tools, so as to encourage reader engagement and gain feedback from the readers, as cited above.

2. **The emerging role of reading communities**, mostly online, has also to be exhibited. Social media have brought about significant changes in the creation and intervention of reading communities that have altered the 'word of mouth'.

3. **The publisher maintains his or her power and always holds a central role**, exploring new opportunities and broadening the borders not only of the book but also of the publishing activity. Although new publishing and business models offer to the author and other stakeholders the opportunity to act without the publisher, the latter not only survives but also is thriving by exploring tools and opportunities provided by information and communication technologies, penetrating thus into new technological environments and new audiences. Providing advanced publishing services and exploiting new publishing and business models are among the main challenges of the publishing companies. At the same time, the publishing house's traditional functions are further enforced by their upgraded role in providing and evaluating information. The added value given by the publisher to the entire life cycle of the publishing process is augmenting. In a world of information abundance, advanced publishing services help to improve and promote the publication and enable the reader to discover and explore reading and knowledge experiences. 'Anyone who assumes that book publishing firms will be pushed aside because of the growth of the self-publishing authors or operations just does not understand the innovative strategies and operational structures that have been crafted in the last few years by a cluster of major publishers …The industry's great traditions, and its unyielding, and at times undisciplined, quest for perfection enables it to handle effectively depressions, recessions, technological convergence, war and social upheavals' (Greco et al., 2013, p. xii, xiv).

4. The use and offer of **personalized publishing services** may be exploited as a strategy by the publishing companies so as to reach new audiences and expand activities promoting as well their titles.

5. The **upgraded role of the literary agent.** As shown in the research done by Canty (2012), the agents were among the key figures for the publication and the success of the authors' work. The ways through which they were introduced to authors vary implying that relationships are more complex depending on the conditions and the personality of the author. Going back in time, the evolution of the literary agent since the second half of the 19th century (Gillies, 2007) further exhibits the relationships and collaborations between stakeholders as well as their roles. Nowadays, the rise of the literary agent is among the main features of the publishing activity (Thompson, 2010, 38–99).

6. **The editor**, although nowadays there is a lot of concern for his presence, is always among the bedrocks of publishing. It is noteworthy that the editorial services are high in the priorities of authors when trying to publish their work through crowdfunding. It is also true that the value added in the publishing chain is strongly connected with the work of the editor; the text is considered to be ready for publishing after being edited. According to the scheme in *Logos* readable vertically and horizontally (2005, p. iv) the keywords for the editor's work are: collaboration, criticism, improvement, and text. It is interesting to note that the word 'text' appears after the editor's work, whereas at the author we read the word 'message'.

Going back in Renaissance, at the emergence of the editor and at the systematization of his activity, we may observe that his role was underlined even from the beginnings of the printed book. The name of the editor appeared often in the title page and in paratext material – usually in introductions, prologues, even letters and poems – so as to reassure the reader for the quality of the text and of the edition in general. Famous scholars worked as editors who had to improve text, compare manuscripts and prepare the text for publication, take care of the paratext material, arrange the notes, proofread, collaborate with other stakeholders, in cases translate: 'A comparable strategy was to include a letter or poem written in the name of the long-dead author, but probably composed by an editor, extolling the printer's concern about the correctness of the edition' (Richardson, 1994, p. 4). Mostly in classic texts, but as well as in the vernacular, the role of the editor was often exhibited and his name at the title page of the edition further promoted and advertised the edition. 'During the first century of printing, an investment in editing came to be seen as one of the keys to success both by ambitious printers and publishers and by authors' (Richardson, 1994, p. 7). Editorial work made the text better and marketable, which also promoted the edition. Publishers, in their turn, demonstrated and exploited the work of the editors: 'they did not want to seem to be employing editors simply in order to increase their profits. They preferred to claim that their concern for accuracy arose from an altruistic desire to benefit their public, with no expense being spared in this honourable cause...But no press could survive on idealism alone' (Richardson, 1994, p. 6).

7. We have to consider the **advanced role of the publishing departments**, both older, such as the marketing and promotion departments, and new such as the departments that have to do with new technologies (information technology, internet development). It is more than noteworthy that strategies focused on audience development take also an upgrading role. In that framework, the role of the audience development director (Harvey, 2016) (and of departments regarding audience) enlightens aspects of the publishing activity exhibiting the central role that communication with the readers as well as reader engagement have on publishing policy and strategies.

8. The **impact of social media on libraries**. Libraries have to exploit the opportunities provided by the social media and the trends in reader participation so as to reach new audiences and to empower the existing ones, to build communities of readers, to interact with the community, offer personalized services and develop the publishing services. Thus, reading policy of the libraries/information services has to be redeveloped and reevaluated enhancing new technologies and exploring the emerging role of the reader in the publishing activity and being a gatekeeper of intellectual capital (Kostagiolas, 2012). 'Yet it's not enough just to collect and organize – we are also growing increasingly social. Libraries have a role to play as participants in socializing information' (Swanson, 2012, p. 8). According to Steiner (2012, p. 18): 'Add social media goals or initiatives to the library's strategic plan…Recommend platforms or services to pursue, suggesting resources, policies and procedures…'. Online book clubs, recommendation technologies, digital storytelling, book blogs are among the opportunities leading to convergence and integration of traditional and digital-online tools. According to Kaplan and Haenlein (2010, p. 62–63) there are six types of social media: Collaborative projects, blogs, content communities, social networking sites and two types of virtual words, virtual game world and virtual social world. Reading communities are not only content communities. Libraries have to develop strategies for social media and social networking by successful use of human resources (time intensive media), otherwise 'social media can be a Trojan horse for libraries' (Solomon, 2013, p. vi).

9. The **author** has a variety of choices. The question that comes next regards the boundaries of his/her choices.

More specifically, regarding the academic publishing chain, the role of the reader has always been more than active as he/she has multiple roles, as he/she may be

- author,
- editor,
- member of the scientific committee,
- member of the editorial board,
- reviewer,
- peer reviewer, etc.
- recommending also the book to students, libraries, colleagues, networks…

Thus, the reader is among those who decide, recommend, share risks, create, intervene and participate; that protagonist role is further enforced by the information technologies. It is in that environment though in which publishers seem often to push forward academics to editing, proofreading, reviewing, collecting, communicating and supervising certain aspects of the publishing activity usually at no economic cost.

Information transforms the publishing chain-circle-circuit from a twofold point of view: convergence (1) upgrades existing departments of the publishing house such as the marketing department, (2) adds new stakeholders, such as game designers, multimedia artists, information scientists, etc. Gamification and the use of multimedia in publishing are more than promising since they imply reader engagement and interaction between stakeholders transforming at the same time the book itself. By widening the borders of the book and of the publishing activity gamification offers a new tool. Publishing companies have begun to buy game companies[3] or to collaborate with

---

[3] For example, Cowdrey, Catherine (16 June 2016), 'Hachette buys mobile game company Neon Play', *The Bookseller*, http://www.thebookseller.com/news/hachette-acquires-neon-play-serious-first-step-towards-more-digital-business-335671.

them. Book-related games combine text (traditional narrative) and games and provide to the reader, apart from interaction and engagement, the opportunity to decide on the plot. That privilege of choice means participation and empathy, and brings the publishing activity a step forward.

Undeniably, the impact of information brings about changes and reconsiderations in the roles of all stakeholders while at the same time the traditional ones are combined. For example, the diachronic role of the publisher who offers selection, judgment, taste is maintained in that new framework.

In conclusion, the added value of the publishing chain is – to a certain extent – due to information which on the one hand brings about changes and on the other creates challenges and opportunities for all stakeholders; especially for publishers, authors and readers. In a world of information abundance, the publisher takes new roles along with the traditional ones which are now further widened.

References

Abrams, D., August 19, 2015. Does the Future of Reading Belong to the Phone? Publishing Perspectives. Available at: http://publishingperspectives.com/2015/08/does-the-future-of-reading-belong-to-the-phone/.

Anderson, P., May 24, 2016. As We Trade Less Neurotically. A Nice Chat about Those UK Numbers. Publishing Perspectives. http://publishingperspectives.com/2016/05/publishers-association-statistics-yearbook-print-digital/#.V1ffXDWLRQI.

Baldacchini, L., 2004. Aspettando Il Frontespizio. Pagine Bianche, Occhietti a Colophon Nel Libro Antico. Edizioni Sylvestre Bonnard, Milano.

Barthel, M., 2016. Around Half of Newspaper Readers Rely on Print Edition. Pew Research Center. Available at: http://www.pewresearch.org/fact-tank/2016/01/06/around-half-of-newspaper-readers-rely-only-on-print-edition/.

Blocklehurst, H., Watson, K., 2015. The Printmaker's Art. A Guide to the Processes Used by the Artists from the Renaissance to the Present Day. National Galleries of Scotland, Edinburgh.

Calasso, R., 2015. The Art of the Publisher (Richard Dixon, Trans.). Penguin, London.

Canty, N., 2012. The expereince of first time novelists in the United Kingdom. Publishing Research Quarterly 28, 218–235.

Chi, Y., 2014. The E-volution of publishing: challenges and opportunities in the digital age. Publishing Research Quarterly 30 (4), 344–351.

Clark, G., Phillips, A., 2014. Inside Book Publishing, fifth ed. Routledge, London and New York.

Darnton, R., 2009. "What Is the History of Books?", In: The Case for Books. Past, Present, and Future, PublicAffairs, New York, pp. 175–206. [first published in Daedalus, Summer 1982, pp. 65–83].

Eisenstein, E., 1983. The Printing Revolution in Early Modern Europe. Cambridge University Press, Cambridge.

Gillies, M.A., 2007. The Professional Literary Agent in Britain. 1880–1920. The University of Toronto Press, Toronto, Buffalo, and London.

Greco, A., Milliot, J., Wharton, R., 2013. The Book Publishing Industry, third ed. Routledge, New York and London.

Gregory, S., 2012. Vasari and the Renaissance Print. Ashgate Publishing, Surrey.

Harvey, E., April 28, 2016. The Rise of Audience Development in the Book Industry: An Interview with PRH UK's Claire Wilshaw. Book Business. Available at: http://www.book-businessmag.com/article/the-rise-of-audience-development-in-the-book-industry-an-interview-with-prh-uks-claire-wilshaw/.

Kaplan, A.M., Haenlein, M., 2010. Users of the world, unite! the challenges and opportunities of social media. Business Horizons 53 (1), 59–68. Available online at: http://www.michaelhaenlein.eu/Publications/Kaplan,%20Andreas%20-%20Users%20of%20the%20world,%20unite.pdf.

Kostagiolas, P., 2012. Managing Intellectual Capital in Libraries. Beyond the Balance Sheet. Chandos Publishing, Oxford.

Lyons, M., 1999. I nuovi lettori del XIX secolo: donne, fanciuli, operai. In: Cavallo, G., Chartier, R. (Eds.), Storia Della Lettura Nel Mondo Occidentale. Edizioni Laterza, Roma and Bari, pp. 371–410.

Lyons, M., 2013. The Writing Culture of Ordinary People in Europe, C. 1860–1920. Cambridge University Press, Cambridge.

Maloney, J., August 14, 2015. The rise of phone reading. The Wall Street Journal. Available at: http://www.wsj.com/articles/the-rise-of-phone-reading-1439398395.

McIlroy, T., 2015. Mobile Strategies for Digital Publishing: A Practical Guide to the Evolving Landscape. Digital Book World, New York. Available at: http://thefutureofpublishing.com/industries/the-future-of-mobile/.

Papacharissi, Z., 2013. A Private Sphere. Democracy in a Digital Age. Polity Press, Cambridge.

Phillips, A., 2014. Turning the Page. The Evolution of the Book. Routledge, Abington, Oxon, and New York.

Rhodes, N., Sadway, J. (Eds.), 2000. The Renaissance Computer. Knowledge Technology in the First Age of Print. Routledge, London and New York.

Richardson, B., 1994. Print Culture in Renaissance Italy. The Editor and the Vernacular Text, 1470–1600. Cambridge University Press, Cambridge.

Smith, M.M., 2001. The Title-Page. Its Early Development. 1460–1510. Oak Knoll Press.

Solomon, L., 2013. Foreword. In: Harmon, C., Messina, M. (Eds.), Using Social Media in Libraries. Best Practices. The Scarecrow Press, Lanham and Toronto, pp. v–viii.

Steiner, S.K., 2012. Strategic Planning for Social Media in Libraries. ALA Tech Source, Chicago.

Swanson, T.A., 2012. Managing Social Media in Libraries. Finding Collaboration, Coordination and Focus. Chandos Publishing, Oxford.

Szepe, H., 1997. Artistic identity in the Poliphilo. Papers of the Bibliographical Society of Canada 35 (1), 39–73.

Thompson, J.B., 2010. Merchants of Culture. The Publishing Business in the Twenty-First Century. Polity Press, Cambridge.

Turner, M., 2014. Reinvention, revolution, and revitalization: real life tales from publishing's front lines. Publishing Research Quarterly 30, 388–400.

Wittmann, R., 1999. Una *rivoluzione della lettura* alla fine del XVIII secolo? In: Cavallo, G., Chartier, R. (Eds.), Storia Della Lettura Nel Mondo Occidentale. Edizioni Laterza, Roma and Bari, pp. 337–369.

Redefining publishing: challenges from the past

5.1 Re-discovering strategies, re-considering values

5.1.1 Rediscovering and reusing

Strategies may be rediscovered and redeveloped having their origins in concepts and features that we recognize as our past. Values may also be rediscovered or reconsidered in a new technological, social and cultural framework identifying as well their diachronic aspect. In the previous chapters we tried to explore the extent to which current trends are 'new', investigating the ways by which every era introduced, developed and then established its own 'new'. Challenges nowadays are undeniably many and often more complicated than expected; they seem to derive from new information and communication technologies but their origins and explanations can be traced beyond tools into more complicated aspects of the publishing activity depending on needs, desires, expectations and aesthetic concepts. Thus, challenges from the past lead us to publishing policies and strategies based not only on history and knowledge in the methodological framework introduced in this book but also on our current needs and desires.

Innovation is undeniably among the keywords for the publishers who in a highly competitive environment have to introduce new elements, forms, terms, models and strategies so as to:

- Further establish their fame,
- Create a recognizable profile,
- Enrich their catalogue/frontlist,
- Revive and exploit the opportunities of backlist in a new concept,
- Reach new audiences,
- Establish a direct relationship/communication with their existing and potential readers,
- Collaborate with other stakeholders of the publishing chain,
- Collaborate and gain partnerships with other stakeholders in the creative/media industries (art, multimedia, music, information industry, etc.),
- Gain feedback from the reader,
- Develop the artistic identity of their editions and exploit the aesthetic capital for marketing reasons,
- Take advantage of social media,
- Take an advantage in a competitive environment,
- Satisfy the reader's needs,
- Introduce the element of surprise.

Already tested and successful strategies and methods may be of value to the publishing industry. The revival of preorders is a good example. As issues considered in this chapter have already been discussed in the previous pages, they will not be repeated but concerned so as to synopsize publishing opportunities, values and strategies that derive from the past and are or can be of use nowadays. The chapter aims to

Re-Inventing the Book. http://dx.doi.org/10.1016/B978-0-08-101278-9.00005-X

outline conclusions, set questions and recognize topics of future research interest in the methodological framework set in the first and second chapter.

5.1.2 The emergence of a converged culture: new reading, aesthetic and consumer experience

Reading on mobiles and tablets alters the book per se as well as reading, aesthetic and consumer experiences. Specific editions are created so as to be read on the devices we usually have with us, mainly mobiles/smartphones and tablets. For example, at 'editions at play' by Google the word 'readtime' is used specifying our available and needed time, helping the reader to define the reading experience.[1] Furthermore, the use of multimedia and of gamification in these editions redefine the borders and the aesthetics of the book.

This convergence of media will be a valuable key concept for:

1. Approaching new audiences,
2. Developing new reading experiences,
3. Developing consumer behaviour,
4. Introducing new elements to the book,
5. Altering the information mechanisms of the page,
6. Altering the typology of the book,
7. Developing the aesthetics of the edition, further empowering the aesthetic capital,
8. Introducing new stakeholders in the publishing chain-circle-circuit altering at the same time the relationships,
9. Creating collaborations, synergies,
10. Further exploring a correlation with other forms of art,
11. Exceeding the borders of the existing reading audience.

Already existed audiences will be interested in the new forms of the book as well as other potential audiences defined by age and information literacy. The question is 'how successful' these editions have been till now. Although there is much concern and discussion about them, sales of printed books and of the 'most traditional' electronic publications that reproduce the aesthetics of the printed page are still high. Apart from the point that these highly experimental forms obviously prepare the audience for the next step, they also set a converged framework for both printed and electronic material emerging issues of reading and consuming, and setting questions about the nature of the book and of the publishing activity.

5.1.3 Aesthetics in publishing: introducing the aesthetic capital of publishing

The artistic identity of the book, whether printed or not, whether in its traditional or emerging forms, is of significance. Aesthetics in publishing still and always matter giving added value to the edition, being part of the book as described in the second chapter. In that framework, the aesthetic capital has to be added to the other capitals of publishing (Thompson,

---

[1] https://www.penguinrandomhouse.co.uk/media/news/2016/april/penguin-random-house-uk-in-partnership-with-lex-and-editions-at; http://www.thebookseller.com/news/hachette-capitalises-euros-buzz-footy-app-attract-reluctant-readers-330666.

2010, pp. 3–14). The book goes certainly beyond content: the desirable, useful, friendly and often interactive book of our digital era has to gain and demonstrate its artistic identity so as to reach new audiences, most of which come from the printed book. The picture and other visual material are a threshold providing precious (not only visual) information and access to knowledge. Furthermore, we have to consider the embellishment of the text and the relationship between content and aesthetics, as discussed in the second chapter.

Thus, the capitals of the publishing industry are as follows:

- Intellectual
- Economic
- Human
- Symbolic
- Social
- Aesthetic

The aesthetic capital is related with the visual identity of the book, whether printed or not, whether tangible or not. This visual, artistic identity is undeniably of value and of specific commercial merit, constantly being transformed nowadays due to new technologies. The aesthetic capital may be additional or not to the text (intellectual capital, intangible asset) and certainly it offers a lot toward marketing strategies. As in the new forms of the book the term 'material object' or 'tangible assets' does not serve well, we can use the term 'artistic identity' or 'visual identity' taking into consideration convergence of media, gamification, multimedia, music, etc.

In that framework, we have also to consider:

- Reader participation in the aesthetic identity of the book,
- The role of aesthetics in personalized publishing services,
- The visual paratext that is further developed in ebooks.

All the above are derived from methods, behaviours, concepts and strategies from the past. Undeniably, reader participation in the development of the artistic identity of the book, whether electronic or printed, whether with the use of multimedia or not, is of significance and may be used as an updated method for getting feedback from the reader, reaching new audiences and developing marketing as well as promotion strategies. Reader engagement leads to direct communication with the readers and, apart from providing data and feedback, can develop the artistic identity through specific tools, platforms often controlled by publishers and social media.

Undeniably, the artistic identity of the new forms of the book has its origins in the printed book. Apart from it, there is inevitably common ground between the two: the printed book's artistic identity (illustration, decoration, visual paratext, mechanisms of the page) influences the new forms of the book (Scheme 5.1) not only due to the needs and expectations of the readers' but mainly due to the taste and enhanced methods established till now. This influence and enhancement can be vice versa; it is also challenging and of further research interest how new technologies and new forms of the book influence the printed one that still thrives.

Ebooks enhance the use of multimedia converging different forms of art and of information technologies. From this point of view, already tested methods, issues and concepts may serve as the basis of 'new' introductions and policies. For example,

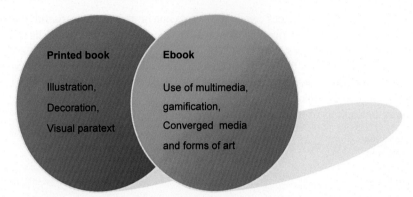

Scheme 5.1 The common ground of traditional (printed) and new forms of the book.

some of these converged editions may bear in mind lavishly illustrated books in a different technological and cultural environment. In that context, the combination of aesthetics of previous decades (that, apart from known and tested, are almost nostalgic, such as covers) with the new technologies may be a decision worth taking.

Additionally, personalized publishing services form a challenging, under development and discussion field that remind us of hand-illuminated books and of Renaissance strategies not only for embellishing the book but also for using it in terms of privilege, prestige, recognition, direct communication, recommendation and patronage. As a method for penetrating into new audiences and satisfying needs and desires of specific readers, these services can be used supplementary so as to augment reader participation and promote titles.

The significance of the artistic identity of the book, whether printed or digital, will further be recognized due to the added value to the edition. As the last lines of this book were prepared, the Global Illustration Award (for five categories) was announced to be conferred in the Frankfurt Book Fair (Anderson, 2016) the director of which, Juergen Boos, stated that 'in today's visually dominated world, illustration and design are of increasing value and particular importance in the process of creating beautiful books.'

Certainly, new forms of the book, often converged, look for their specific identity; publishers and designers–illustrators as well as marketers have to explore the new opportunities based on the aesthetics in publishing. Meanwhile, the revival of the printed book and its augmented sales currently push forward stakeholders to reconsider and redevelop the aesthetics concepts. Reviving older and tested methods and combining them with the new opportunities offers a privileged point of view and strategy.

5.1.4   The addition of colour (and of participation)

The addition of colour in printed as well as in enhanced ebooks and book apps creates different aesthetic experiences trying to overcome the monotony, reminding simultaneously of the choices for coloured illustration during the previous centuries

(Blocklehurst and Watson, 2015, pp. 24–30). Woodcuts were printed in black ink, and occasionally were embellished with the addition of colour (Dackermann, 2002), whereas in unique luxury copies during Renaissance, as discussed in the second chapter, hand illumination was added by miniaturists of the era. Nowadays, new forms of the book offer the opportunity of adding and enjoying colour in books.

In that context, we have to consider the current success of colouring books. These printed books, for which some wonder if they are really books, offer the opportunity to the reader of creating and participating by the addition of colour. This systematization of the colour as a creative and relaxing activity may be of further research interest regarding publishing, reading, social and educational concepts, and promotion methods. Certainly, it may be used in enhanced books and ebooks and may be applied to reader engagement strategies.

5.1.5 Desires of the reader and the element of 'publishing surprise'

Readers desire to

- Have access to information; readers want to be informed not only about new releases but also about activities, news from the industry, discounts and communities of readers. Information is a value and an asset of our era, and publishers have to provide access to it and additionally to evaluate, select and offer it to the readers,
- Read,
- Buy,
- Own the book as content and as object of aesthetic value,
- Discover,
- Be updated,
- Enjoy,
- Share with others; social media play a significant role in building communities of readers and transforming the traditional 'word of mouth',
- Communicate with stakeholders; publishers have to handle it. (For example, providing direct communication with the authors through special platforms, websites, social media.),
- Have privileges/be rewarded/exceed the borders of the member,
- Have advanced roles as discussed in the third chapter focussing mostly on reader engagement.

These desires have to be satisfied on a twofold basis: on the one hand, by the knowledge of the readers' needs, concerns and expectations (marketing, feedback from the readers) and on the other by the element of surprise. The combination and balance between the two will provide an advantage to the publishers, presupposing often new business models.

In that context, keys for the publishers for knowing their audience are:

- Information,
- New information and communication technologies,
- Social media,
- Data,
- Collaborations, synergies,

- Feedback,
- Surveys for reading behaviour, information seeking behaviour,
- Knowledge of the past.

The element of surprise is among the most powerful for the publishing industry. Calasso (2015, p. 54) identifies, regarding the Italian publishing scene in the 1950s, that 'everyone was tired of being taught selectivity. They wanted to find things out for themselves'. Nowadays, the reader seems to be in the centre of the publishing activity; reader engagement, social media, online reading communities and advanced reader copies..., etc., are leading towards a reader-centred approach or what it seems to be like that. The 'audience development director'[2] is created in that context adding a new stakeholder in the publishing chain–circle, as discussed in the fourth chapter, and pushing a step forward the exploitation of the reading audience with the aim to develop publishing policies and strategies.

5.1.6   Reader engagement: readersourcing

According to the above, among the challenges for the publishers is the direct communication with the reader. Regarding reader engagement, the different points of view (publisher's, author's, reader's, etc.) in developing behaviours, methods and policies are of further research interest. From the publisher's point of view, the reader has to be inspired and encouraged in a preset framework with the use of social media and the development of marketing and audience strategies.

The term 'readersourcing', used and introduced in this book, attempts to explain the nowadays emerging role of the reader in the publishing chain-circle-circuit and exhibits the benefits that the publishers obtain through strategies adopting reader engagement. Readersourcing presupposes knowledge of the market and of the audiences, and offers to the publishers feedback from readers, direct communication, book promotion, publicity and sales. Thus, readersourcing can be an effective tool for marketing, exploring interactivity with other stakeholders and also discovering new talents and good books. In that context, online communities and self-publishing platforms owned by the publishers offer the privilege of intervention and of further developing business models.

5.1.7   Back to backlist

New information and communication technologies provide to the publishers the opportunity of reviving an older or classic title. With printing on demand no book is out of print any more. Revised editions of older titles, often with new introductions and other paratext material, new translations and editing as well with a new aesthetic approach offer a 'second life' to the work. Regarding the aesthetics of these revised editions, the publisher has to choose between reproducing the older typology of the book or creating a new one often combining the older with new opportunities. The

---

[2] http://www.bookbusinessmag.com/article/the-rise-of-audience-development-in-the-book-industry-an-interview-with-prh-uks-claire-wilshaw.

former recalls the already tested commercially, emotionally and aesthetically typology, and the other invests on innovation, even surprise. Nostalgia not only for the content but for the book as material object is of significance (such an example is the 'pulpification of classic works'; Abrams, 2016). Redesigning revised older editions is certainly a challenge on the basis of which there is the use and reminding of the previous aesthetics.

5.2 Keep reinventing: challenges from the past for the publishing industry

5.2.1 Transformations of the publishing value chain

In the publishing chain new stakeholders can be observed mainly related to information and communication technologies, coming often from other disciplines (such as multimedia, informatics, game designing, information management, etc.). Collaborations, new technologies and converged material have to be developed in what we can call the 'publishing framework', related thus with books, and obviously with people creating, publishing, offering and reading books. For example, regarding publishing it is not just another app or game that we use but a game adopted and enhanced in the book, a new opportunity and dimension correlated and incorporated into the book and the publishing and reading process as known and developed.

As already discussed in the previous chapter, the publishing chain-circle-circuit has been transformed into an information value publishing chain. In that framework, the roles and responsibilities of the reader, the literary agent, the marketing department and of those related to new technologies have been upgraded. Readers take an advanced role due to a number of reasons – in which information technologies, social media and marketing strategies are included – and publishing companies encourage it as part of their strategies.

In that context, we have to recognize that the publishing company is still the protagonist or among the protagonists. But the roles have to be redefined and reconfined under the magnifying glass of information technologies and of the changing needs, desires and expectations of all stakeholders. There is a lot of concern about the information role of the publishers who do not only provide information but also evaluate, curate and select information. Thus, the traditional values "selection, judgement, taste", that create the privileged and protagonist role of the publisher, are more than valuable and updated. Apart from books, the publisher has to provide information and paths to it, to correlate different forms, to converge media, to take advantage of the new opportunities, to collaborate and gain synergies.

It seems that there is a lot of concern about content. We have though not to forget that publishers mainly publish books/editions, not just content, not just platforms, tools or information – all these are just part of a publishing policy that aspires to create a recognizable profile, to discover and introduce books, to reach and augment readers. The book, in all its forms, is the product. From this point of view, publishers still often set the rules and the scene, offer the opportunities, decide and choose, propose and innovate, satisfy and introduce.

It is true that publishing has always been a privileged field. 'Publishing is a glamorous but low paying profession, and there seems to be an endless supply of exceptionally bright, eager people (mainly English, and history majors) who want jobs in book publishing' (Greco et al., 2013). Inevitably there is a convergence of roles and a widening of collaborations and synergies nowadays. Among other tastemakers, publishers are high in the hierarchy having the privilege to decide and introduce.

Due to recommendation technologies though and social media new tastemakers have emerged including reading communities, social media and book clubs. Electronic bookstores, for example, play a significant role through the services provided (rankings, preorders, recommendations, etc.). In that framework, we may wonder what taste and tastemaker mean; different points of view, such as of marketing or of art history, imply different approaches and methodologies. Obviously, beyond technological tools, business and publishing models, promotion and marketing strategies, concepts of information seeking behaviour, taste, expectations and desires can be found.

5.2.2   Transformations of the book

The boundaries of the book are obviously extended and reset. We read on printed and electronic books, on the paper and on the screen, on tablets, mobiles and ebook devices. Meanwhile, special platforms, apps, etc., are created for the publishing activity due to new publishing and business models as well as to digital marketing and new promotion strategies. In a world of variety and opportunities, the book is constantly being transformed and at the same time transforming reading, writing, communicating, studying, enjoying, living, searching and discovering. Convergence, experiment and innovation set the framework for the new issues taking into consideration the publishing tradition and the art of the era.

In the core though of all these, there is the book in its tested and familiar concept that still influences and defines reading and consumer behaviour. Apart from the fact that the printed book is still preferred at certain kind of texts, the expectations, needs and desires of the reader lead to converged new forms, traces of which can be found in the publishing past. Naturally, questions are raised concerning boundaries, as it will be pointed thereafter.

The life cycle of the book is further widened. The book does certainly not start when published and not finished when its reading is over. Social media and information technologies have extended the borders of 'word of mouth', of reviewing and sharing information. There is an emerging social and bookish role of the reader. Limitations and specific parameters unavoidably exist related to the nature of social media, of the publishing strategies and policies, of the stakeholder's aims. As enlightened in this book though, reader engagement is not so new as we think it is, and lessons from the past, whether from the publisher's or the author's or the reader's point of view, may offer to the development of strategies and policies.

Furthermore, the success of the printed book demonstrates that there is a privileged area for introducing and experimenting combining the older with the new one, the tested with the experimental, the traditional with the innovative. As aesthetic experiences are everyday changing due to a number of reasons (among which the convergence of media and information technologies are prevailing), the development of the aesthetics policy in the publishing company will provide a recognizable profile and the use of specific visual and marketing tools. In that framework, the publishers have to consider as well the transformations of the printed book; though not so revolutionary as those of the digital-electronic these transformations will bring a step forward the publishing company offering new reading and aesthetic experience. From this point of view, information mechanisms of the page can go hand in hand with the aesthetics/visual mechanisms of the page (this is an issue of my future research).

5.2.3   Inside and beyond revolutions

We like to use the word revolution, we are accustomed to thinking that new things happen every day, that technology runs implying thus that we live in a challenging era. The word 'revolution' is indeed used very often for describing or introducing current trends. We want to categorize and characterize things giving added value to them and thus to our lives. In that framework, reality and myths have always gone hand in hand; we think that myths often help us to understand, explain and exploit. We think that the Internet and new technologies have brought about a revolution; but, as discussed in the previous chapters, the printing revolution (Eisenstein, 1983), the Gutenberg revolution, is a continuing, ongoing revolution, its limits exceeding current trends.

We generally like revolutions because they offer innovation and a scope in our lives. 'The beauty of the Web is that it democratized the tools both of invention and of production' (Anderson, 2012, p. 7). Obviously, information offers choice. Choice offers freedom and democracy. Freedom leads to reinventing: the book, content, taste, communication, our lives, etc. Key concepts of the publishing industry, such as access, globalization, discoverability, convergence, engagement, innovation, democratization of taste, are diachronic values proving that the revolution that started with Gutenberg was the first information revolution and is still continuing.

5.2.4   Inside and beyond boundaries: questions, regards and future research

Certainly, there are limitations and borders that we have to recognize and often to exceed. The starting point is that books in all forms have to be viable products ready to be promoted, sold and read. It seems that what Robertson (2013, p. 5) wrote for past periods is of value nowadays: 'although by definition print is a medium for producing multiples, the expansion of the market through industrial means of production also meant significant fragmentation and conflict at this time. Mass markets are made up of competing groups, all vying for status.'

In a hybrid publishing world, questions are raised regarding the boundaries:

· **Between printed and electronic, traditional and new forms of the book**: Although there is much concern about new technologies, the printed book survives, even thrives in specific audiences and kind of texts. Furthermore, the aesthetics of the printed book may create a module, a basis on which several innovative ideas can be introduced. In that framework, enhanced multimedia seem to fulfil older desires and issues developing new ways of reading, enjoying and understanding, whereas colouring books go back in time as well as gamified content. Thus, questions concerning the boundaries of the book, especially its nature and structure, are reset. For example, there is a discussion about the colouring books.

- **Between verbal and visual (converged forms of media)**: Innovations in the visual identity of the book, as well as in visual paratext, introduce new concepts in the aesthetic capital of the book. Text and image, word and picture are further and in new ways combined changing thus the book as an aesthetic object. Experimental and augmented multimedia, the introduction of picture, sound and links to the digital text, the options provided to the reader by new technologies and business models set the framework for the redevelopment of the page and of the book. After Renaissance, this is the first time that the page in its structure, aesthetics and what has been called in the book 'information mechanisms' have been changing so deeply (this is an issue of my future research).
- **Between private and public**. To publish means to make the text (and the information included) public (Clark and Phillips, 2014; Bhaskar, 2013, pp. 16–22). Nowadays, the borders between private and public seem to have been redefined due to social media/networks and new information technologies (Papacharissi, 2013). Even though, this is not something new and surprising as discussed in the case of Pietro Aretino at the third chapter. Publishing, since its beginning, made public the information and the text giving access to it and providing the opportunity of response, collaborations and dialogue. Aretino published his correspondence mainly for reasons of image and prestige, so as to gain privileges demonstrating thus the opportunities provided by printing to communicating and making the private (or the considered to be private) public. Nowadays social networks provide a lot of personalized opportunities and there is a lot of discussion about it.
- **Between globalized and localized** there is no conflict, as it seems. In a globalized world, the introduction and reception of the 'new' trends in the smaller publishing markets is certainly of great research interest; the extent to which the 'new' is adopted and combined with the traditional and with the unique features of each industry is investigated in the bibliography and has to be further investigated (for example, Baensch, 2006; Banou et al., 2013; Banou and Phillips, 2008; Banou, 2011; Musinelli, 2010; Kovac and Squires, 2014; Carrenho, 2015, 2005; Ramos, 2013).
- **Between the expected and unexpected**: readers usually expect the next book according to their profile, needs, desires and other readings; these expectations are often being defined by the author or the publishing company or the kind of text. The already developed tradition influences these expectations for both text and picture/aesthetics of the book. The element of surprise for both text and artistic identity, as already discussed, is significant since it further establishes the symbolic capital of the publishing company creating a recognizable profile and introducing market authors, styles and concepts. The unexpected is a risk but it is the step for sales and success.
- **Between text and paratext**: nowadays due to information technologies and converged forms of the book, the relationship between text and paratext can further be developed or redeveloped. Paratext, both verbal and visual, as discussed in the second chapter, can be more interactive providing, apart from immediate access to links and material, options to the reader so as to decide what and how to read, to enhance, to explore. Thus, the book seems to become more friendly and convenient and provably more personalized.

- **Between public taste and personalized publishing services**. In the second case, the choice and the decisions are of the reader–commissioner; issues of taste are also reconsidered in that framework reminding in a more democratized and systemized framework of a Renaissance patronage tradition. Personalized publishing services are also a step forward for promoting books and encouraging participation of the reader in the publishing activity. Questions regarding taste, prestige, power are raised.
- **Between reader engagement and publishing strategies**: reader engagement is valuable for the marketing and promotion methods of the publishers. The limitations though and the boundaries, although not always visible, have to be set. The role of the reader although active and upgraded in comparison to the past is often defined in an already set framework in which the publisher finally decides. Certainly, there are many cases in which the framework is not set by the publisher, but in a world of abundance of opportunities every trend and tool can be a challenge for different stakeholders.
- **Between recommendation technologies and shared experience**. We live in a world where others seem to recommend, propose, introduce to us because they know our needs due to marketing tools and data collection. Thus, on the one hand, readers share their experiences through social media and online communities of readers redefining thus the "word of mouth" and on the other recommendations are made to them every day influencing and defining their behaviour and taste.
- **Books that were about to print but never published**. Is that just a matter of history? Certainly, but not only. It would be challenging for publishers and editors to look at these cases and take advantage of manuscripts and preparations for the edition. The expectations and sometimes the myths created push forward these editions. In that framework, paratext is of certain value connecting the past with the present.
- **Between ourselves and the others**. The question is never between us and the books, it is between us and the world around us, between us and the others. In a world of abundance and running technology, reading and publishing always mean communication still implying personalized ways of reading, understanding, sharing, thinking, acting and creating. In an often difficult and fragmented world, every book is a promise, reading is an action of freedom, and sharing an action of democracy. These diachronic concepts are not lost but further empowered (and ought to be empowered).

Questions regarding the borders and extending them encourage and inspire us to develop theories, methodologies and strategies. In a changing hybrid world, such as ours, challenges and lessons from the past enlighten current publishing issues.

5.2.5   Challenges from the past. How and why?

The book has always to be a desirable and viable product, being valuable for each reader due to both content and artistic identity, whether printed or digital/electronic. Every book is a different experience for the reader; every book is different for the publisher and other stakeholders. Undeniably, the impact of information and communication technologies, of convergence and social media create certainties and myths, that are related with the realities and the illusions of change (and of revolutions as well). As changes go deeper in the publishing industry, in the nature of the book and in the publishing chain-circle-circuit, challenges from the past meet certainties and uncertainties of nowadays hybrid era providing the framework for understanding and developing (and redeveloping). Rediscovering and adapting these rediscoveries in the current information technologies' context means to introduce, to reimagine, redesign and reinvent the book restructuring in cases the process.

Among the great challenges for the publishing industry nowadays that derive from the past we may recognize the following:

1. Aesthetics of the book: The development of a recognizable aesthetic profile or visual identity by exploiting and converging traditional and innovative (due to new technologies) elements,
   - Reader engagement in the aesthetics of the book (and in the aesthetics publishing chain–circle), as described in the second chapter,
   - Further exploitation of verbal and visual paratext using multimedia and other opportunities (for example, frontispiece – photo or portrait of the author, running titles, page headings, etc.)
   - Reconstructing the page,
   - Use of 'patronage paratext',
   - Introduction of the aesthetic capital in the publishing's capitals.
2. Using converged forms of the book (multimedia, gamification,…)
3. Reader engagement (Readersourcing), as in the third chapter,
4. Further developing online reading communities,
5. Direct communication with the reader; building a relationship of trust between publishers and readers,
6. Use of recommendation technologies,
7. Development of editions for mobiles and tablets,
8. Personalized publishing services,
9. Personalized copies,
10. Short forms,
11. Serialization,
12. Preorders,
13. Crowdfunding,
14. Storytelling,
15. Collaborations, synergies; introducing new stakeholders in the publishing **chain-circle-circuit**,
16. Collaborations with libraries,
17. Exploitation of already used and tested methods. Lessons from the past, which – if studied and understood – will provide the framework for strategies.

Key values of the publishing industry include innovation, selectivity, taste, surprise, convergence, data, experience and engagement. But beyond this, challenges from the past show the road, apart to success, to the understanding of the industry. This book has identified as key issue the creation of a methodological framework based mainly, but not only, on the historical explanations of publishing combining – apart from publishing history, book history, literature and art history – methodology from sociology, media, information science, management and marketing. In that context, 're-' seems in this book to be a key issue: reinvent, reimagine, redevelop, redefine, reuse, reconstruct, reconsider, etc. New terms introduced, such as readersourcing or aesthetic capital, attempt to offer to the study and policy-strategy making of the publishing industry.

But the majority of things has always to be studied. The above are also topics for further research in which we may add questions such as the following:

- Measuring through surveys (qualitative and quantitative) the impact and effect of the all above mentioned issues,
- The use of devices such as the tablet and mobile for reading,
- Hybrid environment and issues of the printed book,
- Colouring books,
- Paratext: new concepts,
- Visual information,
- Different points of view for reader engagement,
- Bookselling cultures and the rise of independent bookstores,
- The impact of recommendation technologies by publishers or bookstores,
- Boundaries of technologies and of social media that are often defined by their use and success,
- The aesthetic publishing chain-circle-circuit in different publishing sectors,
- Role of the reader in academic publishing.

Certainly, there is always something more and better to be studied, and to be written. The above may serve as a challenge for future research, discoveries and rediscoveries.

5.3 A comment as epilogue. Time and the book (or reinventing ourselves)

Approaches in this book resemble sometimes to a poly-prismatic mirror which offers to each issue and feature a privileged image that finally constitutes and reconstructs the phenomenon as a whole. Probably this may be attributed to the fact that each book competes with the time: personal time and objective time, the time of the book and of the author, even of the reader.

Thus, we may talk about the time of the book that is transformed into the book of time. Because the boundaries are not only of information, knowledge, communication, research but also of pleasure, taste, sharing and access to ourselves. Some consider time as a rival, others as a friend. But the luxury of the book further implies a luxury of time, of a time rediscovered, rewon, restructured and redefined. The time of each book we read or write or in which we are somehow involved is a deeply experienced, rewarding and reconsidered time.

From this point of view, every book can be a book of reinvention and of reimagination. Discovering and reading books implies often reinventing ourselves in kaleidoscopic options of time trying to offer to our desires and needs a different approach; these approaches may go back in time to a redevelopment and fulfilment of reconsidered options or towards the future inside issues and options reimagined. Reinventing the book means to a large extent to reinvent ourselves; and before this, reimaging the book means to reimagine the world around us and our lives as well.

References

Abrams, D., May 06, 2016. The UK's Oldcastle Books: Pulping Up the Classics. Publishing Perspectives. http://publishingperspectives.com/2016/05/oldcastle-books-pulp-classics-imprint/#.VzZWReTGD_w.

Anderson, C., 2012. Makers. The New Industrial Revolution. Random House Business Books, London.

Anderson, P., July 11, 2016. Illustration and Design: "Particular Importance". Publishing Perspectives. Also in Digital Book World (11/7/2016) http://publishingperspectives. com/2016/07/illustration-award-frankfurt-book-fair/#.V4VC-KLGD_w. http://www.digi-talbookworld.com/2016/frankfurt-book-fair-announces-global-illustration-award/.

Baensch, R., 2006. The book publishing industry in Brazil. Publishing Research Quarterly 22 (4), 31–36.

Banou, C., Phillips, A., 2008. The Greek publishing industry and professional development. Publishing Research Quarterly 24 (2), 98–110.

Banou, C., Kostagiolas, P., Olenoglou, A.-M., 2013. The organization of the large book publishing houses in a changing era: a case study. Logos 24 (1), 30–40.

Banou, C., 2011. Backlist and frontlist, bestsellers and longsellers in a small publishing market: the case of the Greek publishing industry at a turning point. International Journal of the Book 8, 139–154.

Bhaskar, M., 2013. The Content Machine. Towards a Theory of Publishing from the Printing Press to the Digital Network. Anthem Press, London and New York.

Blocklehurst, H., Watson, K., 2015. The Printmaker's Art. A Guide to the Processes Used by the Artists from the Renaissance to the Present Day. National Galleries of Scotland, Edinburgh.

Calasso, R., 2015. The Art of the Publisher (Richard Dixon, Trans.). Penguin, London.

Carrenho, C., 2005. The Brazilian book publishing industry and its current challenges. Publishing Research Quarterly 21, 77–92.

Carrenho, C., 2015. Brazil: has the country of the future become the country of the present for publishing? Publishing Research Quarterly 31, 54–63.

Clark, G., Phillips, A., 2014. Inside Book Publishing, fifth ed. Routledge, London and New York.

Dackermann, S. (Ed.), 2002. Painted Prints. The Revelation of Color in Northern Renaissance and Baroque Engravings, Etchings and Woodcuts. Pennsylvania State University Press, Pennsylvania.

Eisenstein, E., 1983. The Printing Revolution in Early Modern Europe. Cambridge University Press, Cambridge.

Greco, A., Milliot, J., Wharton, R., 2013. The Book Publishing Industry, third ed. Routledge, New York and London.

Kovac, M., Squires, C., 2014. Scotland and Slovenia. Logos 25 (4), 7–19.

Musinelli, C., 2010. Digital publishing in Europe: a focus on France, Germany, Italy and Spain. Publishing Research Quarterly 26, 168–175.

Papacharissi, Z., 2013. A Private Sphere. Democracy in a Digital Age. Polity Press, Cambridge.

Ramos, G., 2013. Evolution of the Brazilian publishing market. Publishing Research Quarterly 29 (2), 164–174.

Robertson, F., 2013. Print Culture. From Steam Press to Ebook. Routledge, New York and London.

Thompson, J.B., 2010. Merchants of Culture. The Publishing Business in the Twenty-First Century. Polity Press, Cambridge.

Timeline

Key points of publishing
(With emphasis on editions and historical figures referred in the book)[1]

From the Mid-15th Century, Renaissance

c. 1453, Mainz, Invention of printing by Gutenberg, printing of the Gutenberg Bible, the first printed book.

Last decades of the century: development of the typology of the book.

c. 1460–1510, development of the title page.[2]

The hand press[3] was used till the end of the 18th century.

1486, Bernhard von Breydenbach, *Peregrinatio in Terram Sanctam.*

1493, Schedel, H., Liber Chronicarum, Anton Koberger, Nuremberg. Famous edition, known as the "*Nuremberg chronicle*", combining text and image, lavishly illustrated with woodblocks by M. Wolgemut and W. Pleynderwurff.

Aldus Manutius (1449–1515), publishing activity in Renaissance Venice: Introduction and establishment of libelli (libri) portatiles (portable books, pocket-sized books), and of italics. Collaboration with scholars. Aldus Manutius created not only a typographic culture but an everyday culture as well.

Last decade, Florence, publishing activity of the Greek scholar Janus Lascaris and Italian printer Lorenzo de Alopa.

16th Century, Renaissance-Manierism

Venice as a typographic capital.

Illustration and decoration of the printed book developed.

1543, N. Copernicus, *De revolutionibus orbium caelestium libri sex*, Nurember, Ioannis Petrius (beginning of Scientific Revolution).

1545, Conrad Gesner, *Bibliotheca Universalis*, Christopher Froschauer, Zurich (first bibliography—reference work).

---

[1] This is definitely not an extended timeline and does not aspire to cover in detail all developments in publishing. Its aim is A. to provide the general framework with only some of the key points of the evolution of the publishing industry, B. to include historical figures mentioned in the text, whether famous or not, so as the reader to be better introduced to the text. "For more information and for an extended and analyzed "timeline" see Lyons, Martyn (2011). Books. *A Living History*. London: Thames & Hudson. For the title page: Smith, 2006. For technology in publishing: Howard 2009"

[2] Smith, 2006.

[3] Gaskell, Philip (1972), *A New Introduction to Bibliography*, Oxford University Press, distinguishes the hand press and the machine press period.

1550, Florence (Torrentino), first edition of the *Vite* by Giorgio Vasari.
1568, Florence (Giunti), second edition of the *Vite* by Giorgio Vasari.
In the first half of the century, Pietro Aretino published his works in collaboration with the publisher Francesco Marcolini, Venice.
Christoph Plantin, Antwerp, systemization of the publishing process, production of polyglot *Bible* in eight folio volumes, 1568–1572.

17th Century, Baroque

1641, Torquato Accetto, *Della dissimulazione onesta*, nella stampa di Egizio Longo, Naples.
From 1650, emergence and development of subscriptions, preorders in Britain.
Elzevirs, Netherlands: innovative publishing activity.
1684, Moxon Joseph, *Mechanick Exercises on the whole art of Printing*, London.

18th Century, Enlightenment

Reading Revolution, Literacy in the Western world.
From 1751, publication of *Encyclopedie*.
The subscription publishing model flourishes.

19th Century, Industrial Revolution

Systemization in book production and distribution.
New printing techniques (the machine press period). Mechanization of printing (Stanhope press from 1800).
Paper, new techniques for producing it.
New audiences, dynamic reading groups: women, children, working class.
Thriving of novels.
Best sellers (in Victorian Britain), such as the work by Dickens.
Serialization.
Creation of publishing series.
Illustration changed: new techniques.
L. Hachette, second half of the century, bookstores at railway stations in France.
Emergence of the publisher as known nowadays.[4]
Role of the press (newspapers, magazines) in promoting the books.
"Free to all, open to all" public libraries.
Reading societies, reading rooms.
Second half of the century: The emergence of the literary agent in the UK.

[4] See also "History of printing timeline" by American Printing Association, available at https://printinghistory.org/timeline/

Index